Money and the Rise of the Modern Papacy

This is a pioneering study of the finances and financiers of the Vatican between 1850 and 1950. Dr Pollard, a leading historian of the modern papacy, shows how until 1929, the papacy was largely funded by 'Peter's Pence' collected from the faithful, and from the residue the Vatican made its first capitalistic investments, especially in the ill-fated Banco di Roma. After 1929, the Vatican received much of its income from the investments made by the banker Bernadino Nogara in world markets and commercial enterprises. This process of coming to terms with capitalism was arguably in conflict both with Church law and Catholic social teaching, and becoming a major financial power led the Vatican into conflict with the Allies during Second World War. In broader terms, the ways in which the papacy financed itself helped shape the overall development of the modern papacy.

JOHN F. POLLARD is a Fellow of Trinity Hall, Cambridge. He is the author of *The Vatican and Italian Fascism, 1929–1932: A Study in Conflict* (1985).

Money and the Rise of the Modern Papacy

Financing the Vatican, 1850–1950

John F. Pollard

Fellow of Trinity Hall, Cambridge

CAMBRIDGE
UNIVERSITY PRESS

PUBLISHED BY THE PRESS SYNDICATE OF THE UNIVERSITY OF CAMBRIDGE
The Pitt Building, Trumpington Street, Cambridge, United Kingdom

CAMBRIDGE UNIVERSITY PRESS
The Edinburgh Building, Cambridge, CB2 2RU, UK
40 West 20th Street, New York, NY 10011–4211, USA
477 Williamstown Road, Port Melbourne, VIC 3207, Australia
Ruiz de Alarcón 13, 28014 Madrid, Spain
Dock House, The Waterfront, Cape Town 8001, South Africa

http://www.cambridge.org

First published 2005

Printed in the United Kingdom at the University Press, Cambridge

Typeface Plantin 10/12 pt.   *System* LATEX 2$_\varepsilon$ [TB]

A catalogue record for this book is available from the British Library

Library of Congress cataloguing in publication data
Pollard, John F. (John Francis), 1944–
Money and the rise of the modern papacy: financing the Vatican, 1850–1950 /
John F. Pollard.
   p.   cm.
Includes bibliographical references and index.
ISBN 0 521 81204 6
1. Papacy – History – 19th century.   2. Catholic Church – Finance – History –
19th century.   3. Capitalism – Religious aspects – Catholic Church – History –
19th century.   4. Papacy – History – 20th century.   5. Catholic Church –
Finance – History – 20th century.   6. Capitalism – Religious aspects –
Catholic Church – History – 20th century.   I. Title.
BX1950.P65   2004
262'.136 – dc22   2004045811

ISBN 0 521 81204 6 hardback

For Jonathan Steinberg

Contents

Appendices   231

Illustrations

Tables

Acknowledgements

I should like to begin by thanking Ambassador Sergio Romano for bringing the existence of the diary of Bernardino Nogara to my attention, and Ambassador Bernardino Osio for allowing me access to his grandfather's diary and other papers, and thus starting me on this particular research project. I am also grateful to the staff of Anglia Polytechnic University Library, the British Library, Cambridge University Library, the Biblioteca Nazionale Centrale and the library of the Istituto di Storia Moderna e Contemporanea in Rome, the National Archives (formerly Public Records Office) at Kew, the Archivio Segreto Vaticano and the Archive of the Second Section of the Vatican Secretariat of State. Thanks are also due to Julie Satzik of the Chicago Archdiocesan Archives, Fr Ian Dickie of the Westminster Archdiocesan Archives, Dr Dos Santos and the staff of the National Archives in Luxembourg, Prof. Cesarano and Dr Loche of the Archivio Storico of the Banca d'Italia, Dr Francesca Pino and the staff of the Archivio Storico of the Banca Commerciale Italiana in Milan, Dr Ferrucio Ferruzi of the Archivio di Stato di Roma, Prof. Poala Carucci and the staff of the Archivio Centrale dello Stato in Rome, Prof. Michele Abbate and the staff of the Archivio Storico del Ministero per gli Affari Esteri in Rome, the director of the Registre du Commerce, Canton Vaud, Switzerland, the staff of the Archive de Département de Paris, Companies House in London, Mr John Taylor and the staff of the National Archives and Records Administration and the archivists of the National Catholic Welfare Conference, both in Washington DC.

Anglia Polytechnic University History Research Committee, the British Academy and the Scouloudi Foundation all provided funds for the various research trips in Europe and America without which this book would not have been possible.

Several friends, colleagues and students have helped me in the research for this book, or advised me about aspects of it: Max Beber, Anna Bristow, Lucia Faltin, James Seymour Hegelson, Paul Hypher, Susanne Jennings, Ron Machell, Martin Manuzi, Joseph Pearson, Joy Porter, Stewart Stehlin, Clive Trebilcock, James Walston, Brian Williams and

David Wilson. I also owe Brian a debt of gratitude, along with Michael Walsh and Oliver Logan, who read a complete draft of the manuscript and offered some very useful advice. I am especially grateful to Dan Raff and the other members of the University of Pennsylvania, Wharton Business School, Economic History Seminar for inviting me to discuss my work with them; Jonathan Steinberg and Susan Zuccotti were both kind and helpful in their comments as respondents. For any errors of fact, and for opinions and interpretations, the responsibility is, of course, mine alone.

I owe an immense debt of gratitude to Nora Galli dei Paratesi, James Walston and Brian Williams, for their hospitality, friendship and stimulating company in Rome over the years. Finally, I would like to acknowledge the moral support of Pompey.

Currency exchange

1   Exchange rates in 1880 in terms of French francs

Belgian franc, Swiss franc, Italian lira and Spanish peso	1 Ff
Egyptian piaster	0.31 Ff
British pound sterling	25.22 Ff
Dutch florin	2.60 Ff
Austro-Hungarian florin	2.50 Ff
German mark	1.11 Ff
US dollar	5.18 Ff

2   Average exchange rates, December 1926, 1936 and 1950 (in US cents per unit)

Country	Unit	December 1926	1936	1950
Austria	Schilling	14.08	18.79	n.q.
Belgium	Belgian franc	2.78	3.38	1.99
France	old franc	3.95	6.11	0.29
Germany	RM, DM	23.80	RM40.30	DM23.84
Italy	lira	4.44	7.29	n.q.
Netherlands	guilder	39.99	64.48	53.42
Spain	peseta	15.24	12.31	n.q.
Sweden	krona	26.72	25.63	19.33
Switzerland	Swiss franc	19.32	30.19	23.14
United Kingdom	pound sterling	485.12	497.09	280.07

From Charles P. Kindleberger, *A Financial History of Western Europe* (2nd edn, Oxford, 1993), p. 467.

Glossary

ABSS Amministrazione per i Beni della Santa Sede (Administration of the Assets of the Holy See). Main agency responsible for administering Vatican palaces and gardens (prior to 1929), other property in Rome and the capital assets accumulated as a result of the investment of the surplus from Peter's Pence.

Americanism A 'heresy' condemned in Leo XIII's apostolic letter, *Testem Benevolentia* of 1899. It allegedly consisted of such ideas as the rejection of external spiritual direction: the elevation of natural virtues over supernatural ones and a preference for 'active' virtues to 'passive' ones. At bottom, the concern in Rome and France was about the liberal democratic climate in which the Catholic Church lived in America.

Amministrazione per le Opere di Religione/Pias Causas Created by Leo XIII secretly to administer and invest cash funds and stocks and bonds of Italian religious orders and occasionally dioceses.

annates or 'first fruits' The first year's revenue of an ecclesiastical benefice (q.v.), usually a bishopric, which had to be paid to the Papal Treasury.

APSA Amministrazione per il Patrimonio della Sede Apostolica, formed from the merger of the ABSS and the ASSS by Paul VI in 1967.

arbitrage Simultaneous purchase and sale, normally in different places, of currencies, sometimes for delivery at different times, with no price risk.[1]

ASSS Amministrazione Speciale della Santa Sede (Special Administration of the Holy See). Henceforth Special Administration. Vatican agency created by Pius XI in 1929 to administer and invest funds received from the Italian government as laid down in the Financial Convention of that year, whose management was entrusted to Bernardino Nogara.

---

[1] Taken from Charles P. Kindleberger, *A Financial History of Western Europe* (2nd edn, Oxford, 1993), pp. 459–62.

beatification A process carried out by officials of the Roman curia (q.v.) by means of which a dead person is judged to have led an especially holy life in conformity with the Church's teaching, and may even have been responsible for a miraculous cure. The person is then given the title of 'venerable' or 'blessed'.

benefice, ecclesiastical An ecclesiastical office – e.g. that of bishop or parish priest – whose income was originally derived from an endowment.

Camarlengo, Cardinal The cardinal responsible for the administration of the affairs of the Holy See, including finance, during a *sede vacante* (q.v.). He is also responsible for the smooth running of the funeral of the deceased pope and the conclave.

Canon Law, Code of The manual of laws which regulates all aspects of the life of the Roman Catholic Church. The first Code was promulgated in 1917 and a revised version in 1983. There is also a separate Code for the Eastern Rite (q.v.) and Uniate (q.v.) Churches.

canonisation The process, carried out in the same way as for beatification (q.v.), whereby a dead person is declared to have led an especially holy life in conformity with the Church's teaching, to have demonstrated signs of 'heroic virtues' and to have performed miracles and is therefore given the title of 'saint', and is judged to be worthy of veneration by the faithful.

Casa Generalizia The Rome headquarters of a religious order, or alternatively the residence in the city of a religious order whose base is outside of Italy.

catechism A comprehensive manual of Catholic religious belief which, in a simplified form, is used for the religious instruction of children.

chirograph A papal administrative decree of limited circulation within the Roman curia.

clerico-moderates Italian laymen with a more conciliatory attitude towards the Italian state than their intransigent (q.v.) fellow Catholics. Many were businessmen, financiers and large farmers and some became members of the Italian Parliament after the *Non Expedit* (q.v.) was relaxed from 1904 onwards.

commandite (Italian *commenda*) A sleeping partnership in which, as a rule, one or more partners provides the entrepeneurship, and another, the sleeping partner, the capital.[2]

concordat A treaty between the Holy See and the government of a secular state which regulates relations between the Church and the

---

[2] Ibid.

government of that state and guarantees certain rights to the Church in the free exercise of its ministry.

consols An abbreviation for 'consolidated British debt', which is borrowed in perpetuity.[3] In this book it refers to the consolidated debt of the Italian state.

delegate, apostolic A representative of the Holy See to the ecclesiastical hierarchy of a given country or countries. He does not have diplomatic standing but has in the past, nevertheless, frequently performed a secret diplomatic role in relationship to governments.

Eastern Rite Churches Those churches, like the Catholic Copts, Maronites and Melkites, who have different liturgies and discipline (married priests, etc.) from the 'Latin' rite Catholics of the West.

encyclical The most important of all the public communications of the pope, usually addressed to the hierarchy of the whole Church, the hierarchy of a given country or to both hierarchy and faithful together.

ex cathedra Literally 'from the seat'. Only papal pronouncements made solemnly on the basis of the teaching authority of the apostolic see ('seat') are to be regarded as infallible.

exegesis The scholarly study of the Bible, with the purpose of interpreting its content in the light of the times.

Fondo per il Culto The department of the Italian Ministry of Justice which distributed the revenues of the expropriated properties of the Italian Church to holders of ecclesiastical benefices – like parish priests, cathedral canons and bishops – throughout the peninsula from the 1860s onwards. In 1929, it was transferred to the Ministry of the Interior.

forced circulation (Italian *corso forzoso*) Repudiation by a government of central bank obligation to redeem paper notes in circulation in coin, so that the notes are obliged to remain in circulation.[4]

fungible A good, like money or grain, which can be replaced by another in respect of function or use.

Holy See The bishopric of Rome, claimed to have been founded by St Peter who was its first bishop. Because of this connection with the 'Prince of the Apostles', his successors in the see, the popes, claim spiritual primacy and authority over the whole Christian Church. Also known as the papacy.

indulgences A device whereby the temporal punishment due for sin in Purgatory is remitted by authority of the papacy.

Intransigents Catholics who maintained an uncompromising attitude of hostility towards the Italian state after the capture of Rome in 1870.

---

[3] Ibid.   [4] Ibid.

IOR Istituto per le Opere di Religione. Literally 'Institute for the Works of Religion'. The name given to the Amministrazione per le Opere di Religione, which had originally been established by Leo XIII to administer the funds of certain religious orders and Italian dioceses, when Pius XII re-organised it in 1942. Nowadays, it is commonly known as the 'Vatican Bank'.

Lateran Pacts The agreements signed by Mussolini for the Italian state and Cardinal Gasparri for the Holy See, on 11 February 1929, in the palace of the Lateran, Rome. They consisted of the Treaty which brought the Roman Question to an end and created the sovereign and independent State of the Vatican City, the Concordat which regulated Church–State relations in Italy down to 1984 and the Financial Convention which resolved financial questions outstanding between the two signatories.

Law of Papal Guarantees Passed by the Italian Parliament in 1871 to 'regularise' the status and role of the pope in Italy following the occupation of the last remnant of the Papal States, its annexation to Italy and the proclamation of Rome as capital city.

Legations, the The northern territories of the former Papal States (Emilia-Romagna) which were ruled by 'legates'.

letter, apostolic A papal communication having lesser authority than an encyclical and usually addressed to individuals or small groups of bishops.

metropolitan Usually the ordinary of an archbishopric who has a limited supervisory jurisdiction over the (suffragan) bishops in his province.

minutante A junior official in the Secretariat of State and other 'dicasteries', departments, of the Roman curia.

mixed or universal bank A bank which not only made short-term loans, but also bought bonds and shares from industrial companies.[5]

modernism 'The synthesis of all heresies.' A set of ideas condemned by the Holy Office in *Lamentabili* of 1907 and in Pius X's encyclical *Pascendi* of the same year. These statements attacked the ideas of various French and British Catholic scholars that, among other things, the Bible should be subject to historical-critical study, that religious dogma develops within history and that sociological concepts can play a useful role in the study of the history of the Church. Most of these ideas have been generally accepted since the Second Council of the Vatican in the 1960s.

---

[5] Ibid.

motu proprio A decree issued on the authority of the pope to regulate the administration of a given part of the Roman curia.

Non Expedit A papal decree prohibiting Italian Catholics from voting and standing as candidates in the parliamentary elections of the Kingdom of Italy. It was finally abolished in 1919.

nuncio, apostolic The diplomatic representative of the Holy See to the government of a state.

Obolo Italian name for the collections of Peter's Pence. Sometimes used to refer to all offerings received by the pope.

Opera dei Congressi The umbrella organisation of the various organisations of the Catholic movement – youth and adult groups, newspapers, credit and co-operative institutions etc. – until it was dissolved by Pius X in 1904.

ordinary The bishop of a diocese who has 'ordinary' spiritual jurisdiction over the clergy and faithful in that area.

Peter's Pence The name used to describe the major form of monetary contributions of the Catholic faithful throughout the world to the support of the Holy See. It originated in Anglo-Saxon England and was revived in the mid-nineteenth century.

primate The leading metropolitan within a given country or region. The archbishop of Baltimore has an 'honorary' primacy or precedence over all other bishops in the United States of America by virtue of being the occupant of the oldest bishopric in the country. The pope is the primate of Italy.

Prefettura dei Sacri Palazzi Apostolici (Prefecture of the Sacred Apostolic Palaces) The administration of the papal palaces in Rome, including, before 1870, the Quirinale Palace.

Propaganda The Congregation of Propaganda Fide, which was responsible for the Church's missionary activities and which had a budget independent of the rest of the Roman curia.

regio placet et exequatur The power claimed by Italian rulers to give permission to newly appointed ecclesiastics to enter into their benefices (q.v.). The Law of Papal Guarantees (q.v.) promised to abolish this permission, but it was not implemented until 1929.

Roman curia Central government of the Roman Catholic Church situated in the Vatican and in other parts of Rome, consisting of the Secretariat of State and the various other congregations, offices and tribunals.

Roman Question The dispute between the papacy and the Italian state following the latter's occupation and annexation of Rome in 1870 and consequent destruction of the last remnant of the temporal power (q.v.).

sede vacante The interregnum between the death of one pope and the election of his successor.

sedia gestatoria The portable throne on which the popes were carried into St Peter's Basilica. It was abolished by Pope Paul VI.

Sostituto The Substitute or deputy to the Cardinal Secretary of State.

temporal power The pope's political sovereignty over the former Papal States of central Italy.

Uniate A Church of the Eastern Rite, for example the Ukranian, which was re-united with Rome after previously being a part of the Orthodox Churches.

usury The lending of money at excessive rates of interest. Until the nineteenth century, *all* money-lending at interest was regarded as being potentially sinful.

visitor, apostolic A special, temporary representative of the Holy See to the hierarchy of a country. The term is also used about papal 'inspectors' during the reign of Pius X (1903–14) who visited dioceses or their seminaries looking for signs of the 'modernist' heresy.

1 Introduction

This is the story of the development of the financial structures and policies of an institution – the papacy – which in 1850 was an essentially
small, semi-feudal and territorial state with fairly loose spiritual authority over millions of Catholics outside of the Italian peninsula, but which
in the next one hundred years shed the last remnants of the 'temporal
power', became a highly bureaucratic institution, with an increasingly
global diplomatic outreach, and which exercised an increasingly rigid,
centralised and undisputed control over the world-wide Roman Catholic
Church. In the process, the papacy also became a global financial institution, no longer deriving its income from the subjects of the Papal State,
but from the offerings of the faithful throughout the world and also from
returns on a growing portfolio of investments in agriculture, real estate,
manufacturing industry, commerce and finance distributed throughout
the financial capitals of the Old and New Worlds – Rome itself, Milan,
Geneva, Lausanne, London, New York, Boston, Chicago, Buenos Aires
and Rio De Janiero to mention the most important. The Vatican's financial 'journey' from being based on a localised feudal/territorial state,
heavily fiscally dependent upon the revenue from the landed economy
of an essentially rural agrarian society, to being a capitalist 'holding company' with Italian-wide and world-wide financial interests parallels the
rise of the modern papacy as we know it and in part helps to explain that
development.

The finances of the Vatican have long been a matter of speculation,
and in the last few decades journalists in particular have become fasci-
nated by them.[1] In part, this is quite simply because the Vatican has,
until relatively recently, been obsessively secretive about its money, in
part for good reason which will become apparent later. It was Cardinal
Domenico Tardini, Secretary of State to John XXIII, who first broke the
taboo surrounding discussion of the finances of the Vatican in October

---

[1] See R. Della Cava, 'Financing the Faith: The Case of Roman Catholicism', *Church and
State*, 35 (1993), p. 48 fn. 2 for a survey of journalistic articles on the Vatican's finances.

1959, during a dispute over the pay of the Vatican's employees when he held a press conference on the subject with journalists accredited to the Vatican.[2] But it is only since Paul VI's reform of the Roman curia in 1967, and the creation of the Prefecture of Economic Affairs of the Church, to co-ordinate the work of all the Vatican financial agencies except, significantly, the 'Vatican Bank' (see the Conclusion, p. 226) that some of the Vatican's accounts have been regularly available in the public domain.[3] Another reason for the journalistic interest is the discrepancy between the simplicity and poverty of the Christian Church of apostolic times and the splendour, power and apparent wealth of the papacy. One of the consequences of the secrecy surrounding the finances of the Vatican has been the inaccurate and ill-informed speculation about the actual size of its wealth which often fails, among other things, to take into account the fact that the treasures of St Peter's and the Vatican palaces and museums are just that, treasures which the pope is not at liberty to sell any more than the United Kingdom government is at liberty to sell the Crown Jewels or the contents of the British Museum. The most spectacular example of this kind of speculation are the words of George Harrison in the Beatles's song, *Awaiting On You All*:

> While the Pope owns 51% of General Motors
> And the stock exchange is the only thing He's qualified to quote
> But the Lord is waiting on you all to awaken and see
> By chanting the names of the Lord you'll all be free.[4]

Needless to say, while it is almost certainly the case that the Vatican owns shares in General Motors, it is extremely unlikely that it has ever held anything approaching a majority holding.

A further cause of journalistic interest has been the Vatican Bank's involvement in dubious deals, with shady partners – like Roberto Calvi of the Banco Ambrosiano and Michele Sindona's Banca Privata – and Archbishop Paul Marcinkus's alleged role in them as head of the Vatican Bank, has led to a spate of works by investigative journalists like Cornwell, *God's Banker*, Garvin, *The Calvi Affair*, and Raw, *The Moneychangers*.[5] But scandals and crises surrounding the finances of the Vatican and difficult relations with private capitalism are nothing new, as the troubled history of the Vatican's relationship with the Banco di Roma and its president Ernesto Pacelli in the late nineteenth and early twentieth centuries

[2] B. Lai, *Vaticano aperto: il diario vaticano di Benny Lai* (Milan, 1968), pp. 107–8.
[3] T. J. Rees, SJ, *Inside the Vatican* (Cambridge, Mass., 1992), pp. 209–10.
[4] From George Harrison's I-ME-MINE, 'The Lord Loves the One that Loves the Lord' (Richmond, 1980).
[5] R. Cornwell, *God's Banker* (New York, 1983); L. Garvin, *The Calvi Affair* (London, 1984); and C. Raw, *The Moneychangers* (London, 1992).

(see Chapters 3 and 4) and the 'Cippico affair' of 1948 (see Chapter 9) demonstrate.[6]

The purpose of this book, however, is rather more comprehensive; it is to examine the ways in which the Vatican financed itself between the end of the pope's territorial kingdom in central Italy, with the fall of Rome to Italian troops in 1870, and 1950, the highpoint of the reign of Pius XII. As someone who sat at the feet of Geoffrey Elton at Cambridge in the mid-1960s and heard him expound his theory of the 'Tudor Revolution in Government', and in particular his explanations of how the Tudor monarchs' search for the means for their governments 'to live of their own' helped determine the shape of the English Reformation, I am acutely aware of the impact that changes in institutional financing can have on the institution itself. But one of the key elements in the circumstances which helped produce the physiognomy of the Church of England – financial necessity – had already had a dramatic impact upon the unity of Christendom as a whole. German resentment at the papacy's sale of indulgences in order to finance the re-building of St Peter's in Rome was of course a major factor in the earlier Lutheran reformation in Germany, and the Reformation in the German, Scandinavian and other lands, in its turn, reduced the flow of revenue to the papacy in the long term. It is the argument of this book that the changes in the ways in which the Vatican financed itself after 1870 had a similarly powerful effect on the institutional development of the modern papacy in the period down to 1950.

The rise of the modern papacy

From the beginning of the reign of Pius IX (1846), but more acutely from 1850 onwards, when Pius returned from Gaeta with his 'liberal period' firmly behind him, the papacy underwent a process of development which we can plausibly define as the 'rise of the modern papacy'. That development reached its culmination in the papacy of Pius XII, 'the last real pope', as Alberto Spinosa has described him.[7] And if one single year may be regarded as the apogee of the 'modern papacy', then it must be 1950, the Holy Year during which Pius proclaimed the dogma of the Bodily Assumption of the Blessed Virgin Mary into Heaven. Without quite making the claims to universal temporal dominion of Innocent III with his concept of the *plenitudo potestatis* of the papacy or Boniface VIII's in the bull *Unam Sanctam* (1302), the 'modern' popes succeeded in imposing

---

[6] For Pacelli, see B. Lai, *Finanze e finanzieri vaticani tra l'Ottocento e il Novecento da Pio IX a Benedetto XV* (Milan, 1979), and for the Cippico affair see C. Pallenberg, *Inside the Vatican* (London, 1961), pp. 194–5.

[7] A. Spinosa, *L'ultimo papa* (Milan, 1992).

their authority upon the Roman Catholic Church and prescribing how clergy and laity should think and act in ways which were without precedent in the history of the papacy. In addition, they gave the world-wide Church a uniform, *Roman* stamp in organisational and disciplinary matters.

The origins of the trans-formative processes which helped create the modern papacy can largely be traced back to the French Revolution and its aftermath, but it can be argued that the Enlightenment of the mid-eighteenth century, and the ecclesiastical movements to which it gave rise, Josephism in the Habsburg lands and Febronianism in Italy, which both sought to free the local churches from papal control, began to stir the papacy from the baroque, Italianate slumber into which it had fallen shortly after the conclusion of the Council of Trent in the late sixteenth century.[8] Diversity and autonomy had been the hallmarks of the life of local churches in that period, with the Gallican privileges of the French Church being the most extreme example.[9] But the French Revolution, with first the establishment of the Civil Constitution of the Clergy which nationalised the French Church to an extent undreamt of by previous reformers and effectively secularised the French state, was a rude awakening indeed for Rome. While later nineteenth-century popes, especially Gregory XVI in his encyclicals *Mirari vos* (1832) and *Singulari nos* (1834), and Pius IX in the *Syllabus of Errors* (in the encyclical *Quanta Cura*, 1864), would do battle with the novel and dangerous political doctrines generated by the Revolution – freedom of the press, freedom of conscience, freedom of religion – and also opposed the movements towards nationalism, liberalism, democracy, republicanism and secularism, and those Catholics like Lammenais and Montalembert who sought to reconcile them with Catholic teaching and practice, Pius VII was immediately confronted by the horrors of the persecution which the Revolutionaries inflicted on France, and the countries which they conquered in their Revolutionary Wars, after he had rejected the Civil Constitution.

But the Napoleonic Concordat of 1804, while not ideal from Rome's point of view, since it left so much power in the hands of the state, nevertheless provided opportunities for papal intervention in the affairs of the local churches which was unprecedented in the history of the papacy. First, it gave the pope the power to depose bishops, and in order to further Napoleon's policy of eliminating the exiled bishops who had opposed the Civil Constitution, dozens were removed. On the other hand, as long as

---

[8] K.-O. Von Aretin, *The Papacy in the Modern World* (London, 1970), pp. 15–20; and D. Holmes, *The Triumph of the Holy See* (London, 1978), pp. 4–12.
[9] Ibid.

they were in office, bishops in French-controlled territory had considerable powers over the parish clergy, which some of them used ruthlessly
in mass movements of parish priests – 3,500 in France in 1837 alone –
with consequent appeals to the pope in Rome.[10] In Germany, Napoleon
had brought about the abolition of church states (those ruled by bishops
and abbots), the abolition of some bishoprics and the downgrading of
some metropolitan sees, and his *mediatisation* reform (reducing the number of German states from over 300 to about 35, and merging hundreds
of them in the process), plus the territorial changes brought about by
the 1815 Vienna settlement meant the subordination of many Catholic
areas to Protestant princes. All these developments undermined local
church loyalties, and bishops and clergy increasingly turned to Rome for
the redress of their various grievances. A further contributory factor in
the growth of the prestige and power of the papacy over local churches
was the conflicts between the bishops and clergy of those churches and
their governments as the nineteenth century progressed. The civil war
between Catholic cantons and the Protestant Sonderbund in 1847, with
the latter's attempts to limit the power of the Church in Switzerland,
was one such conflict that drew the Swiss episcopacy, clergy and laity
closer to Rome.[11] Another was the so-called *Kulturkampf* between the
Prussian/German authorities and the German Church in the 1860s and
1870s,[12] and a third was the conflict between Catholics and the government in Russian-Poland after 1815 which both welded Catholicism into
Polish national identity and provoked a closer affection between Poles
and the papacy, despite the popes' condemnation of revolts on the part
of Polish Catholics.[13]

One of the longer-term effects of the French Revolution was the emergence in France of the Catholic movement known as Ultramontanism
which sought both a monarchist restoration on *ancien régime* principles,
but also a Catholic revival under strengthened papal authority. The Ultramontane project of many bishops, priests and laity would thus focus
Catholic loyalty, obedience and devotion upon the pope and his government of the Church from Rome. Given France's continuing cultural and
political dominance in early nineteenth-century Europe, French religious
ideas and devotional practices were very influential elsewhere, and thus
Ultramontanism became a powerful force in Catholic circles throughout Europe, and especially in parts of Italy.[14] And the influence of the
movement was re-inforced by the pope's triumphant return to Rome in

---

[10] E. E. Y. Hales, *Revolution and the Papacy, 1769–1846* (London, 1960), p. 153.
[11] O. Chadwick, *A History of the Popes, 1830–1914* (Oxford, 1998), p. 48.
[12] Ibid., pp. 37–8.   [13] Ibid., pp. 417–19.
[14] Hales, *Revolution and the Papacy*, pp. 227–30.

1814 and Cardinal Consalvi's negotiation for of the restoration of the temporal power at the Congress of Vienna in that same year. The papacy, accordingly, enjoyed a new prestige on the international stage, and one which only the policies aimed at repressing national and liberal movements inside the Papal States would eventually destroy. Even before Pius IX embarked upon his classic policies of centralising and 'Romanising' the world-wide Catholic Church, his predecessors – Leo XII and Gregory XVI – had pursued objectives which helped those policies to succeed. Gregory even endorsed the abolition of slavery and the slave trade in 1839 and urged the ordination of native clergy and the consecration of native bishops, a move that was well ahead of its time.[15] Both popes gave a new impulse to Catholic missionary activity in the world, which would be continued by Pius IX, Leo XIII, Benedict XV and Pius XI against a background of the imperialistic expansion of the European powers, and which resulted in the spread of the Catholic Church's influence throughout Africa, Asia and Oceania. During his reign, Pius IX created a powerful and effective Church organisation in five continents, with 206 apostolic vicariates or bishoprics created, and his successor Leo XIII established a further 300, with the consequence that a rich harvest of souls was reaped in the 'missionary' territories of Africa, Asia and Oceania – the Catholic population there rose from 5 to 15 million between 1846 and 1978.[16] This enormously strengthened the authority and power of the papacy over the world-wide Church. The reign of Pius IX, 1846–78, was undoubtedly crucial in the historical development of the papacy. According to Mazzonis: 'It would be no exaggeration to say that the Church of the twentieth century, that which we ourselves have known, saw its foundations solidly laid and its characteristic institutional structures emerge in the difficult years between 1850 and 1870, the period in which the contemporary era of its history began.'[17] Accordingly, a number of factors help characterise the differences between the papacy from Pius IX onwards, and that of the popes who went before. In the first place, there was the development of the *magisterium*, the teaching authority of the Roman pontiffs. The key stages in this development were the proclamation of the doctrine of the Immaculate Conception of the Blessed Virgin Mary in 1854, the proclamation of papal Infallibility at the First Council of the Vatican in 1870 and the proclamation of the dogma of the Bodily Assumption of the Blessed Virgin Mary into Heaven in 1950.

---

[15] F. Coppa, *The Modern Papacy, since 1789* (London, 1998), p. 79.

[16] F. Mazzonis, 'Pio IX, il tramonto del potere temporale e la riorganizzazione della chiesa' in B. Angloni et al. (eds.), *Storia della Società Italiana*, vol. XVIII: *Lo stato unitario e il suo difficile debutto* (Milan, 1981), p. 266.

[17] Ibid., p. 388.

The decisions about the dogmas concerning the role of Mary in salvation history were taken *in consultation* with the bishops of the Roman Catholic Church throughout the world, but were not dependent on their expressed opinions. Indeed, as Owen Chadwick has pointed out, 'He [Pius IX] was sure that in his office as supreme teacher of the Church he was protected by God from error . . . No Pope in previous centuries had made a definition of doctrine quite like this.'[18] Thus, though the doctrine of Infallibility was only proclaimed after the consent of the bishops had been obtained in an ecumenical council placed under great pressure from the pope and the Roman curia, its principle had already been previously asserted.[19] After 1870, the popes took upon themselves more and more the task of laying down to the Catholic hierarchy, clergy and laity of the world rules and regulations regarding not only matters of spirituality, religious doctrine and discipline, but political, economic and social issues as well: in particular, all the popes from Pius IX to Pius XII; with the exception of Benedict XV, used apostolic letters, decretals and encyclicals to reiterate the absolute obligation of the faithful to accept papal teaching.[20]

Like the *Syllabus of Errors* of 1864, the proclamation of Infallibility in 1870 was meant as a definitive and defensive response to the threats posed to Roman Catholicism by the 'modern world' as it was understood in the mid-1800s. The Enlightenment, the French Revolution and the ideologies and political movements to which they gave rise – rationalism, secularism, anti-clericalism, freemasonry, liberalism and nationalism – had all damaged and disrupted the Church of the *ancien régime*, both in France, but also in the rest of Europe as a result of the French Revolutionary and Napoleonic Wars between 1789 and 1815. The expropriation of ecclesiastical property, the abolition of clerical privilege and power and the introduction of civil marriage, divorce, secular education and the separation of Church and State were all 'insidious novelties' that were introduced in many European states, and in a significant number of American states, North and South, as well after 1789. Later on in the nineteenth century, the papacy would also have to confront the emerging ideologies and movements of Socialism and Communism, and in the twentieth it would be faced by the threat from Fascism and National Socialism. In these circumstances, Infallibility was meant to provide a solid, steely core to Catholic resistance to these developments, and a means of preserving Roman Catholic unity.

---

[18] Chadwick, *A History of the Popes*, pp. 199–214.   [19] Ibid., p. 121.
[20] P. Levillain (ed.), *The Papacy: An Encyclopedia* (3 vols., London, 2002), II, p. 964.

In the longer term, Infallibility gave the Roman pontiffs an enormous moral and spiritual authority over the world-wide Roman Catholic
Church and thus created the premiss for the practice of increasingly frequent public interventions of the popes in a wide variety of subjects of
importance to the clergy and laity. There was an enormous increase in
the 'output' of the most important of all papal public documents in this
period, encyclicals, as well as of less formal statements like the *motu
proprio*: whereas Gregory XVI published nine encyclicals in his fifteen-
year pontificate, Pius IX wrote in thirty-seven in a reign of thirty-two years
and Leo XIII a staggering eighty-six in just under twenty-five years. Other
modern popes were less prolific, but Pius XII returned to the practice of
Leo and produced forty-one in nineteen years.[21] Leo XIII wrote three
encyclicals on freemasonry, Benedict XV and Pius XII issued encyclicals on the themes of peace and war during the First and Second World
Wars respectively, Pius XI published an encyclical on marriage, *Casti
Connubi*, in 1930, Leo XIII wrote *Graves de Communi Re*, on political
institutions in 1901, and on particular national situations like those in
France, *Aux Milieu des solicitudes*, 1892, on the *Ralliement*, while Pius XI
wrote *Non Abbiamo Bisogno* on the dispute with Fascist Italy in 1931 and
Mit Brennender Sorge of 1937 on his dispute with Nazi Germany. In addition, two popes wrote major encyclicals on economic and social doctrine,
Leo XIII's *Rerum Novarum* of 1891 and Pius XI's *Quadragesimo Anno* of
1931. Not all were actually written by the popes themselves: increasingly,
they relied upon experts in theological and other matters, but these documents, taken together with some of their public utterances, constituted
a formidable corpus of papal teaching. As Zambarbieri has pointed out,
papal teaching was then passed down to the clergy and laity by means of
bishops' pastoral letters, especially those issued during Lent.[22]

This tendency of modern popes to give regular guidance and direction
to Catholics on every conceivable aspect of their lives was re-inforced by
the establishment of two Vatican press organs whose pronouncements
soon came to be regarded as the mouthpieces of the Vatican 'oracle'. In
response to the rise of a combative, anti-clerical press, especially in Italy,
the daily newspaper *L'Osservatore Romano* was established in 1861, and
the Jesuit fortnightly, *La Civiltà Cattolica*, was founded in 1854, but only
brought under the direct control of the Vatican in the 1880s. With their
editors appointed either by the Cardinal Secretary of State, or often the
pope himself, their key articles scrutinised by both in advance, and in

---

[21] See C. Carlen (ed.), *The Papal Encyclicals* (5 vols., Raleigh, N.C., 1990), I.
[22] A. Zambarbieri, 'La devozione al Papa', in E. Guerriero and A. Zambarbieri (eds.),
    La chiesa e la società industriale (1878–1922), Storia della Chiesa, XXII/2 (Milan, 1996),
    pp. 41–3.

some cases with articles written by the pope himself, along with *Acta Apostolicae Sedis*, these publications became the authoritative 'voice' of the papacy to the whole Catholic world and a guide to its bishops.

Infallibility also assisted the development of two other major characteristics of the modern papacy, their efforts to centralise and 'Romanise' the world-wide Church. Throughout the reigns of Pius IX, Leo XIII, Pius X and Benedict XV and beyond, twenty-eight institutions were established in Rome for the education of the clergy and, primarily, future bishops of the local churches. In the reign of Pius IX eight of these institutions were established, including the French, German, Latin and North American and Polish colleges; under Leo XIII another eight, including the Armenian, Canadian, Czech, Portuguese, Ruthenian and Spanish colleges; under Pius X and Benedict XV only three; but under Pius XI another six, including the Beda (English), Dutch and Russicum (Russian); and under Pius XII three, including the Hungarian and Lithuanian colleges: in addition, commencing in Pius IX's reign, the major religious orders, whatever their national origins, began to set up educational institutions for their members in the Eternal City.[23] The popes were particularly anxious to supply bishops to the 'younger' churches, those of Canada and the USA, Australia, New Zealand and Oceania, and later Asia, especially China, who had been trained in 'Roman ways' in Roman institutions.[24] It was fairly easy to do this as these countries were still essentially 'mission territories', under the control of the Congregation of Propaganda Fide, as were the restored hierarchies in England and Wales, Scotland and the Netherlands, until the mid- to late 1800s, and therefore without established traditions of local election by cathedral chapters. It was frequently the case that 'Romanised' bishops sent the best of their clergy to Rome for training, and upon their return set them on the ladder of ecclesiastical preferment, thus ensuring that Roman influences in the local church would establish and perpetuate themselves, a very clear example of this being William O'Connell, who was rector of the North American College in Rome from 1898 to 1905. He became bishop of Portland in 1905 and started sending his trainee clergy to Rome, including Francis Spellman, later cardinal archbishop of New York. Finally, after 1878, the Jesuit-run Gregorian University in Rome took over from the Sorbonne the role of the premier Catholic university and the chief arbiter of ecclesiological thinking.[25]

---

[23] *Annuario Pontificio*, 1948, pp. 911–14; and Levillain (ed.), *The Papacy*, 1, pp. 380–6.
[24] For an example of the impact of 'Romanisation', see J. N. Molony, *The Roman Mould of the Australian Catholic Church* (Melbourne, 1969).
[25] Zambarbieri, 'La devozione al Papa', p. 14.

From the 1880s onwards, the Eternal City became the centre of scholarly and popular attention. In 1883, Leo XIII opened up the Vatican Secret Archives to Catholic and non-Catholic scholars alike, thereby prompting a new interest in the history of the papacy. In addition, he gave renewed impetus to the archeological excavations of Christian Rome, especially the catacombs. These developments helped focus attention upon Rome and the papacy: as well as scholarly histories of the papacy, historical romances such as *Fabiola* and *Quo Vadis* explicitly or implicitly suggested comparisons between the ways in which the early popes had suffered persecution at the hands of the Roman Empire and their treatment now at the hands of the Italian state. In this way, a strong cultural and literary component was added to Roman Catholic identity.[26]

The increasing intervention of Rome in the life of local churches was intensified by the appointment of papal representatives in more and more countries: apostolic delegates, that is envoys without formal diplomatic functions, in the case of mission territories like the USA and Canada, Australia, etc., and apostolic nuncios, that is envoys who acted as papal representatives to both local hierarchies *and* governments, in most Catholic countries. Following the achievement of independence by various Latin American states in the early nineteenth century, the missionary congregation of Propaganda under Cardinal Cappellari, later Gregory XVI, extended the Vatican's diplomatic net by encouraging recognition of them – initially Chile, Colombia, Ecuador and Mexico and later the rest.[27] A century later, as a result of the First World War, and the Versailles Peace Settlement which followed it, there was again a substantial increase in the number of states with whom the Vatican had diplomatic relations. Many of them were not even predominantly Catholic in population; some like Finland had virtually no Catholic populations, but as 'successor states' to the Austro-Hungarian and Russian empires, they desired recognition from one of Europe's oldest powers as a way of establishing their existence as independent, sovereign states.[28] Not surprisingly, the decision to appoint apostolic delegates and nuncios was frequently resisted by national hierarchies precisely because it was seen as constituting interference in the affairs of local churches; the response to such decisions in the cases of the USA,[29] Canada,[30] the Irish Free

---

[26] Ibid., pp. 47–51.   [27] Chadwick, *A History of the Popes*, pp. 47–8.
[28] J. F. Pollard, *The Unknown Pope: Benedict XV and the Pursuit of Peace* (London, 1999), pp. 157–8.
[29] G. P. Fogarty, *The Vatican and the American Hierarchy from 1870 to 1965* (Collegeville, Minn., 1982), pp. 115–30.
[30] R. Perin, *Rome in Canada: The Vatican and Canadian Affairs in the Late Victorian Age* (Toronto, 1990), pp. 47–55.

State[31] and Great Britain[32] being emblematic of this local unease. More recently, the resistance of the Polish hierarchy to the Vatican's *Ostpolitik* in the 1960s and 1970s provides a fascinating example of a local hierarchy which fiercely defended its right to make its own agreements with a hostile, Communist government without interference from Rome.[33]

Building up its network of diplomatic relations was one of the most important elements in the strategy of a succession of popes to assert the continuing international status of the Holy See as a sovereign entity after the loss of territorial sovereignty in September 1870. Pius IX's intransigent refusal to compromise on the ensuing dispute with Italy, the 'Roman Question', in any shape or form was another. The rejection of the Law of Papal Guarantees of 1871, and the annual financial payment laid down in the law, by means of which the Italian government hoped that the question would be settled, was an essential way of asserting the papacy's absolute independence from the Italian state and the determination of the popes not to be or be seen as 'the chaplain of the King of Italy'. A third important element in this strategy was implemented in 1903 when, after the conclave of that year, the new pope Pius X abolished the right to veto unacceptable candidates for election to the papacy exercised by Catholic states such as Austria-Hungary, France, Spain and Portugal. This was intended as a means of eliminating the power of secular governments to interfere in the politics of the Vatican.

The process of establishing a network of Roman supervisory agents/diplomatic representatives over the local churches was steadily advanced during the reigns of Pius XI and Pius XII, and later John XXIII and Paul VI, and has now reached completion in the pontificate of John Paul II. The Vatican now has papal nuncios or apostolic delegates in virtually every country of the world except China, North Korea and Vietnam, Saudi Arabia, Yemen and a clutch of other Arab states. In addition, it sends representatives to major international organisations like the European Union, the Organisation of American States and the United Nations and its subsidiaries.[34] The fact that both Mussolini in 1929 and Hitler in 1933 sought some kind of legitimisation for their new regimes in the form of concordats with the Holy See is a clear sign of the growing influence of Vatican diplomacy in the inter-war period. By 1950, the Roman Catholic

[31] D. Keogh, *The Vatican, the Bishops and Irish Politics, 1919–1939* (Cambridge, 1986), pp. 155–7.
[32] T. Moloney, *Westminster, Whitehall and the Vatican: The Role of Cardinal Hinsley, 1935–1943* (London, 1985), pp. 94–8.
[33] J. Luxmoore and J. Babuich, *The Vatican and the Red Flag: The Struggle for the Soul of Eastern Europe* (London, 1999), pp. 186–8.
[34] *Annuario Pontificio*, 1999, pp. 1329–60.

Church had become a major player on the world stage in its own right, seeking to influence both the domestic and foreign policies of states, and, where possible, the policies adopted by international organisations.

The Vatican sought increasingly to bring local hierarchies more clearly under its supervision as a means of strengthening the unity of the Church in the face of its enemies, and, to this end, from the beginning of the reign of Pius IX, Rome forbade the holding of councils of local/national churches anywhere without its express permission, very often sending representatives either to preside over them or at least keep an eye on their proceedings.[35] The particularly tight, direct control of the Italian Church by the Roman curia may be explained quite simply by proximity, the fact that Italy was (and remains) the home and hinterland of the Holy See, and by the fact that the pope is, after all, not only bishop of Rome and Metropolitan of the Roman Province, but also Primate of Italy. Yet popes prior to Pius IX did not exercise quite such control: it was the political exigencies of the 'Roman Question' which required the close identification of the Italian episcopate with its head. It is significant that an Italian Bishops Conference (CEI) did not emerge until the 1950s, long after the establishment of such institutions in other countries, and that the Italian Church, via CEI, remains directly answerable to the Vatican Secretariat of State.[36]

The Code of Canon Law promulgated in 1917 was, by itself, probably the greatest instrument of centralisation and Romanisation in the Catholic Church in this period, laying down as it did rules and regulations for all ecclesiastical matters, from hierarchical organisation to sacramental discipline, the law of marriage and annulment and the administration of the property of the Church.[37] Hitherto, it had been necessary to consult a huge, scattered corpus of confusing, and sometimes conflicting, laws dating from different epochs, and varying from country to country and even diocese to diocese. If imitation is truly the greatest form of flattery, then the codification of canon law was the Catholic Church's belated tribute to the spirit of Napoleonic reform. But though many bishops throughout the world welcomed the arrival of the Code as a boon, since it provided all the answers, especially in knotty disciplinary cases,[38] it frequently meant that local traditions and practices had to be abandoned in favour of Vatican-imposed uniformity. Following promulgation of the Code, Benedict set up a college of canon law studies and began the process of creating a code of canon law for the Eastern and Uniate Churches in communion with Rome.[39]

[35] Mazzonis, 'Pio IX, il tramonto del potere temporale', p. 267.
[36] P. Hebblethwaite, *John XXIII: Pope of the Council* (London, 1983), pp. 356–8.
[37] *Code of Canon Law: New Revised English Translation* (London, 1983).
[38] Pollard, *The Unknown Pope*, pp. 194–5.   [39] Ibid., p. 195.

John Cornwell has argued that the role of Msgr (later Cardinal) Eugenio Pacelli as Cardinal Pietro Gasparri's adviser on the commission for the codification of canon law set up in 1907 was crucial in ensuring the insertion of canon 329 reserving the right of appointment of virtually all bishops to the Holy See.[40] He further claims that as nuncio to Bavaria from 1917 and to Germany between 1920 and 1929, Pacelli sought to implement this article of the Code through a series of concordats with the German states and that he continued to pursue this policy as Cardinal Secretary of State from 1929 to 1939 in the negotiation of concordats and other agreements with other European states.[41] In fact, the practice of concluding concordats with secular states was nothing new; on the contrary it had a long pedigree. Pius IX was the real pioneer of a concordatory policy, concluding sixteen concordats in the period 1847 to 1862, and during his reign, in countries like Britain and the Netherlands, the restoration of the hierarchy was achieved without giving the state any rights to intervene in episcopal appointments, and only limited initiative to cathedral chapters.[42]

It is also significant that following the introduction of the Code, Benedict XV launched a further project of uniformity, the development of a 'Catechism of the Catholic Church' to replace various local catechisms.[43] But for reasons which are not clear, the project did not come to fruition until the 1980s, under another centralising pope, John Paul II.[44]

Rome-imposed uniformity was also secured in other areas of the Church's life, in particular by encouraging the development of the Marian cult as part of popular devotion by the proclamation of the dogma of the Immaculate Conception in 1850 and which was assisted by alleged apparitions of the Virgin at Lourdes (1858), Marpingen (1876) and Fatima (1917). It is significant that the latter two visions took place in countries which were riven by Church–State strife at the time. Leo XII made a particular contribution to the development of the Marian cult, devoting no less than three encyclicals to the subject of the rosary.[45] Another important devotion which was encouraged in this period was to the Sacred Hearts of Jesus and Mary.[46] One of the most significant developments in the area of popular devotion was the huge increase in the number of beatifications and canonisations in the reigns of Pius IX and Leo XIII: in

---

[40] J. Cornwell, *Hitler's Pope: The Secret History of Pius XII* (London, 1999), pp. 130–5.

[41] Ibid., pp. 58, 86–93, 130–56.

[42] Mazzonis, 'Pio IX, il tramonto del potere temporale', p. 264.

[43] Pollard, *The Unknown Pope*, pp. 193–4.

[44] *Catechismo della Chiesa Cattolica: testo integrale e commento teologico* (Vatican City, 1992).

[45] Carlen (ed.), *Papal Encyclicals*, I, pp. xxvi–xxx. See also D. Blackbourn, *Marpingen: Apparitions of the Virgin Mary in Bismarckian Germany* (Oxford, 1993); R. Harris, *Lourdes, Body and Spirit in a Secular Age* (Berkeley and Los Angeles, 2000).

[46] Chadwick, *A History of the Popes*, pp. 459–60.

these fifty-seven years, as many canonisations took place – seventy-two – as had taken place in the period since the establishment of the branch of the Roman curia concerned with the processes of beatification and canonisation, the Sacred Congregation of Rites, in 1588.[47] The development of the cult of saints was indeed an important element in popular devotion and in cementing popular support for the papacy from those nations whence the *beati* and saints came. Pope Pius X (1903–14) was especially active in the fields of liturgy and devotion, initiating what were probably the greatest innovations in personal religious practices to take place between the sixteenth-century Council of Trent and the Second Council of the Vatican of 1962–5. Perhaps the most revolutionary were the directives issued in 1910 encouraging frequent reception of communion by lay people and early reception by children – usually at seven. According to one historian of the papacy, the subsequent development of the very widespread celebration of children's first communion 'profoundly transformed the religious and social experience of millions of Christians . . . Pius's own popularity as a pope of the people also grew as a result'.[48]

Both Leo XIII and Pius X also laid down important new guidelines for the training of priests, throughout the Church, and not just in Rome. Leo introduced the study of the philosophy of St Thomas Aquinas, 'Thomism', as a key element in seminary education, and Pius X thoroughly reviewed and tightened up seminary disciplinary imposing the anti-modernist oath upon all priests.[49] That measure, which was again a response to a perceived threat from the evils of the modern world – dangerously rationalist tendencies in the fields of biblical exegesis, ecclesiastical historiography and theology – was probably the single most important exertion of Roman authority and uniformity in the history of the Roman Catholic Church. It was underpinned by the sending of papal 'visitors' to various dioceses to sniff out modernist 'heresy', especially in the seminaries. Again, this overriding of the authority of bishops inside their dioceses, even cardinal archbishops in the case of Italian sees, was an extraordinary, unprecedented exertion of the power of Rome on local churches.[50]

There are three other very important dimensions of the development of the modern papacy that need explaining. The first is the development of the devotion of the faithful to the person of the pope, a sort of papal 'cult of the personality', a close and direct relationship between Catholics

---

[47] Levillain (ed.), *The Papacy*, I, pp. 235–6.
[48] E. Duffy, *Saints and Sinners: A History of the Popes* (New Haven, Conn., 1997), p. 247.
[49] Chadwick, *A History of the Popes*, p. 355.   [50] Pollard, *The Unknown Pope*, p. 24.

and their supreme religious leader which has no precedent in the previous history of the papacy. The second is the 'internationalisation' of the Papal Court, and to a lesser extent of the Sacred College of Cardinals and the Roman curia, which developed in the period 1870 to 1939, but which was not to reach its peak until after the Second Council of the Vatican of the 1960s. The third is an aspect of the second, that is the growing power and influence of American Catholicism in Rome. These three crucial aspects of the development of the modern papacy were largely a result of the changes in the way in which the papacy financed itself between 1870 and 1950. Consequently, it is an important object of this book to explain how money affected the rise of the modern papacy, how the finances and financiers of the Vatican are intimately and inextricably interwoven into the history of the Roman Catholic Church in this period.

Sources

Writing a financial history of the Vatican in this period is not an easy undertaking, largely because archival sources are very fragmentary. The Vatican archives, both the so-called 'Secret Archives' and the archive of the Council of the Public Affairs of the Church (*Affari Ecclesiastici Straordinari*), what is now the second section of the Secretariat of State, have been closed after the death of Benedict XV in 1922 (at the time of writing, records relating to the nunciatures of Berlin and Munich between 1922 and 1939 have been made available). And before that date there is only a limited amount of material available in them which is of use: none of the departments of the Roman curia concerned with financial matters – the Administration of the Assets of the Holy See (henceforth, ABSS), the Fabric (chapter) of St Peter's Basilica, the financial sections of the Congregation of the Propagation of the Faith or the Congregation of the Clergy, or the Commission for the Works of Religion (forerunner of the Vatican Bank) have given their records to the Vatican archives. But one does sometimes come across documents which cast light upon the Vatican's financial dealings, most frequently in the reigns of Leo XIII, Pius X and Benedict XV, especially in the *spogli* or collections of miscellaneous documents relating to the popes and to a group of important cardinals like Rafael Merry del Val (Secretary of State to Pius X) and Giacomo Della Chiesa (later Benedict XV). Another key source is the records of the administration of the Sacred Apostolic Palaces (Sacri Palazzi Apostolici) and the apostolic delegation to the United States. But one cannot say that one has not been warned: a note in Blouin's *Catalogue of the Vatican Archives*, issued in 1998 and thus the first comprehensive guide to the Archives in English, says rather laconically that the records of most of the financial agencies of the Vatican, 'are not generally available'.[51] This is particularly frustrating as some of entries in the catalogue give fairly detailed descriptions of their contents – such as that of the *spoglio* of Cardinal Federico Tedeschini, who was, among other things, head of the ABSS in the 1930s.

As is so often the case for other aspects of the history of the modern papacy, one is forced to turn to other archives and sources for information on the finances of the Vatican: the Archivio di Stato di Roma, the Rome provincial archives, which contain material produced by the pre-1870 administration of the Papal States, including the accounts of the Peter's Pence collections received from the faithful throughout the world, and from the post-1870 Italian Ministry of the Interior, Directorate-General of Public Security files which include reports of the Commissario del Borgo, the police chief of the area around the Vatican who had the task, among other things, of spying on it. The Archivio Centrale dello Stato, the Italian Central State Archives, also contain the reports of the Commissario del Borgo, and other sources in Ministry of the Interior files and the Private Secretariat of the Duce. The Archivio Storico del Ministero degli Affari Esteri, the historical archive of the Italian Ministry of Foreign Affairs, and especially the files on the Italian Embassy to the Holy See, also contains much important material for the period after the *Conciliazione* of 1929. Other national archives, like the French national archives in Paris and also the United States archives in Washington, the National Archives and Records Administration and the Public Record Office in London, have also proved extremely valuable. It has been possible to consult only two diocesan archives, those of the archdioceses of Chicago and Westminster. The archives of banks, especially those of the Banca d'Italia (Italian central bank), the Banco di Roma, with which the Vatican had a long and troubled relationship, and the Banca Commerciale Italiana, one of whose vice-presidents was Bernardino Nogara, Pius XI's very successful financial adviser, have also proved very useful. In addition, the records of the company registration offices in Lausanne, London, Luxembourg and Paris have also been used to track down companies set up by the Vatican outside of Italy during the post-1929 period.

In recent years, however, two other vital sources of information have become available which throw a great deal of light on the finances of the Vatican in this period.

1. The first is the diary of Baron Carlo Monti, who was both the lifelong friend of Benedict XV and his 'go-between' with the Italian government in the years 1914 to 1922. The diary, which was published in

---

[51] G. Blouin, *Catalogue of the Vatican Archives* (Vatican City, 1998), p. 435.

1997, is a rich source for any work on Benedict. It also contains several references to important financial matters in Benedict's reign.[52]

2. The second is the unpublished 'diary' of the Italian financier Bernardino Nogara, who was also financial adviser to Pius XI and Pius XII between 1929 and 1954. The 'diary' is in reality a record of the audiences which Nogara had with Pius XI between 1931 and 1939. As will be seen in Chapters 6, 7 and 8, the diary, and the accompanying papers in the Nogara Archives (AFN), provide an unparalleled degree of detailed information about the finances of the Vatican in the period from 1931 to 1939, and in particular the policies Nogara pursued during the crucial period of the laying down of the Vatican's investment portfolio in Italy, Europe and North America.

Given the paucity of documentary sources, it is inevitable that much of the existing secondary literature on the finances of the Vatican in this period is unsatisfactory and unreliable. Some works, however, are both reliable and useful. One such is Felisini's *Le finanze pontificie e i Rothschild* (Pontifical finances and the Rothschilds) which explores the role of the Rothschild banking family in papal finances between 1830 and 1870.[53] Crocella's *Augusta miseria* (August poverty), while occasionally suffering from minor factual inaccuracies – thus he talks about Newfoundland being a part of the United States on p. 99 and Belgium having a 'Protestant government' in 1823 on p. 120 (he means the government of the Protestant-dominated Kingdom of the United Netherlands of which Belgium remained a part until it became independent in 1830) – is a serious academic study of the development of the world-wide collection of offerings for the pope, known in the English-speaking world as 'Peter's Pence', in the late nineteenth century based on research in the Vatican and other archives.[54] Benny Lai's book on the finances and financiers of the Vatican at the turn of the nineteenth and twentieth centuries, and the accompanying volume of documents, is a well-substantiated account of key developments down to 1918, using both papers in the Vatican archives and the archives of Ernesto Pacelli, the president of the Banca di Roma.[55] Other key texts are the memoirs of Francesco Pacelli, the chief negotiator of the Lateran Pacts on the Vatican side,[56] and the three volume history

---

[52] A. Scottà (ed.), *La Conciliazione Ufficiosa: diario del barone Carlo Monti 'incaricato d'affari' del governo italiano presso la Santa Sede (1914–1922)* (2 vols., Vatican City, 1997).

[53] D. Felisini, *Le finanze pontificie e i Rothschild, 1830–1870* (Naples, 1993).

[54] C. Crocella, *Augusta miseria: aspetti delle finanze pontificie nell'età del capitalismo* (Milan, 1982).

[55] Lai, *Finanze e finanzieri vaticani*; and idem (ed.), *Finanze e finanzieri vaticani tra l'Ottocento e il Novecento da Pio IX a Benedetto XV: atti e Documenti* (Milan, 1979).

[56] F. Pacelli, *Diario della Conciliazione*, ed. M. Maccarone (Vatican City, 1959).

of the Banco di Roma.[57] Giovanni Grilli's book on Vatican finance in
Italy, while frequently rather jaundiced towards the Church in a crudely
Marxist way, is also nevertheless very useful, especially on the period from
1929 onwards; in particular, it provides an insight into Nogara's acquisitions of share-holding in major Italian companies, which complements
Nogara's own diary.[58] Edward Hachey's edition of the annual reports
of the British ministers to the Vatican in the 1920s and 1930s also provides a surprising amount of information on the finances of the Vatican,
and related matters, in that period.[59] Even more unusually, the book published by the *Chicago Tribune* journalist, George Seldes, in 1935[60] actually
contains figures, estimates of the value of the Vatican's investments, its
annual income, etc., in the mid-1930s, and there is a useful pair of articles about the post-Lateran Pact finances of the Vatican by Cipolla in the
Turin daily newspaper *La Stampa* of November 1931.[61] They were based
on interviews with Nogara, and though eventually repudiated by him,[62]
their broad accuracy is supported by other sources. Another important
secondary work is Corrado Pallenberg's book on the finances of the Vatican.[63] Where possible, the original sources from which these books have
been compiled have been consulted.

But other major works on the financial history of the Vatican are not so
good. In particular, Lo Bello's *The Vatican Empire*,[64] which, while it is a
vast compendium of useful information, gleaned from usually unnamed
sources, is seriously flawed. For instance, he claims that Benardino Nogara, who counted two archbishops, the rector of a seminary and a mother
superior among his siblings, was Jewish![65] Another important American
journalistic source which owes a lot to Lo Bello is that of Gollin.[66] Even
quite recent works, like Alvarez and Graham's excellent study of German
espionage against the Vatican during the Second World War, display woe-
ful ignorance about the finances of the Vatican. According to them, during
the Second World War the economy of the Vatican was 'based on pious
donations, museum entrance fees and the sale of postage stamps'.[67] This
is quite simply untrue, as will become evident in Chapter 9.

---

[57] L. De Rosa, *Storia del Banco di Roma*, I–II (Rome, 1982–3); G. De Rosa, *Storia del Banco di Roma*, III (Rome, 1984).
[58] G. Grilli, *La finanza vaticana in Italia* (Rome, 1961).
[59] E. Hachey (ed.), *Anglo-Vatican Relations* (Boston, 1972).
[60] G. Seldes, *The Vatican – Yesterday, Today and Tomorrow* (London, 1934).
[61] A. Cipolla, 'Due giorni in Vaticano', *La Stampa*, 16 and 22 Nov. 1931.
[62] AFN, Nogara's diary, entry for 9 Dec. 1931.
[63] C. Pallenberg, *Vatican Finances* (London, 1971).
[64] N. Lo Bello, *The Vatican Empire* (New York, 1976).   [65] Ibid., p. 125.
[66] J. Gollin, *Worldly Goods: Pay Now, Die Later* (New York, 1971).
[67] D. Alvarez and R. Graham, SJ, *Nothing Sacred: Nazi Espionage against the Vatican, 1939–1945* (London and Portland, Oreg., 1997), p. x.

Another problem is that many of the secondary sources simply repeat each other, thus perpetuating the same factually inaccurate stories over the decades. The classic instance of this is to be found in one of the latest books to be published on the more recent Vatican financial scandals, Mario Guarino, *I mercanti del Vaticano* (The merchants of the Vatican),[68] which takes all of its information about the activities of Nogara from David Yallop's book on the death of Pope John Paul I, 1984;[69] this in turn takes its information (without citing the source) from Nino Lo Bello's *The Vatican Empire*. Yallop is not very reliable anyway: John Cornwell in his book *A Thief in the Night*, convincingly demolishes Yallop's fundamental thesis, his claim that John Paul I was murdered at the instigation of various Vatican personalities whose positions were threatened by the newly elected pope.[70]

One further reason for writing this book is precisely the fact that it is now possible to test many of the claims of the existing body of secondary literature against the newly available documentary sources. We thus have the opportunity, for the first time, to piece together various kinds of evidence in an effort to reconstruct with some accuracy general developments in the financial history of the Vatican, especially between the fall of Rome and the end of the Second World War, even though some of the pieces in the mosaic will, inevitably, be missing until the Vatican becomes more open in its archival policy. In addition, we have sufficient material to make some informed guesses about how the finances of the Vatican affected its international role during the early years of the Cold War.

The major themes

This book will explore a number of major themes, beginning, most obviously, with the ways in which the Vatican financed itself, especially after 1870, when it had lost the revenues of the Papal States but refused the annual compensatory payments as laid down in the Law of Papal Guarantees of 1871, and 1929 when, as an integral part of the settlement of its long-standing dispute with Italy, the 'Roman Question', it received substantial sums of money in compensation for its territorial and fiscal losses between 1859 and 1870. In broader terms, the changes in the various sources of papal financing will be traced through a succession of discrete periods. It will also examine how the Holy See managed its finances, with an especial concern for the financial competence or

---

[68] M. Guarino, *I mercanti del Vaticano, affari e scandali: l'industria delle anime* (Milan, 1998).
[69] D. Yallop, *In God's Name: An Investigation into the Murder of Pope John Paul I* (London, 1985), pp. 145–52.
[70] J. Cornwell, *A Thief in the Night: The Death of Pope John Paul I* (London, 1985).

otherwise of both the individual popes, and their ecclesiastical and lay administrators and how the Vatican spent its money. The Lateran Pacts of 1929 mark as important a watershed in the financial history of the modern papacy as the fall of Rome in 1870. Thus the book will investigate how the Vatican invested the large amount of cash, 91 million dollars at the prevailing exchange rates, which it received under the terms of the Financial Convention, under the guidance of Bernardino Nogara, how its investments were affected by the Wall Street Crash and the subsequent world-wide depression, and how Nogara put the damage right by changes in investment policy from 1932 onwards. Of equal importance will be an examination of the ways in which the Vatican's financial problems and activities affected its relations with the various parts of the Italian Church, the Catholic social and political movements in Italy, and the Italian state itself, and how those activities affected its relations with other states. As well as the 'Italian dimension', the fascinating 'American dimension' of the financial history of the Vatican in this period will be explored, with particular attention paid to its impact upon the development of the papacy as a whole.

In this period, a tension arose between, on the one hand, the tendency of the papacy, in response to the rise of industrial and finance capitalism, to enunciate a corpus of Catholic social teaching, ethical guidelines for Catholics involved in economic and social affairs and, on the other, the speculative activities carried out by investment advisers on its behalf, engaged as they were in efforts to provide financial sustenance for the work of the Holy See. The exploration of this tension is another major theme of this work, especially in the reign of Leo XIII who produced the first major papal encyclical on social matters – *Rerum Novarum* (1891) – and that of Pius XI who commemorated *Rerum Novarum* with his own encyclical, *Quadragesimo Anno* (1931) and issued two more encyclicals on the effects of the 'Great Depression'. How did their strictures on the workings of the capitalist system, especially monopoly finance capital, square with the Vatican's own speculative financial ventures in Italian, and eventually world, markets? Finally, and specifically in this context, what does the history of the finances and financiers of the Vatican between 1870 and 1950 tell us about the development of the relationship between Catholicism and capitalism on both the theoretical and practical plane? How did the papacy in this period come to terms with the realities of capital accumulation, speculation and profit?

2   The reign of Pius IX: Vatican finances before and after the fall of Rome (1850–1878)

Introduction

The pontificate of Pius IX was a momentous one in the history of the modern papacy; indeed, it could be said to have largely inaugurated it. Giovanni Mastai-Ferretti was born in Senigallia, Le Marche, in the northern Papal States and had a fairly conventional career as a papal official, apostolic delegate in South America until becoming bishop of Imola in 1823 and cardinal seventeen years later.[1] His election to the papacy in 1846 was essentially a compromise between liberal and conservative candidates, but to an Italy in patriotic ferment in the mid-1840s he was seen as a 'liberal', reforming pope. The revolutions of 1848/9 changed all that. When Pius returned from Gaeta in 1850, whence he gone to flee the revolution in Rome, he had turned decisively against the key elements in that revolution, liberalism and Italian nationalism. In 1854 he proclaimed the dogma of the Immaculate Conception of Mary; in 1864 he published the *Syllabus of Errors* (in the encyclical *Quanta Cura*) which was a comprehensive denunciation of the errors of the modern world and which concluded with the by now famous declaration that 'The Roman Pontiff could not and would not reconcile himself with progress, liberalism and modern civilisation.' In July 1870, at the end of the First Council of the Vatican, the popes were proclaimed infallible when speaking *ex cathedra* on matters of faith and morals, opening the way to a centralisation and 'Romanisation' of the Catholic Church over the following decades. Yet, if the proclamation of Infallibility marked the highpoint of the pontificate of Pius IX, it was soon followed two months later by its lowest: the siege, occupation and annexation of Rome by Italian troops. When Pius IX died in February 1878, he was still anathematising the 'sub-alpine usurper' (the King of Piedmont-Sardinia who had become monarch of united Italy) and proclaiming himself to be 'the prisoner of the Vatican'.

[1] For a biography of Pius IX in English, see F. Coppa, *Pope Pius IX: Crusader in a Secular Age* (Boston, 1979); and G. Martina's biographical essay in Levillain (ed.), *The Papacy*, II, pp. 1191–7. There is also his full-blooded studies in Italian, G. Martina, *Pio IX (1846–1851)* (Rome, 1974), *Pio IX (1851–66)* (Rome, 1986) and *Pio IX (1866–1878)* (Rome, 1990).

Illustration 1 Pope Pius IX

Papal finances, 1815–46

The financial structure of the papacy was undergoing a long process of transformation before 1870, and momentous changes had already been taking place in the way in which the Holy See financed itself before the collapse of the temporal power. Almost from its very beginnings, the papacy as an institution had derived its income from a variety of sources. With the stabilisation of control over the Papal States in the twelfth century,[2] there were essentially two major sources of papal revenue: first, from the Church as a whole, through such things as first-fruits and annates, Peter's Pence (offerings of the faithful) and fees paid to the various offices of the Roman curia by laity and clergy alike for services rendered (especially the Congregation of the Council), with occasionally special taxes, like those for the Crusades in the Middle Ages and the sale of indulgences to finance the re-building of St Peter's Basilica in Rome in the sixteenth century,[3] and secondly, from the Papal States, whose revenues came in the form of taxes upon property and trade, and other impositions. As the centuries passed, and particularly after the Reformation cut off revenues from the German lands, Scandinavia and the British Isles, the balance moved in favour of revenue from the Papal States.[4] Until 1870, 'as a property-holder par excellence, the Holy See also lived off rents, sales and investments of real estate'.[5]

When Pius IX returned from his exile in Gaeta in 1850, this system of financing was still substantially intact, but was in the process of being undermined by a number of developments which had supervened since the outbreak of the French Revolution. It can be argued that, even before 1789, the ecclesiastical reforms of enlightened despots like Joseph II of Austria had begun to undercut papal authority in various European states, and reduce the flow of revenue to Rome.[6] The Revolution's attack upon the French Church, and especially the National Assembly's law on the Civil Constitution of the Clergy of 1790, which effectively 'nationalised' the Church, and the application of French ecclesiastical legislation to conquered territories, usually led to the loss of property and income by the individual 'national' churches, and the severing of links with Rome, with a consequent drying up of the flow of revenue into the Papal Treasury. Even after the Treaty of Vienna of 1815 and the subsequent restoration of reasonably good relations with most of the European Catholic states, the papacy's income from outside of the Papal States was rather less than it had been before 1789. And in the thirty-five years that followed the Vienna settlement, the earning capacity of the Papal States declined. Despite the

[2] P. Mollat, *The Popes at Avignon: 1305–1378* (London, 1963), pp. 319–26; J. Delumeau, 'Political and Administrative Centralisation in the Papal State in the Sixteenth Century', in E. Cochrane (ed.), *The Late Italian Renaissance in Italy, 1525–1630* (London, 1970); and G. Barraclough, *The Medieval Papacy* (London, 1968), pp. 39–44 and 113–15.

[3] Delumeau, 'Political and Administrative Centralisation', pp. 120–2 and 148–9.

[4] Delumeau, 'Political and Administrative Centralisation', p. 298, where he says that 'as foreign sources of revenue dried up, the Popes were forced to find them in their own domains'.

[5] Della Cava, 'Financing the Faith', pp. 37–61.

[6] Von Aretin, *The Papacy and the Modern World*, p. 11.

Napoleonic reforms in the matter of property rights, commercial law and weights, measures and currency, and Cardinal Consalvi's attempt to carry out administrative and legal reform, and stimulate economic growth in the years following the Congress of Vienna, the economy of the pope's dominions did not flourish.[7] The picture was not all gloom and doom, however; the northern part of the Papal States, that is the Legations region around the city of Bologna, with its fertile plains and production of silk and tobacco, among other cash crops, was relatively prosperous, as was Umbria, the so-called 'garden of the Pontifical state'.[8] But other regions, especially the city of Rome and its surroundings, whose economy has been described as 'stagnant',[9] and half of whose population was essentially dependent upon governmental and Church hand-outs, were much less well off. According to Zamagni, one of the leading economic historians of modern Italy:

> If we turn to the city of Rome, we discover a singular economy with one half of the population begging for a living, while the other half, with the exception of the aristocracy and clergy – who owned all the buildings in the city, together with extensive farmland – included all those who lived from services provided for the rich, as well as visiting pilgrims and foreigners (hoteliers and petty traders), were much less well-off.[10]

In broader terms, the papal administration did little in the Restoration period to encourage economic growth, either through the improvement of agriculture or the development of industry, or through more modern financial institutions. There may even have been a *doctrinal* motive for this: when asked about matters of political economy, a member of the Papal Treasury allegedly replied that 'he refused to study works on that subject as they were pernicious and on the Index of Prohibited Books'.[11] In fact, John Stuart Mill's *Principles of Political Economy* was placed on the Index in 1856.[12] Liberalism, even economic liberalism, was still accursed Liberalism. Demarco actually says that non-agricultural activities in the Papal States declined in the first half of the nineteenth century.[13] In

---

7 Hales, *Revolution and the Papacy*, pp. 249–55; and M. Caravale and A. Caracciolo (eds.), *Lo Stato Pontificio: da Martino V a Pio IX* (Turin, 1978), pp. 625–9 and 689. Delumeau, 'Political and Administrative Centralisation', suggests that the economic malaise of the Papal States was of long-standing: on p. 304 he writes that at the beginning of the seventeenth century they 'lacked a healthy economy and a healthy society'.

8 For a fuller picture of the economy of the Papal States at this time, see Delumeau, 'Political and Administrative Centralisation', pp. 599–606.

9 V. Zamagni, *The Economic History of Italy, 1860–1990: Recovery after the Decline* (Oxford, 1993), p. 21.

10 Ibid.

11 G. Bolton King, *A History of Italian Unity* (2 vols., London, 1909), I, p. 75.

12 Seldes, *The Vatican*, p. 180.

13 D. Demarco, *Il tramonto dello stato pontificio: il papato di Gregorio XVI* (Turin, 1949).

Illustration 2 Map of the Papal States

consequence, as Hearder notes, the finances of the Papal States were in difficulty from the beginning of the Restoration period in 1815: 'Papal state finances were far from healthy, despite the immense wealth of the Papal court.'[14] So even before it was forced to confront the serious financial consequences of the Roman Republic of 1849, the papal government was obliged to resort to loans, frequently with the Rothschilds, in order to

[14] H. Hearder, *Italy in the Age of the Risorgimento, 1790–1870* (London, 1983), p. 102.

balance the books.[15] As a result, the nineteenth-century popes, like some of their medieval predecessors, became dependent upon Jewish bankers for their financial survival, thanks to the continuing Catholic prohibition against 'usury', money-lending at interest, which had been renewed by Pope Benedict XIV in his encyclical *Vix Pervenit: On Usury and Other Dishonest Profit* in 1745.[16] James de Rothschild, the head of the Paris branch of the family bank, became in effect the papal banker, and according to Cameron, 'until 1859 he was the chief financial support and agent of the Papacy'.[17] In 1832 the Rothschilds made a loan of £40,000 to the papacy and Carl Rothschild was received in audience by the pope and received the ribbon and star of the order of the newly founded order of St Gregory as a reward.[18] The Rothschilds tried to use their financial clout as leverage to bring about an amelioration in the condition of the Jews in the Papal States (see also below, p. 29) but as Ferguson points out, 'The paradox of the relationship with the Papacy was that substantial profits could only be made so long as the Holy See did NOT reform its finances, but if it could not reform its taxes, it was unlikely to reform its treatment of the Jews.'[19]

Historians have blamed the papal administration, composed almost exclusively of clergy, for the failure to improve the economic condition of the Papal States.[20] The old guard of cardinals, prelates and their lay hangers-on, those who had faithfully, and sometimes ostentatiously, refused all truck with the French occupying authorities, opposed all reform after 1815, from wherever it came. A narrow, clericalist ecclesiology pervaded the papal administration which, despite Napoleonic reforms, was not very efficient; indeed, many of the old practices were restored after 1815. All this was not helped by the *political* instability experienced by the Papal States in the Restoration period. As in many post-Napoleonic states in Europe after 1815, Italy, and especially the Papal States, saw the development of strong opposition to the system of restored, virtually absolute monarchy, which rulers had great difficulty keeping under control, despite the generous use of censorship, secret police and prison sentences for political activities.[21] In the case of the Papal States, 'vigilante forces', like the notorious *sanfedisti* and *centurioni*,

[15] R. E. Cameron, 'Papal Finance and Temporal Power (1815–1871)', *Church History*, 26 (1957), pp. 132–3.

[16] Carlen (ed.), *Papal Encyclicals*, I, pp. 15–17.   [17] Cameron, 'Papal Finance', p. 133.

[18] N. Ferguson, *The World's Banker: The History of the House of Rothschild* (London, 1998), p. 27.

[19] Ibid. p. 590.   [20] See, for example, Zamagni, *The Economic History of Italy*, p. 21.

[21] Hearder, *Italy in the Age of the Risorgimento*, pp. 103–5.

were also employed to intimidate opponents of the papal administration, especially those recruited from the new middle class in the northern parts of the pope's dominions.[22] In 1831, in the wake of the July Revolution in Paris the previous year, there were serious insurrectionary outbreaks in Bologna and other cities of the Legations, which eventually had to be suppressed by Austrian troops.[23] Even after the election of a new pope in 1831, Gregory XVI, the papal government effectively ignored the memorandum of the European Powers demanding administrative reform, especially the partial laicisation of the bureaucracy.[24] Gregory and his advisers used the 1831 uprisings as an excuse for their continued mishandling of the finances of the Papal States, and the disorder in the finances actually got worse: no budgets or balance sheets were published between 1833 and 1846, nor were there any records from which a balance sheet could be reconstructed.[25] Dissent continued and revolutionary organisations continued to spread through the remainder of 1830s and early 1840s.[26] By the outbreak of the French Revolution of 1848, the Papal States were ripe for revolution, especially its major cities, Bologna and Rome. Not even the election of someone who was thought to be a liberal pope, Pius IX in 1846, and his package of liberal reforms – including a constitution – was able to resolve the deep-seated political conflicts or satisfy the revolutionary movements in Rome, whose agitations finally culminated in the murder of Rossi, the pope's prime minister, the pope's flight from the Eternal City and the formation of the Roman Republic in 1849.

Reforming governments were costly: Rossi imposed a tax on ecclesiastical landed property in order to pay for the papal contingent to the Italian forces fighting to liberate Italy from Austrian rule in the north, and to deal with the financial consequences of the general European economic crisis.[27] Revolutionary government was also costly, more so. Short-lived though it was to be, the rule of Giuseppe Mazzini, the 'father of Italian nationalism', over the Roman Republic was benign, moderate and reforming. Within a few months, the government of the Republic had increased the public debt from 4,920,000 scudi to 8,798,000 scudi or 30 million francs,[28] and issued non-convertible paper currency.[29] In order to eliminate the Republic's paper money, which had declined in value by

[22] S. J. Woolf, *A History of Italy: 1700–1860: The Social Constraints of Political Change* (London, 1979), p. 317.
[23] Ibid., p. 272.   [24] Hales, *Revolution and the Papacy*, pp. 268–9.
[25] Cameron, 'Papal Finance', p. 133.
[26] See M. D'Azeglio, *Gli ultimi fatti della Romagna* (Turin, 1846).
[27] Caravale and Caracciolo, *Lo Stato Pontificio*, pp. 652–4.
[28] Cameron, 'Papal Finance', p. 134.   [29] Ibid.

35 per cent, resort was made to the first of another series of major loans from the Rothschilds.[30]

Giacomo Antonelli as administrator of the papal finances

The return of Pius IX to Rome, in 1850, following the defeat of Garibaldi's defence of the Roman Republic by French troops, quickly brought with it the ascent to power of one of the first major papal financiers, Giacomo Antonelli, later Cardinal Secretary of State, who was to administer the Papal Treasury from 1850 to his death in 1876. Antonelli came from a middle-class family (which he later had ennobled) with long service in the papal administration, and he began his career in 1830 in the courts of Rome. After a period as a delegate or governor in the provinces, he returned to the capital in 1840 and became Under-Secretary for Internal Affairs.[31] Antonelli is a very controversial historical figure,[32] who has frequently been presented as a disreputable character, immoral and at the same time financially rapacious – for example, according to Hearder, 'If Pius IX seemed reminiscent of the age of the Counter-reformation and Tiepolo, Antonelli was an equally anachronistic reminder of the age of the Borgias.'[33] There was certainly something quite unprepossessing about this cleric – he never reached beyond deacon's orders – who seems to have exercised a powerful influence over Pius IX in his later, reactionary years. He has, in particular, been blamed for encouraging the intransigent hostility of Pius IX to Italian nationalism, liberalism and just about everything else that was new and modern about the world in the mid-nineteenth century.[34] In one sense, he was a very appropriate leading representative of the Roman curia of his time, which was run by a clerical elite that was both narrow in its outlook on the world and largely the product of a self-perpetuating ruling oligarchy who grew fat on their enjoyment of office. His brother, Filippo, for example, made a particularly large fortune by creating Rome's first savings bank, the Banca Romana. Whereas the new landed and commercial classes elsewhere in the Papal States, especially

---

[30] Ferguson, *The World's Banker*, p. 590.

[31] F. Coppa, *Cardinal Giacomo Antonelli and Papal Politics in European Affairs* (New York, 1990), pp. 22–3.

[32] For biographies, see ibid., and C. Falconi, *Il cardinale Antonelli: vita e carriera del Richelieu italiano nella Chiesa di Pio IX* (Milan, 1983).

[33] Hearder, *Italy in the Age of the Risorgimento*, p. 119: for a fuller evaluation of Antonelli, see Chadwick, *A History of the Popes*, pp. 92–6.

[34] Coppa, *Cardinal Giacomo Antonelli*, p. 5; and Martina, *Pio IX (1851–1866)*, pp. 227–8, where he says that Pius became markedly less intransigent after the death of Antonelli in 1876.

in the Legations, became increasingly opposed to papal and ecclesiastical rule, the local nobility and middle class of Rome and Latium that worked for the papacy and supplied most of its personnel, ecclesiastical or lay, remained loyal almost to the end.[35]

On the other hand, Antonelli did bring about a reform of the financial administration of the Papal States. He had first demonstrated his financial abilities in 1845, when he organised the 'Leuchtenberg operation', the purchase for the Holy See of a vast land-holding in the Marche provinces of the Papal States.[36] After 1850, he separated the financial administration of the Papal Court and Roman curia from that of the States and commenced a re-structuring of the national debt. In 1858, that is on the eve of the invasion of the Papal States by the victorious armies of Piedmont, the finances of the Papal States still recorded a budget deficit of 2,537,798 scudi, because of the demands of debt-servicing.[37] In attempting to balance the budget, Antonelli was faced by equally unpleasant alternatives – seeking foreign loans, very expensive, or increasing taxation, which was likely to damage further the economy, and increase the grievances of the pope's subjects. But he did it. In 1859, by increasing existing taxation and introducing new ones, he balanced the budget, and with resort once again to the Rothschilds, in 1857 he succeeded in consolidating all of the various debts and loan accounts of the Papal States into a single debt to be redeemed in stages by 1901.[38] All in all, the Rothschilds' gave the loan on very generous terms. Though Pius IX agreed to abolish the ghetto, into which the Jews of Rome had been obliged to return after the pope's return from Gaeta, he successfully resisted other reforms and also refused to pledge the Church's landed property as collateral.[39] Antonelli's success in balancing the budget was achieved despite the extra costs incurred for the building of a thousand kilometres of railway, though this was, admittedly, rather a modest achievement by comparison with railway-building elsewhere. Pius IX rather enjoyed a train ride, whereas his predecessor had condemned railways – Gregory XVI is reputed to have said 'chemin de fer, chemin d'enfer' (roughly translated: 'the iron road is the road to hell').

The effects of Italian unification, 1859–61

The progress which Antonelli had achieved in the financial sphere was soon swept away by the momentous events in Italy of 1859 to 1861. In

[35] Caravale and Caracciolo, *Lo Stato Pontificio*, pp. 605–6.
[36] Felisini, *Le finanze pontificie*, p. 82.   [37] Ibid. pp. 166–71.
[38] Cameron, 'Papal Finance', pp. 134–5.   [39] Ferguson, *The World's Banker*, p. 590.

those years, aided initially by French military support, the Kingdom of Piedmont-Sardinia under Camillo Cavour's premiership succeeded in carrying through the first stage of Italian unification, and in March 1861 the Kingdom of Italy was proclaimed under the sovereignty of Victor Emmanuel II of Piedmont-Sardinia. The Habsburg Empire lost the immensely wealthy region of Lombardy in 1859, and the Bourbons of Naples lost their entire kingdom in 1860, but the papacy was also a sizeable victim of this first stage in the creation of a united Italy: further campaigns brought in the Veneto in 1866, and Rome and its surroundings in 1870. More than two-thirds of the Papal States, including its richest regions, the Legations and Umbria, and 76 per cent of its population, were taken from the pope, and his sovereign possessions were reduced to Latium, the largely agriculturally stagnant region around the city of Rome, also known as the 'Patrimony of St Peter'. As Cameron describes it:

The position of the finance minister in the government of the Pope in the 1860's was not an easy one. In a state with an area and population less than that of a small German duchy, he was called upon to service a debt which ranked in size with that of some of the major powers of Europe.[40]

In fact, his comparison is a little exaggerated: most German duchies were considerably *smaller* than the remnant of the Papal States in population and area. This despoliation of its territory had serious effects on the finances of the papacy. Clearly, the loss of the commercially and agriculturally rich northern regions of the Papal States drastically reduced its tax revenue figures, and to make matters worse, it was not until 1864 that the Italian government secretly agreed to take over responsibility for two-thirds of the debts of the Papal States, in line with its occupation of territory, but this arrangement was not to commence until 1868.[41] On the other hand, the actual expenditure of the remaining Papal States was increased as a result of the need to provide for their security against a further Italian military threat. In this, Monsignor Merode, the pope's 'minister of war' was zealous in seeking to create a large papal army, partly of volunteers and partly of mercenaries. Again, it was not until the convention of 1864, by which Italy agreed not to attack the pope's remaining territory, a guarantee underwritten by the French, that the pope could have any military security and consequently reduce military spending. An additional cost was the continued payment of the former servants of the papal government in the provinces now under Italian rule, which Pius IX insisted on as a matter of honour, but which also indirectly bolstered his claim to the lost territories of the Papal States. Meanwhile, the

---

[40] Cameron, 'Papal Finance', p. 137.   [41] Ibid., p. 136.

generosity of Catholics throughout the world came to the rescue: from 1860 onwards, the revival of Peter's Pence, the goodwill offerings of the faithful helped bridge the huge gap that had opened up between income and expenditure in the papal budget.

Peter's Pence

The revival of Peter's Pence, or the *Obolo*, as it is called in Italian, was a largely spontaneous response of the Catholic clergy and laity throughout the world, to the pope's plight in 1860. Credit for first launching the appeal for funds for the pope has been claimed on behalf of Montalembert, whose speech in the Chamber of Peers in 1848 is said to have been the first appeal for Catholics to rally financially to the pope.[42] Given that Peter's Pence originated in Anglo-Saxon England, appropriately enough another theory is that it was a London Catholic journal, probably *The Tablet*, which first urged Catholics to help the beleaguered pontiff.[43] Similar appeals in the capitals of Catholic states, Vienna and Paris, other European countries and even in parts of North and South America were made by bishops, clergy and laity alike.[44] The contributors to Peter's Pence included both clergy and laity, rich and powerful, sometimes so rich and powerful that they included the Comte de Chambord, pretender to the throne of France, the Emperor Maximilian of Mexico and other Austrian archdukes, Roman princes, the bourgeoisie, but also the poor: sometimes it really was a case of the 'widow's mite'.[45] And it was not only individuals who gave; religious communities, Catholic associations and Catholic journals all organised collections. Given the origin of the pope's unhappy plight, the invasion of Piedmontese forces, the revival of Peter's Pence was inextricably linked to the appeals for *military* support to defend the last remnant of the Papal States from the threat of a further Italian invasion. At the same time as appeals were made for financial support for the pope, Catholic men were also being asked to enrol as volunteers in his armed forces. Frequently, offerings were made specifically to equip, feed or pay these volunteers, and some of the money was deducted in the country of origin to defray the expenses of the young bent on going to Rome.[46] A classic refrain in the notes which accompanied the offerings of

---

[42] Crocella, *Augusta miseria*, p. 93: much of this section is based on Crocella's work.
[43] M. De Leonardis, *L'Inghilterra e la questione romana: 1859–1870* (Milan, 1981), p. 89.
[44] Crocella, *Augusta miseria*, pp. 95–9.
[45] See the examples cited in B. Horaist, *La dévotion au papa et les catholiques français sous le pontificat de Pie IX (1846–1878). D'après les archives de la bibliothèque apostolique vaticane* (Rome, 1995), pp. 52–3.
[46] Ibid.

the faithful was the words 'for the maintenance of the Zouaves', volunteer papal soldiers.[47] Increasingly, Peter's Pence offerings sent to Rome were directed to the support of the Belgian monsignor De Merode's Ministry of War.[48]

Over the next few years, the collection of Peter's Pence was put on an increasingly organised basis in many countries and according to Crocella, 'The collection for the *Obolo*, spread rapidly in a kind of competition which involved the whole Catholic world.'[49] Initially, the chief contributors to Peter's Pence were Catholics in European states, with French Catholics way ahead, as can be seen from Table 1. France's outstanding primacy in this table was due both to her still being, in some measure, 'the eldest daughter of the Church' and also to her being the wealthiest country on the mainland of Europe, in the period before Germany became fully industrialised. Belgium, though very much smaller in population, was also industrialised and prosperous, as well as being an overwhelmingly Catholic country. The pattern of industrialisation at this time also helps to explain why Germany, and even Austria-Hungary, which as yet had few major industrial areas, contributed so little in proportion to the numbers of Catholics which they contained, and especially in relation to their role as major contributors to Vatican finances by 1914.

The change in the picture for the United States of America between 1864 and 1870 was thanks to the US bishops, gathered together in the Second Plenary Council of Baltimore in 1866, who 'expressed the need of the present pontiff for his patrimony. Furthermore, the bishops condemned those who had sacrilegiously taken away from the patrimony and they decreed an annual collection for the Pope's needs.'[50] After 1870, America made an increasingly large contribution to Peter's Pence, as befitted a country with a growing Catholic population.

The full significance of the growing phenomenon of Peter's Pence needs to be grasped. It was not simply a financial expedient that helped keep the central government of the Catholic Church afloat, contributed to the defence of the remaining Papal States and thus upheld the honour and dignity of the pope. It did all of those things, but it also had a profound effect upon the role of the pope himself, and his relation to the faithful. Crocella has made the point that the motives for the faithful sending money varied from country to country: for many French Catholics, for instance, it was a way of protesting against Napoleon III's equivocal policy towards the papacy and its temporal power: for Italian Catholics, too,

[47] Ibid., p. 99.   [48] Ibid.   [49] Ibid., p. 108.
[50] T. T. McAvoy, CSC, *A History of the Church in the United States* (South Bend, Ill., 1969), p. 201.

Table I *The source and the amount of Peter's Pence*

Nation or geographical area	1864 amount in scudi	Percentage	1870 (Jan.–Aug.) amount in francs	Percentage
France	510,995,781	47.13	2,589,671.65	40.90
Italy	134,430,009	12.40	502,204.59	7.93
Spain	110,934,562	10.23	211,680.49	3.34
Belgium	38,460,310	3.55	545,330	8.61
Holland	37,460,310	3.44	348,718.37	5.51
Germany	15,980,381	1.47	79,855.25	3.12
Austria	31,847,1852.94	2.94	79,885.80	1.26
Ireland	14,055,185	1.30	122,058.80	1.93
Breslau and Poland	16,930,000	1.56	34,926	0.55
Other European states	17,627,761	1.63	87,143.45	1.38
Total for Europe	928,605,647	85.65	4,718,844.49	74.53
Chile	10.93	—	20,880	0.33
Argentina	—	—	15,015.37	0.24
Brazil	2,087,125	0.19	31,835.30	0.50
Mexico	16,777,200	1.55	15,000	0.24
USA	826,400	0.08	96,587.09	1.52
Canada	12,045,765	1.11	71,984	1.14
Other American states	794,000	0.07	69,370.05	5.06
Total for the Americas	32,541,420	3.00	320,671.81	5.06
India	1,692,440	0.15	17,557.25	0.28
Other Asiatic countries	—	—	65,638.10	1.04
Australia and Oceania	94,900	0.01	36,690	0.58
Africa	2,359,360	0.22	2,625	0.04
Total Non-European	4,146,700	0.38	122,510.35	1.94
Anonymous and uncertain nationality	118,906,269	10.97	1,169,250.62	18.47
Total	1,084,200,063	100.00	6,331,277.27	100.00

Source: Crocella, *Augusta miseria*, pp. 126–7.

it was a way of registering their opposition to the ecclesiastical policies of the Liberal regime. In consequence, Liberal-radical political forces, especially in Italy, strongly opposed the collections and sought by means of legislation to impede their despatch to Rome.[51] It was also the first opportunity for the Catholic faithful to play an active, and usually public, part in the life of their Church; it thus represented a kind of 'democratisation' of the Church, which was an interesting and ironical response to the French Revolution and all its works, liberalism, nationalism and democracy itself. In this way, Pio Nono was also effectively appealing over the

[51] Crocella, *Augusta miseria*, p. 169.

heads of Catholic monarchs and other heads of state who had responded in a lukewarm way, if at all to his plight. Thus contributing to the collection of Peter's Pence constituted a first form of mass 'Catholic action', portending the emergence of a mass Catholic movement which, in its various forms would later in the nineteenth and in the early twentieth centuries become a major auxiliary to the activity of the hierarchy and especially of the pope.

It was in a broader sense a means for the faithful to assert their Catholic identity in a new way, that is by expressing solidarity with the earthly head of their religion in a very tangible form. Pilgrimages to Rome would later also play their part, the development of railways and steamships making it much easier for large numbers of pilgrims to reach the Eternal City and, ironically, this was assisted by the new Italian state's policy of nation-building by 'stitching up the boot' through the completion of Italy's railway system.[52] This inevitably meant that the relationship between the pope and the faithful, even before the formal proclamation of Infallibility at the First Council of the Vatican in 1870, changed markedly. Whereas, hitherto, the pope in Rome had been a very insubstantial figure, more of a symbol than a real person, now he acquired real personality and the faithful, by making their offerings to him, developed emotions and feelings towards him in an individual way.[53] Pius IX, at least in regard to the more generous and munificent donors, reciprocated: papal benedictions, framed letters and papal titles of nobility and knighthoods began to be distributed well beyond the confines of the Roman provinces, and the numbers of non-Italians awarded the coveted honorary post of papal 'chamberlain' grew rapidly after the beginning of the 1860s (see below, Chapter 3, pp. 48–9). The fortuitous invention and spread of photography around mid-century aided the process. Pictures of the pope were now widely circulated, some individuals receiving signed copies, all of which strongly contributed to the 'personalisation' of the relationship between the believer and the head of his/her religion. The process would take a further twist after 1870 when the myth of 'the prisoner of the Vatican' was disseminated to the poor faithful by means of very graphic illustrations. Some less savoury aspects of this phenomenon were the genuine belief of some of the faithful that the pope was chained to the wall by Italian shackles and 'An enterprising fraud even sold as relics straw from the palliasse of his cell.'[54] Thus began the cult of the 'victim-pope' that was

[52] Horaist, *La dévotion au pape*, pp. 57–9.
[53] A. Vecchi, 'Linee di spiritualità nei documenti pontifici da Pio IX a Pio XII sull'azione cattolica', in anon., *Spiritualità e azione del laicato italiano* (2 vols., Padua, 1969), I, pp. 97–8.
[54] Chadwick, *A History of the Popes*, p. 24.

to endure until 1929, and to re-appear at times of crisis thereafter, as in 1931, during the conflict between Pius XI and Mussolini, and in 1948, during the heavily polarised Italian general elections of that year when Pius XII feared a Communist victory and its consequences.

At the very time that the Vatican was seeking to 'Romanise' the daughter churches, and especially the new ones like those in North America, Australia and Oceania, the development of Peter's Pence was bringing about a parallel process of the 'internationalisation' of the Church as a community and organisation. Thus Rome's success in demanding obedience from local hierarchies on matters of Infallibility, disciplinary and organisational, and to a lesser extent, liturgical uniformity, was assisted by a growing sense on the part of the laity that they belonged to a truly *universal* Church, embodied in its head, the pope.

Making ends meet between 1859 and 1870

It has been estimated that between 1859 and 1870, the offerings of the faithful of the world brought about an average of 8 million lire a year into the Papal Treasury.[55] Admittedly, this varied according to events. Thus when the pressure seemed to be off the Papal States, such as in 1864 when the Italian government signed the September Convention with France guaranteeing the pope's possession of Rome, or after Garibaldi's failed attempt to attack Rome at Mentana, 1867, the size of offerings temporarily declined. Despite the fluctuations, Peter's Pence quickly became a major prop to the normal financing of the government of the Papal States: by 1864 it was providing a large part of the overall revenue of the state. However, the total revenue from Peter's Pence in the years 1859–62 was barely sufficient to plug the annual deficit.[56] And though it had originally been intended for *special* purposes, like the increased military expenses (mainly for the Zouaves or volunteer army) and Pius IX's charitable funds (300,000 lire), it was more and more used to cover the normal expenses of the state – including public works, welfare relief and day-to-day administration.[57] In addition, the regularity of its receipt inevitably turned it into a sort of collateral for the various loans which were contracted or launched in the period between 1860 and 1864. The first, of the usual, rather old-fashioned type, was contracted with Rothschild's bank, and it was to be the last with that Jewish financial institution.[58] Indeed, it is surprising that the loan got off the ground at all considering the background against which the negotiations were conducted. Two years earlier,

[55] Felisini, *Le finanze pontificie*, p. 183 fn. 35.
[56] Cameron, 'Papal Finance', p. 13.   [57] Crocella, *Augusta miseria*, pp. 114–15.
[58] Letter to the author from the keeper of the Rothschild archive, London, 27 Nov. 1998.

Pio Nono's insistence that a Jewish boy from Bologna, Edgardo Mortara, baptised secretly by his parents' Christian maidservant, be taken away from his home and brought up as a Catholic, caused a scandal.[59] By the end of 1858, the case had become an international *cause célèbre* with even Christian sovereigns and governments calling for the restitution of the child, which the pope stubbornly refused.[60] It is not known whether the Rothschilds used their strong bargaining position in an attempt to obtain the release of Mortara, but they did seek to ameliorate, without success, the notoriously bad living conditions of the Jews of Rome, who unlike Jews virtually anywhere else in Western Europe, were still strictly confined to their over-crowded ghetto.[61] Another factor that contributed to an attenuation of relations between the Rothschilds and the Vatican was the financial support given by the Jewish banking family to the Kingdom of Piedmont-Sardinia, later the Kingdom of Italy, which reflected their growing sympathy with the Liberal-nationalist cause.[62] But the Rothschilds were fairly canny in political terms and sought to avoid public clashes with the Church as in the saga of assisting in the operation to liquidate the ecclesiastical property taken over by the Italian state in the 1860s.[63]

Though Pius IX had tried to raise money in 1860 without recourse to bankers, by a direct appeal to the laity of France, the main burden of organising the 1860 loan was carried by two Catholic bankers, Blount and Bouillière, supported by the Rothschilds,[64] because Napoleon III's government would not allow such an operation outside of French banking regulations.[65] The 1860 loan would not suffice, and within two years, it was necessary to raise another loan. This time the French bishops preached up the loan, urging Catholics to subscribe on the grounds that 'in doing a good work, the faithful . . . will at the same time be making an advantageous investment' and the bishop of Autun went so far as to assure them that the 'Pope is a good risk'.[66] Rarely have religious faith and capitalistic speculation been so closely inter-twined! In 1864 yet a third loan, whose 'selling' to European Catholic faithful, according to Crocella, 'bore a close resemblance to the preaching of a crusade' was launched.[67]

[59] For the full story, see D. Kertzer, *The Kidnapping of Edgardo Mortara* (New York, 1997).
[60] Chadwick, *A History of the Popes*, pp. 130–1.
[61] D. Kertzer, *The Popes against the Jews: The Vatican's Role in the Rise of Modern Anti-semitism* (New York, 2001), pp. 118–25.
[62] Ferguson, *The World's Banker*, pp. 403–4.   [63] Ibid., pp. 686–7.
[64] Cameron, 'Papal Finance', p. 137.   [65] Ibid.   [66] Ibid.
[67] Crocella, *Augusta miseria*, p. 42; and V. Viaene, 'Catholic Mobilisation and Papal Diplomacy during the Pontificate of Pius IX (1846–1878)', in E. Lamberts (ed.), *The Black International, 1870–1878: The Holy See and Militant Catholicism in Europe* (Leuven, 2001), p. 149.

Cameron says that the French bishops 'insisted on making this a test of religious faith', yet there is evidence that some French bishops were unhappy with the constant appeals for Catholics to subscribe to loans in support of the Papal States.[68] The plea for Catholics to subscribe to the papal loan rather undercut appeals for them to contribute to Peter's Pence. Even worse, the 1864 loan subscriptions were rather fewer than had been expected and hoped for.[69]

During the course of the 1860s, Catholic financiers made several proposals to replace this rather precarious loan-financing basis to the finances of the Papal States by more 'modern' capitalistic schemes. The first proposal was for a massive, world-wide lottery that would replace Peter's Pence itself: instead of making their offerings to the pope, the faithful would buy tickets in the lottery which the authors of the schemes believed would raise 50 million francs per year, 40 million of which would go into the Papal Treasury.[70] The Vatican said 'no' to a fundraising device which, however, in the simpler form of Bingo, became the financial mainstay of many Catholic parishes in the late twentieth century. Though the revenues from Peter's Pence fluctuated from year to year, they were well established and assured. In any case, they very effectively mobilised the support of the Catholic faithful, which a lottery might not have done. A similar scheme was proposed by the Belgian banker, Langrand-Dumonceau, who had been largely responsible for the 1864 loan to the papacy. By the end of the 1850s he was something of a Catholic financial tycoon, with twenty banks, other credit institutions and insurance companies to his name, and was in the process of negotiating a scheme with the Catholic hierarchy of Hungary to sell the landed property of the Church there in exchange for bonds issued by the Agricultural Credit Bank of Brussels.[71] One of Langrand-Dumonceau's other ambitious schemes was to capitalise the landed property of the Church in the Papal States, on the lines of the scheme he was negotiating in Hungary.[72] This too was rejected. Finally, in 1868, Langrand-Dumonceau and his friends came up with the idea of issuing 'Roman Bonds' as a way of investing the revenue of Peter's Pence on a world-wide basis, with no more success than for the earlier proposals.[73] One obvious danger was that this scheme, were it to be successful, might have given quite the opposite impression to the faithful: that the pope, far from being necessitous of financial support, was actually rich. Even more modest proposals

---

[68] Ibid., pp. 148–9.
[69] Cameron, 'Papal Finance', p. 138.   [70] Crocella, *Augusta miseria*, p. 62.
[71] G. Jacquemyns, *Langrand-Dumonceau: promoteur d'une puissance financière catholique* (5 vols., Brussels, 1960–5), V, pp. 343–4.
[72] Ibid., p. 291.   [73] Ibid.

in 1863 to help stimulate the economy of the Papal States by establishing a credit bank for agriculture and a joint stock company to take the burden of carrying out necessary infra-structural works in the pope's dominions were rejected by the papal administration.[74]

What was the underlying cause of the rejection of these various attempts to draw the capital of Catholic ecclesiastical institutions, and especially of the papacy, into more productive channels of investment, in other words to insert the Church into the capitalist system? Ecclesiastical indifference, indolence or inertia? There was almost certainly an element of all of these, but as Crocella suggests, the strongest factor was probably a deep-seated suspicion and hostility in Vatican circles towards capitalistic devices.[75] Langrand-Dumonceau, as well as underlining the enormous financial benefits that his schemes would bring to the Church, enunciated a very idealistic rationale for them as well. With pointed reference to the financial power of successful Jewish and Protestant competitors, the Belgian banker urged 'that his gigantic dream of a true Christianity would be realised and religion would be regenerated'.[76] He and his colleagues were trying to do nothing less than to reconcile Catholicism and capitalism, trying to persuade the papacy to come into the nineteenth century and embrace the modern, capitalistic world, or in the case of his schemes, a sanitised, Christian version of it, but he failed. Rome remained conservative and cautious and that was probably the best policy because in 1870 Langrand-Dumonceau went catastrophically bankrupt. Had it agreed to any of his schemes, the finances of the Vatican would have suffered with him. But things would ultimately change. The papacy's attitude to involvement in capitalist ventures would eventually become more relaxed as will be seen in the next chapter.

The Papal States and Latin Monetary Union

The Papal States had to endure one more humiliating episode, thanks to their virtually bankrupt condition, before their final elimination in September 1870. One hundred and forty years before the emergence of the European Monetary Union, a smaller precursor appeared on the scene – the Latin Monetary Union.[77] Bringing together the French,

---

[74] Ibid.

[75] Crocella, *Augusta miseria*, pp. 59–60; and Viaene, 'Catholic Mobilisation', p. 148.

[76] Jacquemyns, *Langrand-Dumonceau*, v, pp. 468–72, 'Mémoire secret sur la piussance catholique financière a former'.

[77] The most up-to-date study of the LMU is to be found in L. Einaudi, *Money and Politics: European Monetary Unification and the International Gold Standard (1865–1873)* (Oxford, 2001).

Belgian and Swiss francs, and the Italian lira, the Union came into force in 1866 and provided that the gold and silver coinage of the three states should be inter-changeable. Anxious not to suffer the economic (especially commercial) effects of exclusion from the LMU and espying a possible way out of the Papal States' financial difficulties, in June 1866 Antonelli hurried through an abandonment of the scudo in favour of the decimal lira, and adhesion to the Union.[78] Relying on the goodwill of Napoleon III's government in Paris, and with a ruthlessness and unscrupulousness unusual even for him, Antonelli embarked on a massive increase in the coining of silver coins with less than the prescribed amount of the necessary metal: 'The Pontifical State with a population of between 500 and 700,000, had coined as much as Belgium which had a population of five million.'[79] In the short term, the excess circulation of debased papal coinage in the other countries of the Union was tolerated, and brought considerable benefits to the Papal States, but it inevitably prompted Swiss and French banks to reject papal coins, and eventually led to the ejection of the Papal States from the Union. Indeed, it could be argued that the financial difficulties of the Papal States, along with those of its neighbour the Kingdom of Italy, which had made its currency unconvertible, ultimately led to the collapse of this the first serious attempt towards the achievement of a common European monetary system.

The fall of Rome

By 1870, notwithstanding Peter's Pence and the foreign loans, the Papal Treasury still could not make ends meet. With a public debt of 20 million lire,[80] the financial problems of the Papal States were insoluble, short of a miracle or an equally miraculous massive regeneration of the economy, like the reclamation of the Roman *campagna*, the countryside surrounding Rome, and the conversion of the Church's remaining landed property into more profitable investments. More fundamentally, it was due to a refusal on the part of the ecclesiastical rulers of one of the last theocracies in human history to come to terms with the modern world, and in particular the increasingly capitalistic organisation of the world's economy. The capture of Rome by the Italians came, therefore, as a blessed release from an impossible burden; it was, as Crocella says 'an advantageous defeat' from the financial point of view.[81]

[78] Ibid., p. 9.   [79] Ibid., p. 104.
[80] Crocella, *Augusta miseria*, p. 66.   [81] Ibid., p. 155.

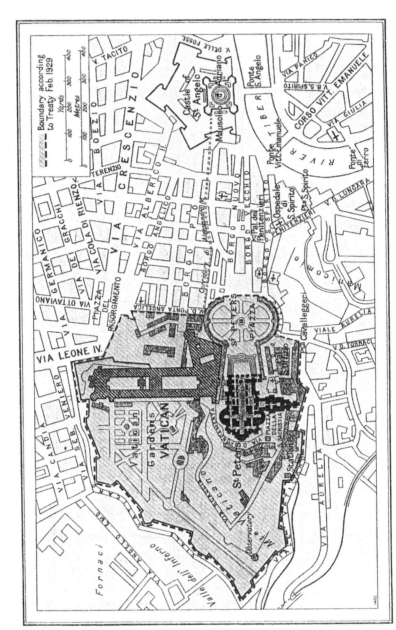

Illustration 3 Rome and the Vatican

On 20 September 1870, Italian troops led by General Cadorna breached the walls of Rome at Porta Pia. The papal forces, under orders from the pope, quickly laid down their arms. Papal Rome was no more, the more than a thousand-year-old pontifical state had finally been destroyed. Surrounded by the foreign ambassadors to the Holy See, Pius IX waited anxiously in the Vatican and declared himself to be its 'prisoner': thus a great myth was born, and with it, a new era in the history of the papacy, and its relations with the Italian state. In particular, a new chapter would be written in the story of the 'Roman Question', that great conflict between them which would complicate Italy's foreign relations and poison its domestic politics for nearly sixty years.[82] But a new chapter in the financial history of the papacy also began in 1870. Stripped of the income from the former Papal States, the pope would henceforth be almost wholly reliant upon the offerings of the faithful throughout the world, and upon the successful investment of those offerings.

The aftermath of 1870 and the Law of Guarantees

In the aftermath of the Italian capture of Rome, it became clear that the Italians had orders *not* to enter the Leonine City,[83] that is the area of Rome between the Tiber and the Vatican itself, sometimes referred to as the Borgo but not exactly coterminous with it, which was enclosed by walls. This was presumably in an endeavour to persuade the pope to resign himself to accepting this area as his new 'kingdom'. One can only speculate that had the Italians stuck to their orders, then history might have been different, and much of the pain and anguish of the 'Roman Question' might have been avoided. But it was not to be so. Whether because he presciently realised that the loss of the temporal power was complete and probably desirable, or for his stated reason that only the presence of Italian troops in the Borgo would prevent anti-clerical tumults threatening the Vatican, Antonelli asked Cadorna to occupy the Leonine City. Filippo Mazzonis has argued that their subsequent complaints and demands for a restoration of the temporal power notwithstanding, Antonelli and the pope saw the loss of the Papal States as an inevitable but necessary opportunity for the Church to adjust to the modern world by becoming a wholly international institution.[84] With Italy and the Italians (not always very pleasantly) now under his very windows in the Vatican, Pius IX embarked upon an intransigent policy towards the 'despoiling', 'usurping' Italian

---

[82] J. F. Pollard, *The Vatican and Italian Fascism, 1929–1932: A Study in Conflict* (Cambridge, 1985), p. 1.
[83] Chadwick, *A History of the Popes*, p. 217; and Martina, *Pio IX (1866–1978)*, pp. 237–8.
[84] Mazzonis, 'Pio IX, il tramonto del potere temporale', pp. 260–2.

state and its rulers, whom he regularly excommunicated for their 'sacrilege'. In particular, he absolutely rejected the Law of Papal Guarantees which the Italian Parliament passed in May 1871 to regulate relations with the papacy after the fall of the temporal power.

It is arguable that Pius's policy was nothing new, merely a continuation of his policy prior to Rome's capture: previous attempts to persuade him voluntarily to renounce the temporal power, in 1860, had failed. The application of a modified form of the Piedmontese ecclesiastical legislation of 1853 to the newly conquered territories between 1859 and 1870, as a result of which most of the property of religious benefices, including collegiate churches, cathedral chapters and bishoprics, plus the religious orders, was transferred to the management of the state in return for a fixed annual payment, simply confirmed him in his hostility towards the new Italian state.[85] Fortified by the support of the bishops of the world in the First Council of the Vatican (1869–70), and in particular their nearly unanimous acclamation of the doctrine of papal Infallibility, Pius felt invulnerable against the slings and arrows of outrageous fortune. Between 1860 and 1878, he made no less than six formal, public protests against the loss of the temporal power, including three encyclicals.[86] There was also an element of the 'martyr' or 'victim-pope' about him, as he faced his enemies across the Tiber: not unlike the defiance of Pius XII when threatened by a possible victory of the Marxist Left in the Italian general elections of 1948 and his prediction of the consequent likely arrival of the Cossacks in St Peter's Square.[87] After all, this was merely entering into the logic of the history of the papacy since St Peter and some of his early successors had been physically martyred.

Yet the Law of Guarantees was an honest effort on the part of Cavour's political successors, the liberal-conservative government of the Right, to achieve a resolution of the Roman Question conflict, following his fundamental principle 'A Free Church in a Free State.'[88] Though, of course, Pius rejected in principle the right of a secular state to limit his sovereignty, and though he might suspiciously regard the Law as an attempt to turn him into 'the chaplain of the King of Italy', it contained a number of clauses that came close to satisfying his needs as the head of the Roman Catholic Church throughout the world. His status as 'sovereign pontiff' was recognised by Italian law and he was to be accorded the same honours and privileges as the Italian king, and the inviolability of his person was protected by the same sanctions as protected the king. The

---

[85] A. C. Jemolo, *Church and State in Italy, 1850–1950* (Oxford, 1960), p. 25.
[86] Carlen (ed.), *Papal Encyclicals*, I, p. xxvi.
[87] O. Logan, 'Pius XII: Romanità, Prophesy and Charisma', *Modern Italy*, 3 (1998), p. 237.
[88] Jemolo, *Church and State*, pp. 34–9.

Vatican, the papal summer villa at Castelgandolfo in the Alban Hills to the south-east of Rome and various other palaces and buildings in Rome used by the Roman curia were granted for his exclusive use and, moreover, were exempt from the jurisdiction of the officials of the Italian state (in effect, they therefore enjoyed the *extra-territorial* status of embassies and other diplomatic buildings). The pope was guaranteed free communication with the Church throughout the world, and diplomatic envoys to the Holy See were granted the same immunities and privileges as those enjoyed by diplomats accredited to Italy: all this was also to apply during the *sede vacante*, the vacancy in the office of the Holy See between the death of one pope and the election of his successor.[89] In addition, the Italian state abandoned various privileges in relation to its control over the functioning of the Church in the Italian peninsula like the *regio placet* and *exequatur* in the matter of appointment to bishoprics.[90]

As far as the financing of the papacy was concerned, the Law of Guarantees made provision for the losses of the Holy See resulting from the ending of the temporal power: in addition to a generous annual subsidy of 3.225 million lire in perpetuity (to replace the 'civil list' previously granted by the government of the Papal States), exemption from all forms of Italian taxation was granted to the congregations, offices and administrations of the Roman curia and to their dependencies.[91]

This was a law which the anti-clerical Left in the Italian Parliament had regarded as generous, and they opposed it with appropriate zeal during the debates on the bill.[92] But for Pius, it had certain crucial defects:

1. It did not restore a substantial element of territorial sovereignty, in fact, no sovereignty at all. This, as he had re-iterated in the *Syllabus of Errors*, was the only effective basis on which he believed he could freely exercise his spiritual authority over the Roman Catholic Church world-wide. Furthermore, the Vatican, as it was defined in 1870 (see the map on p. 40) was very small: it was what Falconi describes as a 'royal palace, a ministerial omnibus and a haven for refugees', and as such too small to meet all the needs of the Holy See.[93]

2. The Law was not a bilateral treaty, an agreement between equals binding in international law, but an arbitrary, unilateral act of the Italian Parliament which could just as easily, and arbitrarily, be repealed by that same Parliament, which was precisely what several leading politicians of the Left hoped would happen after their party came to power in 1876.

---

[89] For the text of the Law, see Appendix I, p. 231.   [90] Ibid., p. 232.
[91] Ibid., p. 231.   [92] Jemolo, *Church and State*, pp. 48–51.
[93] Falconi, *Cardinale Antonelli*, p. 488.

3. Despite the good intentions of the men who framed the Law, there were some serious ambiguities and lacunae in its wording; in particular, it was not clear what the precise nature of the Holy See's 'enjoyment' of the Vatican, etc., consisted of. Was the Holy See the owner of the 'property'? Was it a tenant? Again, what was the legal status of the pope, the Holy See and, consequently, the various offices of the Roman curia, outside of their extra-territorial enclaves, in other words, in Italian law? This uncertainty, which was highlighted in various parliamentary debates, and in the press over the years, was to pose some serious problems for the management of the Vatican's finances in subsequent decades (see Chapter 4, pp. 95–7).

Some attempt was made to meet the concerns of the Holy See: in particular, over the years suggestions were made that the Law of Guarantees should be 'internationalised', that is turned into a bilateral treaty between the Holy See and Italy, with additional guarantees from other powers. But the proposal foundered on Italian objections that this arrangement would constitute interference in Italy's internal affairs.[94] And though Pius frequently, and vocally, denounced the Law of Guarantees, it is notable how equally frequently the Vatican invoked its clauses to defend its interests, and denounced breaches of the Law by Italian officials after 1870, as in the so-called Martinucci case of 1882. In this case the Court of Appeal for the Roman district held itself competent to adjudicate on a matter connected with the internal administration of the Vatican (and thus) negatived the whole system of immunities and sovereign rights which the Law of Guarantees was supposed to ensure to the Holy See.[95]

Again, the sequestration and sale of the assets of the missionary congregation Propaganda Fide, an integral if semi-detached part of the Roman curia for financial purposes, whose funds were provided by Catholics all over the world, suggested that none of the agencies of the Holy See was truly safe from the operation of Italian law.[96] Even more seriously, in 1915, following Italy's declaration of war upon the Central Powers, the ambassadors of Germany and Austria-Hungary were banished to Switzerland and in 1916, when the Italians seized Palazzo Venezia, the embassy of the Austrian Empire, Pope Benedict XV and his Secretary of State, Cardinal Pietro Gasparri, vehemently protested to the Italian government.[97] And for the rest of the First World War, the Vatican must have deeply regretted the decision of Pius IX to reject Italy's offer to allow the Holy See to set up its own postal and telegraph services; throughout the war, Vatican mail

[94] Pollard, *The Vatican and Italian Fascism*, p. 84.
[95] D. A. Binchy, *Church and State in Fascist Italy* (Oxford, 1970), p. 44.
[96] Ibid., pp. 44–5.   [97] Pollard, *The Unknown Pope*, p. 99.

and telegrams, routed via the Italian government's system, were routinely intercepted and decoded by the Italian High Command, thus revealing all the secrets of its diplomacy and compromising the Vatican's claim to neutrality and impartiality in the struggle.[98] Leaving aside the Palazzo Venezia incident, which took place at a particularly difficult time for the Italians in the course of the First World War, the government of Italy did in fact seek very strenuously and conscientiously to observe the letter of the Law of Guarantees, especially during the conclaves of 1878, 1903 and 1914.

As a consequence of the intransigent position which it had taken up in relation to the Law of Guarantees, the Holy See could not in all conscience accept the annual subsidy. Though Antonelli accepted an original, provisional *assegnazione* (a sort of temporary civil list) from the Italian government in the rather confused and uncertain circumstances of October 1870, all efforts by the Italians to persuade the Vatican to accept the annual payment of the subsidy stipulated in the Law of Guarantees were resisted. Henceforth, the financing of the papacy would be solely dependent upon the goodwill offerings of the faithful throughout the world, Peter's Pence, and the income derived from the investment of the surplus from those offerings. As Antonelli explained to the government official who tried to persuade him to accept the annual indemnity laid down in the Law of Guarantees, '(the Holy Father) will always prefer to survive on the generous charity of the faithful, rather than receive, in whatever form, a cheque from the Government to which you belong'.[99]

The finances of the Vatican after 1870: expenditure and income

Though now spared the responsibilities of civil government consequent upon the fall of the temporal power, the Holy See still had considerable outgoings after 1870. Its annual expenditure on the organs of government of the universal Church, and the Papal Court amounted to roughly 3.6 million lire per annum, and few of these establishments, with the exception of the Congregation of the Council, the tribunal of the Sacra Romana Rota (matrimonial court), which charged fees for various of their services, and the missionary congregation of Propaganda Fide, which received offerings from around the world, enjoyed much in the way of independent income. In total, the following bodies had to be financed:

[98] D. Alvarez, 'Vatican Communications Security 1914–1918', *Intelligence and National Security*, 7 (1992), pp. 443–53.
[99] Falconi, *Cardinale Antonelli*, p. 487.

1. The Papal Court and the Papal Family (Household), including the 'armed forces' of the pope and the administration of the Sacred Apostolic Palaces including the stables.
2. The Sacred College of Cardinals.
3. The various congregations of the Roman curia, the central government of the Roman Catholic Church, including the Secretariat of State.
4. The apostolic delegations and nunciatures abroad.
5. The Vatican museums and galleries (partly offset by entrance charges).
6. The other papal palaces and the major basilicas of Rome – St John Lateran, St Mary Major, St Lorenzo and St Paul's Without-the-Walls.
7. The pensions of former employees.

In addition, money had to be found for the pope's charitable work, including several schools for poor Roman children, and for the building of new churches in Rome.[100] For the court of a non-existent state, the Papal Court was considerable in its personnel and costs. A panoply of both lay and ecclesiastical figures, not to mention *four* military corps – the Noble, Palatine and Swiss Guards and the Papal Gendarmerie – all made claims upon the papal purse. The Noble Guard was especially costly: in the 1883 income and expenditure accounts for the Sacred Apostolic Palaces, nearly 188,000 lire, virtually 10 per cent of expenditure, was devoted to the Guard, whereas the costs of maintaining all the other three corps amounted to just less than 300,000 lire. Papal ceremonies, especially beatifications and canonisations, were hugely costly – though some contribution might reasonably be expected from the promoters of such causes, and a national pilgrimage for someone raised to the altars might bring substantial offerings from the pilgrims (see Chapter 3, pp. 58–9).

The survival of the Papal Court, in all its pomp and circumstance, and costliness, was not, however, a mere accident; a product of ecclesiastical inertia, or vanity on the part of the pontiff, it was a very clear and deliberate act of political policy after 1870, and one followed by nearly all of Pius IX's successors. At its most mundane, it was a question of keeping up appearances: the trappings of sovereignty had to be maintained in the eyes of the Great Powers of Europe to whom the pope so frequently addressed his protests about the loss of the temporal power, and to the faithful. Even if he was no longer the 'pope-king', Pius IX, and his successors down to 1929, claimed to be 'sovereign pontiff', and they were determined to let no one forget that. In order to do so, in their eyes it was necessary to maintain to the full the outward trappings of monarchy. Some of Pius IX's successors, like Leo XIII and Pius X, were perhaps a little careless

---

[100] ASV, Sacri Palazzi Apostolici (SPA), Amministrazione, b. XIII, 2, 1, Tabella Preventiva, 1884.

Table 2 *Income and expenditure accounts of the administration of the Sacred Apostolic Palaces, 1883*

Income		Expenditure	
Payments to Sacred Apostolic Palaces	Lit. 30,637.50	Personal expenses of the pope	23,112.50
Rental income from Rome	83,737.70	Fixed payments	32,027.43
Rental income from Castelgandolfo	945.91	Papal 'chapels' and other liturgical function	28,471.70
Miscellaneous income	23,303.51	Furnishings etc. for the papal apartments	36,663.33
		Salaries and honoraria	461,713.41
		Clothing allowances, medical assistance and funerals of employees	39,663.80
		Pensions and other payments	270,637.86
		Maintenance work	188,514.50
		Gardens etc.	48,968.50
		Stables	62,078.16
		Heating, lighting and stationery	47,344.20
		Noble Guard	187,820.04
		Palatine Guard	57,103.79
		Swiss Guards	152,925.26
		Pontifical Gendarmerie	94,319.59
		Vatican museums and galleries	15,400
		Gifts and donations	10,903.12
		Taxes and imposts	30,045.03
		Miscellaneous expenses	141,304.42
		Decoration of the museum of the 'Candelabri'	135,000
Total income	143,674.62	Total expenditure	2,064,021.65

Excess of expenditure over income covered by Peter's Pence Lit. 1,920,347.03

Source: ASV, SPA, Amministrazione, b. XIII, 2, 1 Tabella Preventiva, 1884.

about keeping up this game, the former for intellectual reasons, the latter out of natural humility, but when Benedict XV came to the papal throne in 1914 he restored many of the ceremonies and spectacle of the papal monarchy which had briefly gone out of use.[101] After 1870, the Papal

[101] Pollard, *The Unknown Pope*, p. 76.

Court actually expanded, as a process of the 'internationalisation' of its lay element got under way.

Originally, the lay element in the court had consisted of the Roman aristocracy, supplemented with a few representatives of the various nobilities and patrician elites of the Papal States. After 1870, the Roman nobility was divided with the majority of the great families spurning the new king's court in the Quirinale Palace and remaining faithful to the pope in the Vatican, the so-called 'black aristocracy', the more intransigent of whom, like Prince Lancellotti, closed the doors of their palaces and refused to open them again until the *Conciliazione* (the reconciliation between the Holy See and Italy) in 1929.[102] As contributors to both local Catholic charities and to Peter's Pence, the noble or bourgeois layman, in Europe, and increasingly in North America and even Australia, increasingly expected, and were led to expect, a reward in the form of a papal honour for their generosity.[103] By the end of the nineteenth century, it had become an established practice for local bishops to recommend the appointment of worthy laymen to titles of papal nobility – mainly marquis and count (the papal financiers Langrand-Dumonceau, Blouin and Blumensthil were among early recipients) – to papal chivalrous orders, and in this regard Pius IX actually instituted a new order in his own name to add to that of St Gregory the Great, and to the lesser honour of a papal 'chamberlain' or gentleman of the chamber.[104] As Seldes wrote in 1934:

> Those [chamberlains] who are able, come to the Vatican to serve the pope for a week, then depart for their homes, in the Ukraine [sic], or in Wisconsin, or in Africa, with the medal of the pontificate which commemorates four important events of the year gone by and which will remain a souvenir forever of their eight days in Rome in the very heart of Christendom.[105]

The powerful impact of the Papal Court on the American mind in particular was the object of a bitter complaint by the Italian ambassador to America in 1903, and he explained it that it was 'largely due, I fear, to the Vatican habit of bestowing titles of nobility on rich Americans who help the Church financially. Because they have no aristocracy, the Americans are particularly susceptible to this form of flattery. The rich Protestant Mellon of Philadelphia has just been made a Papal Marquis.'[106]

---

[102] Levillain, *The Papacy*, I, p. 627.
[103] Ibid., 'The Papacy extended its influence into an economic and social elite that was not sparing in its generosity.'
[104] *Annuario Pontificio*, 1948, p. 873.
[105] Seldes, *The Vatican*, p. 227: precisely how Seldes thought anyone would have been able to escape the Soviet Ukraine in the middle of the 1930s is not clear.
[106] ASMAE, Ambasciata d'Italia agli Stati Uniti, Pacco 33, 1903–7, report of 17 April 1903.

Two of the non-Italian members of the Papal Court, Henry De La Garde Grissel, an Englishman who served in the pontificate of Leo XIII, and Francis MacNutt, an American who served both Pius X and Benedict XV, have left interesting memoirs of their experiences of the Papal Court.[107] This new element in the Papal Court had almost all contributed substantially to the Church's finances and their presence helped to consolidate the attachment of local populations of Catholics to the Holy See.

Pius and his successors had another financial burden to carry, which arose out of policy: he insisted on paying the salaries/pensions of those officials who had either been sacked by the new Italian rulers, or who had refused to serve them out of loyalty to him. The last-named remained a major burden for the Holy See for decades to come. As late as the beginning of Pius X's reign in 1903, the Vatican was still paying out 658,884 lire for pensions and other subsidies, mostly for former employees, over 15 per cent of its budget at that time.[108] The Vatican further insisted on making up the difference between what the new government paid in salaries and pensions and what these employees would have received in papal employment.[109] This may have played a useful part in the propaganda war with the Italian state, and the 'pope's pensioners' frequently played an important part in noisy anti-government demonstrations in Rome, but it was expensive. Another cause of financial difficulties was the failure of Pius IX to reform the Roman curia which still contained offices and office-holders whose functions were now redundant after the end of the temporal power. As Seldes points out: 'The disappearance of temporal power (1870) produced almost no change [in forms of administration]. The temporal budget of the pope disappeared, but the habits and practices of absolute monarchy and of unlimited power remained in their entirety.'[110] The increasing expenditure of the Holy See was also caused by another form of 'modernisation', the fact that Pio Nono felt obliged to meet the challenge of the modern world, and in particular the resort of the liberal, anti-clerical enemies of the Church to mass movements and to the media, i.e. the press. Antonelli may not have been so impressed by the utility of such organisations as the Società della Gioventù Italiana di Azione Cattolica (GIAC), an association of Catholic youth which had emerged

[107] H. De La Garde, Grissel, *Sede Vacante: Being a Diary Written at the Conclave* (Oxford, 1903); and F. A. MacNutt, *A Papal Chamberlain* (London, 1936).
[108] ASV, Segreteria di Stato(SdS), Spoglio di Pio X, b. 4, fasc. 16, Pensioni, no date; see also Martina, *Pio XI (1866–1878)*, p. 247 fn. 33.
[109] Lai (ed.), *Finanze e finanzieri vaticani: atti e documenti*, p. 25, Antonelli to the nuncios, 9 Oct. 1870.
[110] Seldes, *The Vatican*, p. 245.

with the express objective of defending the Holy See from attack and vindicating its rights and the rights of the Italian Church generally.[111] The pope did and he began a policy of subsidising Italian lay Catholic organisations which has persisted down to today.[112] Again, in an age of newspapers, it was important for the Holy See to possess its own with the result that in 1861 it bought a Roman daily, *L'Osservatore Romano*, and brought the Jesuit fortnightly *La Civiltà Cattolica* from Florence to Rome. Henceforth, these two journals, though publicly described as 'semi-official' organs, would become the authoritative mouthpieces of the Holy See. But this venture into modern journalism, however essential to the future of the Church, was expensive, and when the Holy See began to support wider, lay journalistic initiatives throughout Italy, the *stampa buona*, the 'good', Catholic, press (see Chapters 3 and 4), it became very expensive indeed.

Italy, as the homeland and hinterland of the Holy See so to speak, was inevitably of particular importance, especially given the difficult relations with that country's liberal-conservative governments. One consequence of Pius IX's refusal to accept the Law of Guarantees proved costly, because the Italian commitment to reforming its ecclesiastical legislation and abolishing the *regio placet* and *exequatur*, the state's right of preventive veto in the matter of nominations to Italian episcopal sees, thereby lapsed. So the Italian government retained a veto on major ecclesiastical appointments, most importantly of bishops, and frequently refused such appointments where the candidate was not deemed suitable, that is was regarded as openly hostile to the state. Just as important, in order to receive their salaries and cover for their expenses from the state, they officially had to show the bull of appointment by the Holy See, in effect, recognising the authority of the state over the Church, something which Pius IX and Antonelli were unwilling to let them do.[113] When the said bishops could not claim their temporalities, the income deriving from their office, the Holy See had to subsidise their expenses – Falconi estimates that 500,000 lire was expended by the Vatican in this way between 1870 and 1878.[114]

Building a patrimony for the Holy See – Antonelli's investment of the residues of Peter's Pence

At his death in 1878, it is estimated that Pius IX left the Holy See a 'fortune' of 30 million lire; since it took various forms – bank deposits, stocks

---

[111] R. A. Webster, *The Cross and the Fasces: Christian Democracy and Fascism in Italy* (Stanford, Calif., 1959), p. 20.

[112] Martina, *Pio IX (1866–1878)*, p. 267.   [113] Jemolo, *Church and State*.

[114] Falconi, *Cardinale Antonelli*, p. 494.

and bonds and IOUs, and probably some gold – it could more correctly be described as a patrimony.[115] Assuming that there was no large-scale increase in expenditure through inflation, since the major expenses of the Holy See remained stationary, this would suggest that the Vatican had managed to save 4.3 million lire per year from its income from Peter's Pence. At first sight, this seems inconceivable, though there's no way to disprove the suggestion since figures for the income from Peter's Pence in the seven years between the fall of Rome and the pope's death do not exist. However, it seems more likely from other evidence that the figure of 30 million lire was also the result of the intelligent investment of the annual residues from Peter's Pence in those years, after the expenses of the Vatican had been met.[116] In large part this meant the investments made by Antonelli.

In broad terms, Antonelli seems to have been not a little chary of most Italian financial and commercial institutions, perhaps because he realised that Italy suffered both from state financial instability and industrial backwardness; by comparison with other countries in Western Europe – Belgium, France, Germany and Great Britain – Italy in the 1870s had barely been touched by industrialisation.[117] There would also, presumably, have been some resistance to too much financial involvement in Italy on political grounds – hostility to the 'usurping state'. Much of the Vatican's money was deposited in foreign banks, especially Rothschilds in Paris, the Société Général in Brussels and the Bank of England; little or no money was sent to the United States at this juncture, though there is evidence that Antonelli did contemplate depositing money there.[118] Antonelli used the papal nuncios as the agents of his financial operations abroad, especially in the matter of seeking attractive bank accounts and stocks and bonds, rather than company shares.[119] Two Roman financial middlemen, Feoli and Cerasi, also performed various necessary operations, smuggling in Peter's Pence when the Italian governmental authorities showed hostility, exchanging currencies, cashing stocks and bonds which formed part of Peter's Pence and selling precious objects donated by the pious faithful.[120]

Antonelli's investment policy would, to some extent, have been influenced by his brother's banking experience, and also by the activities of

[115] P. Levillain and F.-C. Uginet, *Il Vaticano e le frontiere della Grazia* (Milan, 1985), p. 100; and Falconi, *Cardinale Antonelli*, p. 496.
[116] Lai, *Finanze e finanzieri vaticani*, pp. 59–60.
[117] J. F. Pollard, 'Religion and the Formation of the Italian Working Class', in R. Halpern and J. Morris (eds.), *American Exceptionalism: US Working Class Formation in an International Context* (London, 1997), pp. 158–9.
[118] Lai, *Finanze e finanzieri vaticani*, pp. 59–60.
[119] Ibid., p. 169.   [120] Crocella, *Augusta miseria*, pp. 177–8.

those leading lay members of the Papal Court with business interests in Rome. Like the Church itself, the Roman aristocracy had suffered badly in economic terms from the impact of Porta Pia. In particular, they had suffered the loss of lucrative feudal dues which were abolished by the new rulers in their capital and the surrounding areas.[121] The great Roman aristocrats continued to draw the bulk of their income from landed property in both city and countryside for some time after 1870, and indeed made use of Vatican 'licences' to acquire ecclesiastical property after the Italian state had extended its legislation for the sale of Church lands in the region of Latium in 1873, on condition that they made restitution to the original owners at the 'restoration' of the temporal power.[122] But after 1870 the black aristocracy increasingly invested their spare capital in Roman financial institutions, like the Banca Romana, the French-based Banque Union Générale, the Cassa di Risparmio (Savings Bank of Rome), etc., a process that gathered pace in the last two decades of the century.[123] They also increasingly invested in the local utility companies – water, gas and later electricity – of the new and burgeoning Italian capital city.[124] A series of names, whom one might describe as 'the usual suspects', appear with regularity on the boards of such companies as the Società Acqua Pia Marcia (water, named after Pius IX), the Società Roma Illuminazione e Gas (gas and electricity) and Società dei Molini e Magazzini (flour-milling) and all of them had close and direct links to the Vatican – the princes Borghese, Chigi, Giustiniani Bandini, Rospigliosi, the marquis Theodoli and counts Blumensthil and Soderini.[125]

Antonelli seems to have been wary of new, speculative or even entrepreneurial initiatives. In particular, he very wisely abstained from getting involved with any of the very many would-be entrepreneurs who asked him to invest the money of the Holy See in their wonderful new business ventures. Indeed, Antonelli made it a rule of his financial administration that 'The Holy See cannot involve itself, either directly or indirectly in commercial operations.'[126] But the term 'indirectly' was applied loosely, because Vatican money soon followed that of the leading papal courtiers and was invested in Roman business enterprises listed above.[127] The one thing which Antonelli did not do was to supply what might be called 'venture capital' in new enterprises, this rule of thumb spared him the losses which Leo XIII was to suffer as a result of investing in the Roman building fever of the 1880s (see Chapter 3, pp. 67–8). Nevertheless,

[121] A. Caracciolo, *Roma capitale. Dal Risorgimento all crisi dello stato liberale* (Rome, 1956), p. 143–4.
[122] Ibid., 142–3.   [123] Ibid., p. 144.   [124] Ibid., pp. 146–8.
[125] Ibid., pp. 148–9.   [126] As quoted in Falconi, *Cardinale Antonelli*, pp. 494–5.
[127] Caracciolo, *Roma capitale*, p. 149.

thanks to Antonelli's policy of investment, by the end of Pius IX's reign, the Vatican, like the Catholic aristocracy of Rome, had already begun to make the important switch from relying financially on the exploitation of an essentially feudal system of landed wealth to investment in capitalist credit and commercial enterprises. This was a process that would be accentuated during the reign of this successor.

The death of Pius IX

The death of Antonelli in November 1876 marked a watershed. The appointment by Pius IX of Cardinal Simeoni as the new Secretary of State and as administrator of the 'property of the Holy See' was the first public admission that the Holy See now possessed its own considerable financial assets, a not entirely wise move to make in the new Italian political climate created by the advent to office of the Left through the so-called 'Parliamentary Revolution' of 1876. The death of Pius IX, in January 1878, was an even more momentous event than that of Antonelli. Apart from the fact that the provisions of the Law of Guarantees in relation to the freedom of conclaves would be tested for the first time, his passing raised in an acute form the unresolved question of the legal status of the Holy See in the Italian courts. The issue arose because in 1877, disgusted with the quarrels and litigation which had arisen in his family, Papa Mastai changed his will.[128] Instead of his relatives, the pope made Cardinals La Valletta (Vicar of Rome), Simeoni and Mertel his sole heirs with the power to distribute his estate as they pleased.[129] Furthermore, in order to protect the financial interests of the Holy See, he specifically disposed that 'the large sums of money and negotiable items, plus the credits which are administered by the Cardinal Prefect of the Sacred Palaces be given to the Holy See as its property, for the free disposal of the Supreme Pontiff *pro tempore*'.[130] Despite the efforts of the three cardinals to settle the matter with generous payments, the Mastai family, and in particular the Princess del Drago would not be satisfied and took them to court. This case dragged on for over three years, until it reached the Italian Supreme Court where it was finally settled in the cardinals' favour, though they were still paying members of the family some income from Pius IX's investments as late as 1887.[131] Even this was not enough, and the princess then sued the Italian state, laying claim to the unpaid arrears of the annual payment to the pope as set out in the

---

[128] ASV, SPA, Eredità di Pio IX, fasc. 43.
[129] Ibid.   [130] Ibid.   [131] Ibid., fasc. 42, p. 22.

Law of Guarantees. The Italian courts made short shrift of this claim.[132] Nevertheless, Pius IX's death demonstrated that the financing of the Vatican rested on very precarious *legal* foundations, and this issue would not be resolved until the pontificate of Pius X, nearly thirty years later (see Chapter 3).

---

[132] See AAES, SdS, Italia e Principato di Monaco, 826, Roma, 1910, Sulla condizione giuridico-patrimoniale del Sommo Pontefice e della Santa Sede in Italia, p. 52.

3   The pontificate of Leo XIII (1878–1903)

Introduction

Despite the undoubted intentions of the cardinal electors assembled in the conclave of 1878 that the man whom they would elect should not reign as long as his predecessor, the reign of Gioacchino Pecci turned out to be one of the longest in papal history: twenty-five years.[1] He did not immediately go back on the intransigent policies of his predecessor, but over the years there was a definite movement away from them. Leo ultimately managed to make peace of a sort with the new German Reich and thus bring to an end the *Kulturkampf*, the struggle unleashed against the Church there by Bismarck. He similarly tried to bring about a reconciliation between French Catholics and the new Third Republic, though his call for French Catholics to 'rally' to the Republic was less successful, as the Dreyfus Affair at the end of the century demonstrated. In broader terms, papal diplomacy in his reign, and especially under the direction of Cardinal Rampolla del Tindaro, who became Secretary of State in 1887, was successful in taking the Holy See out of the international isolation to which Pius IX had condemned it. In the 1880s, for example, by mediating in a colonial dispute between Germany and Spain over the Caroline Islands, Leo established an international role for the papacy as an 'honest broker' between the powers.[2] He made notable innovations in Catholic attitudes in social and political matters: the encyclical *Rerum Novarum* of 1891 was a landmark in the development of Catholic social doctrine, firmly rebutting the claims of Socialism and Communism while denouncing the evil results of unrestrained industrial capitalism, and *Graves de Communi Re* (1901) began the process of disentangling the Church from centuries of reactionary alliances of 'throne and altar' by declaring that all forms of state organisation, including democratic and

---

[1] For good surveys of Leo's reign see Chadwick, *A History of the Popes*, ch. 7, Coppa, *The Modern Papacy*, chs. 8 and 9; and Levillain (ed.), *The Papacy*, II, pp. 933–6.
[2] Chadwick, *A History of the Popes*, pp. 287–8; and J.-M. Ticchi, *Aux frontières de la paix: bons offices, médiations, arbitrages du Saint-Siège (1878–1922)* (Rome, 2002), chs. 1–3.

republican ones, might be legitimate, so long as they conformed to fundamental Catholic principles.[3] Leo, a more 'intellectual' pope than his predecessor, made notable efforts in the fields of biblical studies, the re-introduction of Thomism as a basis for Catholic philosophy, especially in the seminaries, and more generally in the fields of missionary endeavour and relations with the Oriental Churches in communion with Rome. Among the lesser things that he will be remembered for were his abolition of the *castrati* (eunuchs) in the Vatican's Sistine Choir and the opening of the Vatican Secret Archives in 1883. His greatest endeavour, and in the short term his greatest failure, was probably with Italy. His efforts to isolate her diplomatically failed with the advent of the Triple Alliance with Germany and Austria-Hungary in 1882 and his relations with her government were made difficult by the consolidation of the power of the Left after their triumph in 1876 and in particular, by the rise of Francesco Crispi, former lieutenant of Giuseppe Garibaldi in 1860. The growth of the *Estrema*, the extreme left of radicals and republicans, underpinned by the intensely political Masonic lodges, with their unremitting anti-clerical hostility to the Church, posed an even more serious threat. Such were the consequent ups and downs of relations with Italy that on four occasions Leo XIII very seriously made preparations for a possible flight from Rome. All this, as will be seen, had a very significant impact upon Vatican financial policy in his pontificate.

The new financial regime

There is some dispute about the state of the Vatican's finances after the death of Pius IX. On the one hand, some historians of papal finances claim that Pius left a reserve of 30 million lire at his death,[4] on the other, Grilli talks about 'the destruction of the assets' of the Vatican[5] and Msgr Ernesto Folchi claimed, rather less dramatically, that some of the Vatican's assets were worthless (see below, p. 60). Guido Manfroni, who as Commissario del Borgo was paid to inform himself about what was going on inside the Vatican, also gives the impression that all was not well with the finances of the Holy See in 1878: 'I have been told in confidence that because of the condition of the pontifical treasury, the new pope has had to suppress much of the largesse traditionally associated with the occasion of the Conclave', and he cites the abolition of the *mesata*, the custom of giving

---

3 Carlen (ed.), *Papal Encyclicals*, II, pp. 480–1.
4 Lai, *Finanze e finanzieri vaticani*, p. 76; and Levillain and Uginet *Il Vaticano*, p. 100.
5 Grilli, *La finanza vaticana*, p. 75.

Illustration 4 Pope Leo XIII

three months' pay to many Vatican employees.[6] He also mentions that this led to a mutiny of some Swiss Guards: the mutineers were paid one year's salary and sacked.[7] There seems to have been a continuing problem during the early years of Leo's reign, and in order to balance the budget 'a system of the most rigid economy has been introduced', and he also says that Leo abandoned the project to build a new garden walk in the Vatican when he discovered how much it would cost.[8] This is confirmed by Chadwick who says 'Personally he [Leo] lived a simple life, and he hated paying money out unnecessarily, so that some of the Vatican staff disliked him because they received fewer tips', and that Leo was 'famous for his penny-pinching, if not avarice'.[9]

It seems likely that the real problem with the finances of the Vatican in the early years of Leo's reign was not so much a lack of reserves as a temporary falling off in the regular income from Peter's Pence, which could, of course, have had very serious consequences in the longer term. Manfroni cites a fall in the offerings from France, Germany and Spain in particular after the death of Pius IX.[10] Later on in his reign, Leo's policy of the *Ralliement* also affected the income from Peter's Pence; offended by his attempts to reconcile the Church and the Republic, many monarchist Catholics reduced their contributions.[11] This makes a lot of sense: Pius IX, whatever his policy mistakes, had a great deal of charisma, and a strong cult of the personality had been built around this over the thirty-four years of his reign. A new pope would need to get known and get established in the affections of the faithful. One of the best ways to do this was to encourage the growth of pilgrimages to Rome. An example of the way in which pilgrimages and Peter's Pence combined in the process of developing the cult of the pope is provided by a pastoral letter which Cardinal Vaughan of Westminster sent to the people of his diocese in 1901:

We have only to add that the Holy Father graciously sends his apostolic blessing to you all, while thanking you for the gift of Peter-pence (£1,175), collected in the Diocese and duly handed laid at his feet by the noble leader of the English pilgrimage. That pilgrimage was eminently satisfactory: it gave the greatest consolation to the aged Pontiff, while incidents connected with it have rejoiced the hearts of Catholic Christendom by once more bringing forward its undying claim to the temporal independence of its august Head.[12]

---

[6] G. Manfroni, *Sulla soglia del Vaticano, 1870–1901: dalle memorie di Guido Manfroni*, ed. C. Manfroni (2 vols., Milan, 1920), I, p. 354.
[7] Ibid.   [8] Ibid.
[9] Chadwick, *A History of the Popes*, p. 277.
[10] Manfroni, *Sulla soglia del Vaticano*, II, p. 28.
[11] E. Soderini, *Il pontificato di Leone XIII* (2 vols., Milan, 1932–3), I, pp. 402–3.
[12] H. Vaughan, *A Lenten Letter on Penance and Other Good Works by Herbert Cardinal Vaughan, Archbishop of Westminster* (London, 1901), p. 1.

With the development of railways, particularly in the Italian peninsula, where they had been strongly encouraged by the government as part of the process of nation-building, the Vatican was to exploit the increasing number of pilgrimages. During the course of his reign Leo proclaimed no less than three jubilees, in 1879, 1882 and 1886, as well as the *anno santo* of 1900 and a special celebration for the silver jubilee of his pontificate in 1903, which meant large-scale pilgrimages to Rome. As in Pius IX's reign, so in that of Leo XIII, some of these pilgrimages had a decidedly political motive to them as well. Thus, in 1888, the Comte de Mun, a French Ultramontanist, brought a pilgrimage of 20,000 French workers to render homage to the sovereign pontiff. The pilgrims' hailing of the 'pope-king', and other offensive gestures against the Italian government, resulted in a riot.[13] But pilgrimages also brought in a lot of money from the faithful, and the Vatican was assiduous in Leo's reign in organising them, as in 1884, on the thirtieth anniversary of the proclamation of the doctrine of the Immaculate Conception.[14] Holy Year 1900, was, of course, the high point of the pilgrimage 'season', when a total of 1,300,000 pilgrims flocked to Rome, 150,000 of them in September alone, with significant numbers from both North and South America.[15] All these pilgrimages, plus beatifications and canonisations, must have brought in a tidy profit to the Vatican's coffers, yet in 1888 the Vatican was still so strapped for cash that it seriously considered making a 'Universal appeal for every Catholic to contribute one cent per day to Peter's Pence'.[16]

The financial Administration of Msgr Folchi

Leo XIII took a very direct and personal interest in the management of the Vatican's finances and during the course of his reign he produced a series of measures to reform their administration. The inauguration of Leo's reign also coincided with a new administrator in charge of the Vatican finances, Msgr Enrico Folchi, the first 'dedicated' ecclesiastical head of the Vatican's finances. From a family which had served the Holy See for many years, Folchi was also an acquaintance of Leo when he had been Cardinal Camarlengo of the Holy Roman Church, and it was the latter who brought him into the ABSS, the administration of the property of the Holy See in 1878.[17] Folchi first worked with a consultative commission composed of the Secretary of State and two other cardinals. Then, in 1880, in one of Leo's many re-organisations of the bureaucracy of the Roman curia, the administration of the Sacred Apostolic Palaces

---

[13] Manfroni, *Sulla soglia del Vaticano*, II, p. 191.   [14] Ibid., p. 19.

[15] Ibid., pp. 271–5, but as Manfroni also points out, pilgrimages could be costly ventures; he estimates that in 1900 the Vatican housed and fed several thousand pilgrims.

[16] Ibid., p. 28.   [17] Lai, *Finanze finanzieri vaticani*, p. 86.

was separated from that of the management of the Holy See's property and investments and Folchi was given greater powers as 'commissario' of the latter under an enlarged commission of cardinals. Finally, in 1887, as a sign of Leo's confidence in him, Folchi was made vice camarlengo of the Holy Roman Church, an important post during a *sede vacante*, the interregnum between the death of one pope and the election of his successor.[18] But Folchi's experience of the Vatican's financial administration, despite his undoubted talents, was not ultimately a happy one. Leo operated as an absolute, autocratic monarch; the appointment of Folchi was, indeed, largely motivated by his desire to circumvent the Roman curia in the matter of financial administration and keep it in his hands, via a fairly low-ranking prelate, which Folchi initially was. In his memoirs, Folchi complained about the pope's methods of government, not to say accounting, and also about the state of the patrimony which he found on his appointment: close to a million lire of the securities and loans in the Papal Treasury had to be written off within a year of Leo XIII's election.[19] Nor was Folchi in sole charge of the Vatican's finances. Apart from Leo's repeated interference in the choice of investments, and particularly in the matter of making loans, including giving one to his nephew Count Pecci, he reserved control of his personal finances to a trusted member of his 'personal secretariat', Msgr Nazareno Marzolini.[20] In addition, any real estate acquired by the pope himself, both before and after his election, was entrusted to Msgr Serafino Cretoni, who worked in the Secretariat of State.[21] The control of the key element in the papal finances, Peter's Pence, along with the offerings received at pilgrimages, also remained in the pope's hands throughout his reign. Money, negotiable instruments and jewellery and gold were then were deposited in a iron chest which was kept under his bed throughout his reign.[22] Though Folchi assisted in the emptying of the white velvet bags in which pilgrims placed their offerings at the end of papal audiences, and had the task of banking cash and changing foreign currencies and other negotiable instruments, the pope himself decided how much would be allocated to the financing of the Papal Court, the curia and the other administrations of the Holy See – 4.5 million lire per annum until it was increased to 5.5 million at Folchi's request because of inflation.[23] Though all the popes in the

---

[18] Ibid.   [19] Ibid., pp. 87 and 89 fn. 2.
[20] Soderini, *Il pontificato di Leone XIII*, II, p. 398.
[21] Lai, *Finanze e finanzieri vaticani*, p. 117.
[22] R. Chernow, *The House of Morgan: An American Banking Dynasty and the Rise of Modern Finance* (New York, 1990), p. 285: 'At the turn of the century, Pope Leo XIII had simply filled a trunk with gold coins and stored it under his bed.'
[23] Lai, *Finanze e finanzieri vaticani*, p. 90 fn. 2.

modern period – with the exception of Pius X – had their own sources of income, and given the fact that most came from noble families their private wealth could have been considerable, all were obviously housed and fed at the expense of the Holy See.[24]

Folchi's principal function was to invest the surplus from Peter's Pence and to look after the existing investments of the Holy See, in which task he combined some speculative activity with a large dose of caution. Because of the very limited extent of industrialisation in Italy, compared to other Western European countries, large-scale industrialisation only began to take off in the 1880s, and then suffered a setback due to the economic crisis, and due to the underdevelopment of the country's financial sector,[25] opportunities for investment were still limited in Italy and Folchi was accordingly forced to speculate with government stocks and bonds, both foreign and domestic.[26] In this regard, neither the Church's ideological antipathy to the Italian ruling Liberal elite, nor the encumbrances of the Roman Question prevented the Vatican from investing in Italian state loan stock as long as it was convenient.

Folchi's caution was exhibited most strongly during the Union Générale affair. This French bank created an important branch in Rome, establishing relations not only with members of the Papal Court, but with the Secretary of State, Cardinal Jacobini, and the pope himself.[27] The head of the Union, Eugène Bontoux, was another Catholic financier with grand visions; indeed, he sought to resurrect the plans of Langrange-Dumonceau of a decade earlier, by offering to take over the management of the Vatican's capital and create two foundations which would then finance all the Vatican's needs through re-investment.[28] Like the Belgian banker before him, the Frenchman also exploited the papacy's continuing ideological and political struggle with Liberalism by offering to create a network of newspapers in Italy and abroad to combat freemasonry and anti-clericalism.[29] Leo and Jacobini were all for handing over the Vatican's millions but were fiercely resisted by Folchi who, among other things would have been put out of a job had the deal gone through.[30] He was right and his superiors wrong. Bontoux went bust in 1881 and the Union Générale with him, so the Vatican would have lost *all* its capital but for Folchi's stand; as it was, it took all of Folchi's efforts to recover sums of money which had already been invested in the bank.[31]

---

[24] See the entry under 'Trattamento della Sacra Persona di Sua Santità,' in ASV, SPA, Preventiva, 1883–4, Spese, where 23,112 lire were assigned to this heading.
[25] C. Seton-Watson, *Italy from Liberalism to Fascism* (London, 1967), pp. 141–3.
[26] Levillain and Uginet, *Il Vaticano*, p. 103.
[27] Lai, *Finanze e finanzieri vaticani*, pp. 97–9.
[28] Ibid., p. 98.   [29] Ibid.   [30] Ibid.   [31] Ibid.

Another sector of the Roman economy in which the Vatican became involved was property. By the 1890s, it is clear that the ABSS was earning a modest but useful income from property lettings in Rome and at Castelgandolfo, the location of the pope's former summer residence, nearly 46,000 lire in 1895, though it is interesting to note that most of the property of the Holy See – 1.4 million lire's worth – was used rent free by religious, educational and charitable institutions.[32] Property rentals must also have become a more significant part of the Holy See's revenues as a result of the intensification of the policy of buying up property around the Vatican itself in the reign of Pius X, 1903–14 (see Chapter 4, pp. 86–7). Under Folchi's administration, there was also some limited Vatican investment in other sectors of the Roman economy, including the buying of further shares in the established lighting and water companies, flour-milling and shares in new ventures like a mechanical workshop, a mining company and several insurance companies.[33]

The Vatican and the Roman building boom of the 1880s

Some of Folchi's investment activity consisted of what could be described as high-class money-lending, the giving of loans to many of the sixty families of the 'black' aristocracy of Rome and other hangers-on of the Papal Court. When he took over the Vatican's finances, he had found that this practice was already well established and, what is more, that in many cases no collateral/security had been asked or given for these loans.[34] Frequently, it was the pope himself who intervened with Folchi to lend money to some indigent aristocrat, sometimes even members of his own family (see above, p. 68). For example, in 1913, the Prince and Princess Borghese were still paying interest to the ABSS on a 4.5 million lire loan secured on their property.[35] It would be no exaggeration to say, therefore, that indirectly, the offerings of the faithful poor of the whole world came to be used as a form of out-door relief for unfortunate, and sometimes feckless, members of the Roman aristocracy. This money-lending element of Folchi's activities also demonstrates that the relaxation of the long-standing ban on 'usury' by various Roman congregations

---

[32] ASV, SPA, Titoli, fasc. 48–521, 'L'Elenco di alcune proprietà appartenenti all prefettura dei Sacri Palazzi Apostolici e loro valore dedotto dalla rendita attuale effetivo o reperibile.'

[33] See Lai, *Finanze e finanzieri vaticani*, p. 127 fn. 2.

[34] Ibid.: not all such loans were made at interest, see ASV, SdS, Spoglio di Cardinale Della Chiesa, busta 1, letter of 13 Dec. 1900, which is essentially an 'IOU' for 6,000 lire of one Sabatino (rest of signature illegible), who was an employee of the Vatican.

[35] Ibid., Spoglio di Pio X, fasc. 7, Rendiconto del Secondo trimestre del 1913.

during the reign of Gregory XVI had percolated into the investment policy of the Vatican,[36] and it is equally significant that it was precisely in the 1880s that the Vatican-sponsored and controlled Banca Artistica Operaio began to charge interest on its small loans to artisans, shopkeepers and workers.[37]

But some of this money-lending was only a paper transaction, a convenient cover, dictated by political and legal concerns, for the Vatican's massive investments in the Roman economy.[38] And the biggest element in this kind of hidden Vatican investment policy was involvement in the Rome building boom of the 1880s. Encouraged by both Leo XIII and his friends in the papal aristocracy – it is no accident that Folchi was close to the princely Buoncompagni Ludovisi family who were especially active in the boom – Folchi invested large sums from the receipts of Peter's Pence in property and building speculation, through *commandites*, 'sleeping partnerships' with the speculators.

The steady development of Rome as a capital city, complete with monumental government buildings, was paralleled by a massive development of residential quarters, both inside the Roman walls of the city which until 1870 had contained large open spaces, the *ville* or parks of the great Roman families, and outside. Among the prime sites were Castro Pretorio, the Esquiline Hill and the Villa Ludovisi inside the walls, and Prati, the area to the north of the Vatican, and Borgo, the area beyond Porta Pia, and what is now the Parioli district outside the walls. Those members of the Roman aristocracy, especially 'the blacks', who found themselves in financial straits often sought a remedy for their pecuniary difficulties in the sale and development of their Roman estates. One such major operation was the sale and development of the Villa Ludovisi, into which the Buoncompagni family invested massively, largely it has to be said with loans from the Vatican totalling over 2 million lire.[39]

A key precondition of the successful involvement of both the black aristocracy and the Vatican in the boom was the *political* power which Catholics had established for themselves in the city by the beginning of the 1880s. In 1879, the candidates of the Unione Romana, the organisation of the Catholics of Rome closely linked to the Papal Court, had won over 40 per cent of the vote in municipal elections and consequently an increasingly influential position in the council.[40] By 1883, Catholic

---

[36] For this change in the Church's attitude towards 'usury' during the 1830s, see the *New Catholic Encyclopedia*, XIV (2nd edn, New York, 2003), pp. 345–4.
[37] Grilli, *La finanza vaticana*, p. 26.   [38] Caracciolo, *Roma capitale*, p. 151.
[39] Lai, *Finanze e finanzieri vaticani*, p. 187 fn. 7.
[40] Caracciolo, *Roma capitale*, pp. 156–7.

councillors formed part of the *giunta*, the body which along with the mayor exercised executive authority, and between 1887 and 1888, they exercised a powerful influence in municipal affairs.[41] This Catholic dominance rested on two factors, the acquiescence of the Vatican in Catholic voting in municipal elections, to which the *Non Expedit* did not apply, and close co-operation with the liberal-moderate councillors. The Vatican's benevolence was assured by the need to protect the interests of the Church in the panting heart of Catholicism, not least its financial ones, and the clerico-moderate alliance was determined by the common financial interest of Catholics and liberal-moderates. Thus a Catholic-influenced council was able to negotiate in strength with the Italian government which introduced laws on the development of its capital city between 1881 and 1883, granting 150 million lire for infrastructural works and public buildings. The council also supervised the granting of concessions to property speculators and construction firms, and monopolies to public utility firms – like the Catholic/Vatican controlled Società Azienda Trasporti Municipale providing bus and tramways.[42]

The building boom really took off in 1883 and for the next four years it manifested all the feverish symptoms of a 'gold rush'.[43] Great fortunes were made – and later lost – and among those who benefited were members of the Papal Court, like the Boncompagni Ludovisi, the Blumensthil and Borghese families and the Giustiniani Bandini, as well as the Vatican itself.[44] Among the property and construction companies in which Peter's Pence money was invested was the Società Generale Immobiliare, which thus entered into the financial orbit of the Vatican for the first time, as the largest company responsible for the construction of new residential accommodation.[45] The Vatican took a large share-holding in the Generale and the company would assume much greater importance for the Vatican from the 1930s onwards (see Chapter 8, p. 171).

If its contribution to the 1880s' building boom is added to all its other financial activities in Rome between 1870 and 1914, then it is likely that in this period the Vatican was investing an average of 5 million lire of the income from Peter's Pence in the Roman economy. So, irony of ironies, the millions given by the faithful in support of 'prisoner of the Vatican' was going to support the development and embellishment of the capital city of the pope's 'jailer', the usurper of his temporal power.

---

[41] For a full-blooded study of the role of Catholics in the Rome municipality in the reigns of Pius IX and Leo XIII, see A. Ciampani, *Cattolici e Liberali durante la trasformazione dei partiti. La 'questione romana' e la politica nazionale e progetti vaticani (1876–1883)* (Rome, 2000).

[42] Caracciolo, *Roma capitale*, p. 164.   [43] Ibid., pp. 161–5.

[44] Ibid., p. 164.   [45] Lai, *Finanze e finanzieri vaticani*, p. 187.

The Vatican and the Banco di Roma

Another great Roman financial institution with which the Vatican was to establish relations for the first time in Leo's reign was the Banco di Roma and that relationship was to be an extremely difficult one over the years, with much financial loss being inflicted upon the Holy See as a result of the frequent crises which the bank was to endure in its troubled history (see below Chapters 4, 5, 6 and 7). Again, the relationship was, as usual, born out of the connections between the pope and key members of the 'black aristocracy', in this case the *fedelissimi* princes Borghese, Giustiniani Bandini and Rospigliosi, who formed the Banca di Roma as a 'secession' from Bontoux's Union, before it went bust in 1884.[46] Leo established relations with the bank from the beginning; indeed, there is evidence that he helped its launch,[47] as Folchi discovered when the pope asked him to transfer into Folchi's name an investment of 3 million lire at 5 per cent for three years which he had made with the bank.[48] As Zamagni explains, the Banco di Roma was one of a new generation of Italian, 'mixed' banks which arose in the 1880s; in the absence of a large and wealthy class of capitalist entrepreneurs, these banks accumulated capital through deposits and then invested it in industrial ventures.[49] The problem with the Banco di Roma was that it was 'The only mixed bank to operate outside the industrial triangle.'[50] This meant that scope for investment in industrial manufacturing companies was extremely limited, because Rome was not to become a major centre of manufacturing and commerce until after the Second World War. Apart from the Società Generale per le Ferrovie Complementari (railways), the Società dei Molini e Magazzini Generali (flour and food) and Società Romana degli Omnibus (transport), the Banco di Roma invested in mainly real estate and building speculation.[51] Folchi soon realised that the Vatican's finances were becoming too closely linked to the bank – even many of the loans to the Roman aristocracy were secured on Banco di Roma shares.[52] Even worse, a lot of the money entrusted to the Commissione dell'Opera per le Pie Cause by religious orders was also invested in the bank.[53]

The Commissione was born out of the difficult and deteriorating relations between the governments of the Left and the Vatican during the 1880s and early 1890s. The parliamentary Left because of their Mazzinian and Garibaldinian origins were more strongly anti-clerical and

---

[46] Ibid., pp. 97–8.   [47] De Rosa, *Storia del Banco di Roma*, I, pp. 28–9.
[48] Ibid.; Lai, *Finanze e finanzieri vaticani*, p. 98.
[49] Zamagni, *The Economic History of Italy*, p. 146.
[50] Ibid., p. 154.   [51] Lai, *Finanze e finanzieri vaticani*, p. 98.
[52] Ibid.   [53] De Rosa, *Storia del Banco di Roma*, I, p. 30.

Masonic than their rivals on the Right. Two figures in particular, the ex-Garibaldian Red Shirt Francesco Crispi, a true Sicilian firebrand, and Giuseppe Zanardelli, the Brescian radical who was if anything even more hostile to the Church, came to play an increasingly important role in Italian politics in the 1880s. Crispi rose to be prime minister twice, between 1887 and 1891 and between 1893 and 1896. Though the Left as a whole, and even Crispi, came to accept the necessity of the Law of Guarantees,[54] from time to time they sought to implement legislation further restricting the power and property of the Italian Church. Thus, a series of incidents in Rome, including the attack on the procession taking Pope Pius IX's coffin for burial in the Basilica of St Lorenzo,[55] prompted Leo to threaten to leave the city in 1881, 1887, 1889 and 1891. The motive of governments of the Left in initiating such legislation lay in a very real fear of being electorally outflanked by the *Estrema* which had consistently advocated a much tougher policy towards the Church.

In 1873, the Italian law decreeing the liquidation of the property of bishoprics, cathedral chapters and religious orders was extended to Rome and its surrounding provinces,[56] and in 1884 the property of the Congregation of Propaganda Fide, which was the curial office responsible for missionary activity throughout the world, was sequestrated and sold off, despite the clearest of evidence that its wealth had been accumulated from the offerings of Catholics throughout the world.[57] In 1887, the obligation on Italian farmers to pay the tithe to the parochial clergy was abolished.[58] In 1889 the new Penal Code made it an offence for clergy to 'publicly attack or insult the institutions and laws of the State or the acts of the authorities' or 'incite others to disregard them'.[59] In that same year, Crispi introduced legislation to take control of Catholic charitable trusts away from their managers, priests and the leaders of lay confraternities.[60]

Leo feared that the government would lay its hands on what remained of the property of the Italian Church, and especially the religious orders.[61] He sought to provide some means of protection, and so on 11 February 1887 he created a Cardinatial Commission to hold, administer and invest the wealth of religious orders and confraternities, converting gold and real estate into stocks and bonds, where necessary, and put the day-to-day operations into the hands of Folchi.[62] The existence of the Commission was necessarily a closely guarded secret until, that is, there was a theft

[54] Jemolo, *Church and State*, p. 69.   [55] Binchy, *Church and State*, p. 40.
[56] Caracciolo, *Roma capitale*, p. 144.   [57] Binchy, *Church and State*, p. 44.
[58] Ibid.   [59] As quoted in ibid., p. 42.   [60] Jemolo, *Church and State*, p. 46.
[61] Ibid., p. 46.   [62] Lai, *Finanze e finanzieri vaticani*, pp. 112–14.

of stocks and shares from their hiding-place, a vault in the appropriately named *buco nero* (the 'black hole') in 1900.[63]

In 1889 Folchi was presented with another important task, attending to the financial side of the preparations for Leo's flight from Rome. This renewed threat had been prompted by a further deterioration in relations between the 'two Romes', ironically, by the consequences of a failed attempt to bring about a reconciliation.[64] In an atmosphere of tension, which was made worse by the danger of a war between France and Italy, Leo communicated his decision to go abroad to the Italian government via an unofficial channel. When the reply came back that if he abandoned the Vatican, he would not be allowed to return, he swiftly changed his mind and the crisis passed over, though the passage through Parliament of the law on the charitable trusts in 1890 and a riot by French pilgrims in 1891 again almost convinced Leo to leave.[65] But Folchi carried through the agreed financial arrangements, which provided for cash and gold to be transferred to Rothschild's, and his decision to sell Italian government stocks and bonds belonging to the religious orders contributed to the worsening of the economic situation in Italy and to the tensions between Church and State.[66]

The fall of Folchi

Folchi's fall from grace and his departure from the administration of the Vatican's financial affairs in 1891 was as sudden as it was brutal and was in large part due to the bursting of the Rome property boom from 1887 onwards and also the result of the over-exposure of the Vatican to the Banco di Roma. But it can only be fully understood in light of the economic crises which affected Italy, and particularly Rome, in the late 1880s and early 1890s. In part, the crises were cyclical, the first real signs that a world economy was emerging from which no national economy could effectively be isolated, least of all that of Italy.[67] It was also more specifically the result of the economic and foreign policies of Francesco Crispi. The prime minister's hostility towards France, a long-standing prejudice of the parliamentary Left of which he was a member, was re-inforced by the French take-over of Tunisia in 1881 and Italy's conclusion of the Triple Alliance with Germany and Austria-Hungary a year later.[68] By

---

[63] Manfroni, *Sulla soglia del Vaticano*, II, p. 19.
[64] See Jemolo, *Church and State*, pp. 80–1.
[65] Seton-Watson, *Italy from Liberalism to Fascism*, p. 222.
[66] Lai, *Finanze e finanzieri vaticani*, p. 111.
[67] Seton-Watson, *Italy from Liberalism to Fascism*, pp. 141–4.   [68] Ibid., pp. 108–13.

1887, Crispi had entered into a trade war with France, imposing tariffs on Italian imports with the result that the French inflicted much more damage on Italian agricultural exports and withdrew their credit from Italian financial institutions.[69] The effects of the latter move were especially felt in Rome and in 1887 the building boom collapsed,[70] and the Banco di Roma suffered severe losses (for the resolution of this, the first crisis of the bank, see below, p. 72). Other major players in the Roman economy, like the Immobiliare, also suffered heavy losses and had to be restructured.[71]

The finances of the Vatican were, inevitably, badly damaged by the collapse. Levillain and Uginet estimate that the administration for the property of the Holy See lost one third of its capital.[72] Even allowing for the fact that most of the available information about the circumstances surrounding Folchi's dismissal comes from his own memoirs,[73] it does rather seem that he was made a scapegoat by Leo XIII and the commission of cardinals, some of whom, like Rampolla, the Cardinal Secretary of State, appear to have been hostile to him.[74] This version of events is supported by Manfroni and by Caracciolo.[75] In fact, Leo was as much to blame as anyone, having made unwise investments and loans since his election. Later he showed some remorse and attempted to compensate Folchi for his loss of office.[76] It is also possible that Folchi was quite simply a casualty of one of those power struggles which convulse the Vatican from time to time, especially in anticipation of the demise of an ailing pope.

Unlike his successor, Nogara, forty-eight years later (see Chapter 8, p. 181), Folchi was not given a serious chance to defend himself, though his memoirs suggest that his eleven-year management of the Vatican's capital was a good one. In particular had he not changed many of the investments left by Pius IX, the Holy See would have lost much more than a third of the value of its capital; whereas original investments yielded 3.5 per cent, which would have produced a total of 12.4 million lire, he had achieved a return of 24 million lire, nearly 7 per cent.

So Folchi was cast out, and was to be one of only two ecclesiastical administrators of Vatican finances (the other was Archbishop Paul Marcinckus in the 1980s) who did not receive the red hat for his services

---

[69] Ibid., pp. 134–6.   [70] Ibid., p. 110.
[71] Caracciolo, *Roma capitale*, p. 203.   [72] Levillain and Uginet, *Il Vaticano*, p. 104.
[73] For a detailed account of the fall of Folchi, see Lai, *Finanze e finanzieri vaticani*, pp. 123–31.
[74] Ibid. Levillain and Uginet, *Il Vaticano*, p. 104, also blame Folchi for the Vatican's losses.
[75] Manfroni, *Sulla soglia del Vaticano*, I, p. 195; Caracciolo, *Roma capitale*, p. 151.
[76] Lai, *Finanze e finanzieri vaticani*, p. 131.

Table 3 *Vatican expenditure and income accounts, 1878–87*

Income		Expenditure
Peter's Pence	Lit. 54 million	Lit. 78 million
Investment income	Lit. 24 million	
Total	Lit. 78 million	Lit. 78 million

Source: Lai, *Finanze e finanzieri vaticani*, p. 128 fn. 2.

(Nazareno Marzolini died suddenly and prematurely, in 1917). He was replaced by Msgr Mario Mocenni whose rather less controversial administration of the papal finances continued until his death in 1904. Ironically, Mocenni used more or less the same methods as Folchi in his endeavours to keep Peter's bark financially afloat. In particular, he followed a no-risk policy as far as the granting of personal loans was concerned, always insisting on collateral.[77] Otherwise, he continued to follow the advice of the nuncios in the purchase of foreign loan stock, and occasionally company shares.[78] He was equally careful on the expenditure side, making himself as unpopular for his economies during the 1903 conclave as Leo had during the one which elected him twenty-five years earlier, so much so that several of the Palatine Guard resigned their commissions in disgust.[79] Mocenni's success in charge of Vatican finances was rewarded with promotion. Apart from being made a cardinal in 1893, by the end of the century he was effectively 'Governor' of the Vatican, with the delicate responsibility of liaising with the Italian government's representative, the Commissario del Borgo,[80] a role not very dissimilar from that of Cardinal Nicola Canali forty years later (see Chapter 9, p. 208). Ultimately, however, Mocenni was overshadowed in his work as manager of the papal finances by Ernesto Pacelli, but if for nothing else he will be remembered for a rather interesting dictum which demonstrates both the anti-Semitic proclivities of the Roman clergy and their ambivalent attitude to money: 'If money had a religion it would be Jewish, but fortunately it doesn't have one, as a result of which it can be venerated by everybody.'[81]

The advent of Ernesto Pacelli

Folchi's exit from the Vatican stage in 1891 coincided with the arrival there of the first of the great laymen to be associated with the finances of the Holy See, Ernesto Pacelli. Members of the Pacelli family were among

---

[77] Ibid., p. 157.   [78] Ibid.   [79] Manfroni, *Sulla soglia del Vaticano*, II, p. 1.
[80] Lai, *Finanze e finanzieri vaticani*, p. 178.   [81] Ibid., title page.

those papal officials who had refused to serve under the new Italian rulers in 1870. Their association had begun under Marcantonio, who was Under-Secretary in the papal Ministry of Finances and then Secretary for the Interior between 1851 and 1870, and editor of *L'Osservatore Romano* from 1861, and Pietro, who was a customs official, but later also turned to journalism.[82] Marcantonio's youngest grandson, Eugenio, was ordained priest and introduced into the Vatican Secretariat of State in 1901, almost certainly with Ernesto's backing, rising to Under-Secretary of State in 1911. He played a key role in the commission which, under Cardinal Pietro Gasparri, brought about the codification of Canon Law.[83] Sent as nuncio to Bavaria in 1917, he was also central to Benedict XV's peace efforts in that year.[84] He became the first papal nuncio to the German Reich in 1920, Cardinal Secretary of State in 1930 and was elected pope as Pius XII in 1939. Cornwell has criticised his role in the negotiation of the *Reichskonkordat* of 1933 with the Germans and condemned him as 'Hitler's Pope' for his alleged silence during the Holocaust.[85] Whether that is a fair description or not, the pontificate of Pius XII was undoubtedly one of the most important in the twentieth century (see below, Chapter 9).

Marcantonio's eldest grandson, Francesco, also played an important role in the affairs of the papacy; in particular, he was the main negotiator on the Vatican side of the Lateran Pacts of 1929 (including the Financial Convention) which finally brought an end to the Roman Question (see Chapter 5). Thereafter, he remained the Vatican's principal legal adviser and one of its representatives on those companies in which it had a major share-holding (see below, Chapter 8).

Ernesto was Eugenio's and Francesco's cousin, and his role in the history of the modern papacy was also very important; between 1891 and 1903 he was the confidant, investment adviser and banker of Leo XIII, and until 1916 he remained the president of the largest financial institution with which the Vatican had dealings. In addition, he was the Vatican's link with the Italian government for most of that period. It would therefore be no exaggeration to say that the Pacellis were the most important family to be associated with the papacy since the Borgias.

Pacelli's entry into the Vatican and into the confidence of Leo XIII was largely a consequence of his handling of the fall-out from the Banca Romana scandal, in which a number of leading Italian politicians, including heavyweights like Crispi and Giolitti had been involved.[86] Pacelli was

---

[82] Pallenberg, *Inside the Vatican*, pp. 13–15.   [83] Cornwell, *Hitler's Pope*, pp. 41–5.
[84] Pollard, *The Unknown Pope*, p. 125.   [85] Cornwell, *Hitler's Pope*, chs. 7 and 9.
[86] Seton-Watson, *Italy from Liberalism to Fascism*, pp. 154–7, 163–4, 171–4.

Illustration 5 Ernesto Pacelli

able to secure from the Italian government considerable compensation for those affected by the collapse of the former bank of the Papal States, including the pope.[87] Leo was impressed, and Pacelli soon became his confidant and right-hand man in financial matters and, as will be seen later, his intermediary with the Italian government. He was soon *persona grata* in the papal apartments, with a right of almost unlimited access

[87] Lai, *Finanze e finanzieri vaticani*, pp. 150–1.

to the pope similar to that granted to Carlo Monti, Benedict's intermediary with the Italian government between 1914 and 1922.[88] Pacelli
was unobtrusive, discreet and immensely useful to the ageing pontiff.
He was also very successful in avoiding doing anything that would have
aroused envy and resentment on the part of Vatican officials; in particular,
though his bank, the Banco di Roma, profited hugely from his relationship with the pope, Pacelli never permitted himself any personal benefit,
not even in the form of the smallest gift or honour, award or decoration.[89]
Moreover, to protect his privileged relationship with the pope, which was
unprecedented for a layman, he made himself useful to all in the pope's
entourage, supplying favours of one kind or another, like financial advice,
bank loans, jobs for relatives, to the likes of the Cardinal Secretary of
State, Rampolla, and his subordinates Msgr Giacomo Della Chiesa and
Pietro Gasparri, who were becoming more and powerful in the Vatican
in the last years of Leo's pontificate.[90] Lai makes the particular point that
Gasparri was forever asking favours of Pacelli on behalf of relatives and
friends, a trait which worked against him in the conclave which followed
the death of Benedict in 1922 when his election was opposed by many cardinals because of their hostility to his known nepotistic tendencies.[91] In
the light of Leo's age and infirmities and the growing power of Rampolla
and company, this would have seemed a wise, long-term investment at
the time, even though, in the event, after the death of Leo, Rampolla and
his subordinates were to lose out to the protégé of the new pope, Pius X,
Cardinal Rafael Merry Del Val.

Given the continuing uncertainty and anxiety surrounding the legal
status of the Holy See and the pope himself in Italy, and the constant
fears of further Italian legislation against Church-held property, Pacelli
was particularly useful to Leo XIII by virtue of the fact that real estate
and stocks and shares, including those Banco di Roma shares possessed
by the pope and the Holy See, could be kept in his name, a legal fiction
which protected them from prying and hostile eyes, and possible legal
action. Even more important was his role as Leo's banker, providing him
with financial advice on a number of investment options both for his
own accounts and those of the Holy See, and in particular for ABSS.
Ultimately, Pacelli provided the living and authoritative link with the
Banco di Roma itself, into which he persuaded Leo to invest more and
more of the Vatican's capital.

[88] Pollard, *The Unknown Pope*, p. 71.   [89] Lai, *Finanze e finanzieri vaticani*, p. 162.
[90] Ibid., pp. 162–3.   [91] Ibid.

The Vatican 'discovers' American Catholicism

If Christopher Columbus discovered America in 1492, then it could be argued that the Holy See only truly 'discovered' American Catholicism four hundred years later. The growth of Catholicism in the American Republic had proceed apace since the establishment of the first see, Baltimore, in 1789. By the 1880s, the 10 million Catholics in the United States were served by eighty-two archbishops and bishops, and had been given their first cardinal, Archbishop McKloskey of New York, in 1875.[92] Not only were American Catholics numerous and growing, thanks to German, Irish, Italian and Polish immigration, but they were, generally speaking, more devout and faithful than many of their European co-religionists, as the French ambassador in Washington noted.[93] In 1886, taking advantage of the need ceremonially to convey the red hat to Archbishop Gibbons of Baltimore, the 'primate' of America, the Vatican sent Msgr German Straniero to America to draw up a report on American Catholicism.[94] He would not be the last Vatican envoy to be sent to North America in the 1880s and 1890s. As the Vatican sought to come to terms with divisions in both the US and Canadian hierarchies provoked by ethnic differences, the schools question and conservative-liberal tensions, a series of apostolic visitors and delegates were sent to the continent.[95]

In the case of the United States, a further two major questions attracted the concern of the Vatican: what was perceived as American Catholic involvement in organised unionism of a semi-masonic nature – the so-called 'Knights of Labour' – and the alleged heresy of 'Americanism'. The Knights of Labour question was handled by the Vatican to the satisfaction of most of the American bishops, thanks to Cardinal Gibbons's intervention in 1887.[96] And it is a further indication of Gibbons's influence in Rome at this point that he was able to intervene in like manner to persuade Leo XIII to insert a short but significant clause into his 1891 encyclical *Rerum Novarum* permitting Catholics to form associations of workers, thus giving papal approval to trade unionism. But 'Americanism' was a more serious problem and Gibbons's influence would be of no avail in seeking to prevent a papal condemnation of it. Conservatives in the American Church, in France and in the Vatican believed that American

---

[92] Fogarty, *The Vatican and the American Hierarchy*, pp. 9–10.
[93] A. Rhodes, *The Power of Rome in the Twentieth Century: The Vatican in the Age of the Liberal Democracies 1870–1922* (London, 1983), p. 131.
[94] Fogarty, *The Vatican and the American Hierarchy*, pp. 38–40.
[95] See also Perin, *Rome in Canada*, chs. 3–7.
[96] Fogarty, *The Vatican and the American Hierarchy*, pp. 86–92.

Catholicism was infected by heresy, a form of industrious, enterprising, 'muscular' Christianity born of the peculiar political and social conditions of the Land of the Free. The ideological child of the Enlightenment, America seemed to be the very antithesis of traditional, Catholic Europe, glorying in democracy, republicanism, separation of Church and State, egalitarianism (except where the Blacks and Native Americans were concerned) and unrestrained capitalistic individualism. Thus American democracy, individualism and the formal secularism posed worrying dangers for elements in the Roman curia and more generally Catholics in the Old Continent. Another problem for Rome was that American Catholics were not, apparently, very sympathetic towards the pope in his repeated protests against the loss of the temporal power: Fogarty, talking of the opening of the Catholic University of America and the celebrations of the centenary of the founding of the American hierarchy in 1889, speaks of, 'a paper on papal independence prepared by Fr Thomas O'Gorman, recently appointed professor of Church history at the new University. The paper was the substitute which Gibbons and others had arranged for "spontaneous" mass demonstrations against the loss of the temporal power, which the Vatican had requested.'[97]

Leo XIII eventually condemned the 'heresy' in his papal letter *Testem Benevolentiae* of 1899.[98] In doing so, he was rejecting in principle some of the key features of the success of American Catholicism, the separation of Church and State and religious liberty. The fact was that the Catholic Church had prospered and burgeoned under the aegis of American democracy. Large swathes of the United States might still be 'mission territory' in Catholic Canon Law and therefore under the formal jurisdiction of the Propaganda congregation, but hundreds of American Catholics were now going out to other mission territories in Africa and Asia, and by the 1890s, hundreds of thousands of American Catholics were contributing to the missionary effort. In broader terms, American Catholics were now making a major contribution to the financing of the Vatican through their offerings to Peter's Pence. In the conclusion to his report of 1886, Msgr Straniero urged the establishment of a permanent apostolic delegation in Washington, a clear recognition of the importance and vitality of the American Church, and he explained that it could be financed if each of the bishops contributed $100 a year, 'which even the least of the eighty American bishops can pay without the least difficulty'.[99] Confirmation of the growing importance of American Catholics to the finances of the Vatican comes from Count Soderini, one of Leo's closest confidants. According to his memoirs, 'In the pontificate of Leo XIII, there was a notable increase in the flow of offerings from the United States of America, to the point that it compensated for a lesser inflow of French contributions to the Obolo.'[100]

Rerum Novarum, 1891

In 1891, Leo XIII published one of the most important encyclicals in the modern history of the papacy, *Rerum Novarum*, literally 'The New Order', or as it is known in English, 'On the Conditions of the Working Classes'. The publication of *Rerum Novarum* was a landmark in the development of Catholic Social Doctrine, papal teaching on the ethics of economic and social life; indeed, it was effectively the origin of modern Catholic Social Teaching, the first major set of pronouncements upon such questions since the work of St Thomas Aquinas back in the fourteenth century. Subsequent popes have also published major encyclicals on social questions, especially Pius XI (*Quadragesimo Anno*, 1931), John XXIII (*Mater et Magistra*, 1961), Paul VI (*Popolorum Progressio*, 1967) and John Paul II (*Centesimus Annus*, 1981) which have sought to build on and update Leo XIII's pronouncements on the responsibilities of Catholics and the Church in the economic and social spheres.[101] The genesis of *Rerum Novarum* and its appearance in the 1890s may be ascribed to a number of factors. By 1891, industrial capitalism had taken hold not only in Britain and America, where in the latter case immigrant Catholics constituted the bulk of the urban, industrial workforce in the north-eastern and mid-western states, but also in Catholic Europe, in northern France, the Wallonian provinces of southern and eastern Belgium and the Ruhr and Silesia in Germany. Italy, however, was still largely untouched by industrial capitalism. In the 1890s, only the north-western cities of Milan, Turin and Genoa – the later 'industrial triangle' – had begun seriously to feel the effects of industrialisation. Of all of these experiences, only the Belgian case had been a personal one for Leo when he was nuncio there from 1843 to 1846, and it would have had its influence upon the pontiff. Certainly, the experience of such great 'social bishops' as Kettler of Mainz, and their experiments in Catholic social and economic organisations, would have been known to him, and influenced the thinking which led to *Rerum Novarum*.[102] Another reason was quite simply Leo XIII himself. Unlike his predecessor, Leo was a man keenly interested in ideas and

---

[100] Soderini, *Il pontificato di Leone XIII*, II, pp. 402–3.
[101] Carlen (ed.), *Papal Encyclicals*, IV.
[102] P. Misner, *Social Catholicism in Europe: From the Onset of Industrialisation to the First World War* (London, 1991).

in particular, in the theology of St Thomas Aquinas which, in the *Summa Theologica*, supplied the first systematic and comprehensive summary of Catholic theology.[103] It also provided considerable guidance on the Christian ethics of the market place with such concepts as the 'just price' and the 'just wage', which are clearly in evidence in *Rerum Novarum*.[104] This was hardly surprising: Leo saw the theology and philosophy of Aquinas, one of the great 'Doctors of the Church', as constituting the best basis for a resurgence of Catholic theology and philosophy in the face of the dangerous ideas at large in the modern world; hence he saw in Aquinas's ideas about the ethics of social and economic life a good antidote to dangerous economic and social ideas, like laissez-faire economics on the one hand, and Marxian Socialism on the other.

Rerum Novarum reflects this balance exactly: while it condemned Socialism and Communism, arguing in line with Thomist theology that private property was a natural human right, it also condemned the exploitation of the working class and their inhuman working and living conditions. The bottom line of *Rerum Novarum* is that industrial capitalism, like Communism, was inspired by materialism, so both were bad.[105] Another consideration was the underlying philosophy of capitalism, which was essentially liberal and secularist. In Italy, at least, churchmen continued to see capitalism as the evil child of philosophical and political liberalism and condemned it as the result of the 'Manchester (School) of Economics',[106] and the fruit of an 'unrestrained thirst for profit'.[107] Elsewhere, other Catholic writers condemned capitalism as the 'economic system based upon the productivity of money', and still barely tolerated the earning of interest despite the Church's shift in attitude towards this.[108]

How, one might ask, did the Vatican's new investments in banks, construction and utility companies square with the strictures about the operations of capitalism as cited above? That is a very difficult question to answer. There is certainly no clear evidence that Leo XIII's statement of Catholic teaching on economic and social matters affected the Vatican's investment policy. At this stage in the development of papal financial policy, the Vatican had only very limited share-holdings in companies employing large numbers of manual workers. It is not known whether

---

[103] See R. Barry OP, 'The Contribution of Thomas Aquinas', in J. A. Dwyer (ed.), *The New Dictionary of Catholic Social Thought* (Collegeville, Minn., 1994), pp. 940–51.

[104] Carlen (ed.), *The Papal Encyclicals*, II, pp. 241–61.

[105] Misner, *Social Catholicism*, p. 215.

[106] As quoted in A. Gambasin, *Gerarchia e laicato in Italia nel secondo ottocento* (Padua, 1986), p. 151.

[107] As quoted in F. Renda, *Socialisti e cattolici in Sicilia* (Palermo, 1972), p. 67.

[108] Misner, *Social Catholicism*, p. 238.

the Vatican showed any particular concern about the wages and working conditions of those workers or whether it simply took on trust the policies of the management of these companies on these matters.

The effect which the encyclical did have was to prompt the emergence of a network of Catholic economic and social organisations offering assistance to poor workers and peasants alike in Italy, on the lines of those which had already developed in other parts of Europe and which had certainly influenced Leo in his writing of *Rerum Novarum*.[109] In the 1880s and 1890s, Italy went through the first stages of industrialisation with the consequent emergence of the so-called 'industrial triangle' around Milan, Turin and Genoa in north-western Italy, with smaller industrial centres elsewhere. Industrialisation produced an industrial working class and that in turn contributed to the development of a Marxian-dominated working-class movement comprising the Italian Socialist Party and its affiliated co-operatives, trades unions and peasant leagues.[110] The parallel rise of the Catholic movement at this time was very much a response to this development.[111] From the beginning of the 1890s onwards, embryonic Catholic trades unions and peasant leagues, consumer and production co-operatives and mutual insurance societies and small banks and credit unions – the *banche popolari* and the *casse di risparmio* – began to develop in northern and eastern Italy, in the Veneto and Lombardy especially.[112] The organisers were the Catholic lay intelligentsia and priests whom Leo XIII admonished 'to go forth from the sacristy' if they were to save the souls of the working classes and combat the evil of a growing Marxist working-class movement which was already building its own network of economic, social and recreational organisations to attract working-class and peasant support.[113]

The small Catholic banks were based on mutualistic principles not dissimilar from those underlying the organisation of British building societies. They gathered the savings of mainly peasant farmers, but also the Catholic lower middle class of the small towns, and joined them together with capital contributed by wealthier Catholics and provided loans and mortgages for chiefly agricultural purposes. A classic example of them was the Roman Banca Artistica Operaio, which Leo XIII induced Pacelli to save from collapse in 1889.[114] By 1904, forty-four Catholic banks and

---

[109] Ibid., chs. 7, 8 and 9.
[110] Pollard, 'Religion and the Formation of the Italian Working Classes', pp. 158–60.
[111] D. Howard Bell, *Sesto San Giovanni: Workers, Culture and Politics in an Italian Town, 1880–1922* (New Brunswick, N.J., 1986), pp. 60–1.
[112] Pollard, 'Religion and the Formation of the Italian Working Class', p. 171; and Misner, *Social Catholicism*, ch. 13.
[113] Pollard, 'Religion and the Formation of the Italian Working Class', pp. 169–70.
[114] Lai, *Finanze e finanzieri vaticani*, pp. 182–3.

nearly a thousand *casse di risparmio* were joined together under the aegis of the Opera dei Congressi, the umbrella organisation of the Italian Catholic movement.[115]

The rise of Catholic lay capitalism in Italy

But mutualism was not the only basis on which Catholic economic and financial activities had begun to develop in Italy by the turn of the century. The 'blacks' of Rome were not the only Catholic aristocracy to move from traditional agricultural and land-holding activities to building speculation and other commercial activities. In northern and central Italy, men of the Catholic aristocracy, like Count Grosoli, who became president of the Opera, Cesare Nava and Count Soderini, who was an intimate friend of Leo XIII, began to move into commercial and banking spheres in the late nineteenth century, taking with them the capital accumulated through improved, capitalistic farming.[116] By the turn of the century, the Catholic 'plutocracy' in Lombardy, Emilia-Romagna and Tuscany had become prominent not only in the traditional agricultural sector, but in banking, insurance, food processing and other manufacturing sectors.[117] Banking was the key to their success. The leading lights in the Italian Catholic movement, men like Count Grosoli and Nava, sat on the boards of such Catholic banks as the Banco Ambrosiano and the Piccolo Credito di Ferrara, and through their networks of contacts in the broader Catholic movement were able to channel the deposits of the small Catholic saver in the local *casse di risparmio* into capitalist investments on a larger and sometimes national scale.[118]

In the pontificate of Pius XI, these three separate Catholic econ-omic/financial forces – the Catholic small banking network, the capi-talistic activities of the Catholic plutocracy and the financial power of the papacy – would be brought together and become a major factor in the Italian economy. In the reign of Pius XII, they would be welded into a powerful instrument for Catholic economy hegemony in Italy to parallel the political power of the Church as exercised on its behalf after 1948 by the governing Christian Democratic Party.

[115] A. Caroleo, *Le banche cattoliche dalla prima Guerra mondiale al fascismo* (Milan, 1976), p. 25.
[116] M. G. Rossi, *Le origini del movimento cattolico in Italia* (Rome, 1977), pp. 38–40.
[117] Ibid.   [118] Ibid., p. 286.

4   Vatican finances under the 'peasant pope', Pius X (1903–1914)

Introduction

The conclave which followed the death of Leo XIII in 1903 marked an historic milestone for the papacy because it was the last time that a secular power attempted to influence the election of a pope by exercising a veto against a candidate. The declaration by Cardinal Puzyina of Cracow of a veto against Cardinal Rampolla on behalf of the Austrian Emperor Franz Josef undoubtedly helped to clear the way for the success of Giuseppe Sarto, cardinal patriarch of Venice who until that point seemed to have little chance of being elected.[1] In the end, Sarto won convincingly, but because of his natural humility it was only with some difficulty that he was persuaded to accept the papal throne. This was typical of the man who was to be beatified in 1951 and canonised three years later, the first pope to become a saint for over three hundred years. But as pope, he ruled sternly and vigorously, belying the meekness and humility ascribed to him.

Pius was also of humble origins, born of a peasant family in Riese, Treviso province of the region north of Venice, and his ecclesiastical career was an example of how the Roman Catholic Church at its best can provide remarkable opportunities for upward mobility. Curate, priest in a country parish, chancellor of the diocese of Treviso and spiritual director of its seminary, he was appointed bishop of Mantua in 1885 and then cardinal and patriarch of Venice in 1894. He was thus the first of three patriarchs of Venice to become pope in the twentieth century (the others were John XXIII and John Paul I) and was a classic product of that northern Italian Catholic milieu which was to provide a total of five popes before the end of the millennium.[2]

---

[1] Chadwick, *A History of the Popes*, pp. 333–41.
[2] For the life of Pius X, see Levillain (ed.), *The Papacy*, II, pp. 1197–9; C. Falconi, *The Popes in the Twentieth Century* (London, 1967), pp. 1–88; and Duffy, *Saints and Sinners*, pp. 245–53.

Illustration 6 Pope Pius X

By contrast with Leo XIII, ever the aristocratic intellectual and diplo-mat, Pius X was the humble pastor, so much so that he has been nick-named the 'parish priest pope' and certainly, his pontificate was marked by a commitment to pastoral ministry of all kinds. He has been remem-bered for his encouragement of frequent communion for lay people and early communion for children (from seven upwards), as well as the restoration of Gregorian Chant to a central place in Church music, thus marking some of the most important liturgical and devotional reforms since the Council of Trent.[3] He was also a great reforming pope, carry-ing out a major reform of the training of priests, including the setting up of regional seminaries, the administration of the Roman curia and the setting up of a commission in 1907 to codify Canon Law.[4] But he will be remembered most of all for his campaign against 'modernism', encap-sulated in his statements *Lamentabili* and *Pascendi* of 1907, which set in train a witch-hunt against all clergy suspected of 'modernist' opinions in theology, biblical exegesis and Church history,[5] and for his ferocious reaction against the anti-clerical legislation of the Combes government in France which led to a bitter Church–State dispute and the rupturing of diplomatic relations with the 'eldest daughter of the Church'.[6] Indeed, by the end of his reign, thanks to the intransigent policies of himself and his Secretary of State, Cardinal Merry Del Val, the Vatican found itself isolated on the international plane as never before, unable to exercise any influence to prevent the outbreak of the First World War which Pius is alleged to have frequently prophesied.[7]

Pius X as a financial manager

Initially, at any rate, Pius seemed to have inherited a less than promising financial situation. The conclave of 1903 was, as usual, costly, despite attempts at economies on the part of Mocenni and, as usual, there were protests on the part of Vatican employees at the less than munificent 'bonuses' handed out after Pius's election, so much so that some of the Swiss Guards threatened to leave, whereupon the new pope in reply threatened to dissolve the corps, which put an end to the mutiny.[8] The problem was that when Leo's apartments were unsealed only 82,000 lire in cash and a collection of assorted jewels were found,[9] whereas

---

[3] Ibid., pp. 247–8.   [4] Ibid., pp. 245–6.
[5] Chadwick, *A History of the Popes*, pp. 346–59.   [6] Ibid., pp. 391–402.
[7] Pollard, *The Unknown Pope*, pp. 58–9.   [8] Duffy, *Saints and Sinners*, p. 253.
[9] C. Snider, *L'Episcopato del Cardinale Andrea Ferrari, Contributo allo Studio delle condizioni religiose nell'età contemporanea* (2 vols., Vatican City, 1974), II, p. 45.

the conclave had cost more than ten times that amount,[10] giving rise to serious apprehensions about the financial viability of the Holy See. These concerns were dissipated a month later when Marzolini came forward with Leo's brass chest, explaining that he had been given precise instructions by Leo to delay surrendering it to the new pope in order, as Leo requested, to impress upon his successor the need for wise management of the papacy's money.[11] Leo could have spared himself the trouble. Throughout the whole of his previous career, from curate to cardinal, Pius had had to contend with money problems.[12] Consequently, he tackled the financial problems of the Holy See with the same thorough, methodical and practical organisational approach as he had done with his financial responsibilities as priest, bishop and patriarch. He even kept his own records of the receipts and outgoings of Peter's Pence and practised stringent economy.[13] Like Leo XIII before him, Pius handed over a cheque from Peter's Pence to Marzolini as secretary of the ABSS, which in 1907 averaged between 200,000 and 300,000 lire a month.[14]

Pius X's tidy, reforming mind led him to embark on a reform of the Roman curia, including the financial agencies of the Holy See. That reform was also motivated by the desire to render the centralised bureaucracy of the Holy See more efficient in its essential task of ruling the world-wide Church. He even attempted to re-organise the structures of Italian national ecclesiastical administration, in an effort to eliminate the extraordinary variations in the size of dioceses between north and south. Whereas the average southern diocese had less than 100,000 souls, and some many fewer than that, the average northern diocese had two or three times that number, but abandoned the attempt.[15] Neither Pius IX nor Leo XIII had done much to bring about a rationalisation of the Roman curia following the abolition of the temporal power. As a result, the central government of the Church was a chaotic welter of congregations, offices and tribunals, some rendered quite redundant by the fact that the pope no longer exercised territorial sovereignty, and a few duplicated the functions of others. In addition there was enormous financial waste, nepotism

---

[10] F. Martini, *Diario: 1914–1918*, edited by G. De Rosa (Milan, 1966), p. 48.

[11] Majoloni, *Il Giornale d'Italia*, 19 June 1925.

[12] G. Dal Gal, *Il Papa santo* (Padua, 1954), p. 10, where he tells the story of Sarto going around his neighbours in Riese begging for money to pay his seminary costs, and *Acta Pio X, Summarium*, pp. 381–2, detailing Sarto's need to ask for a loan from Mocenni in order to buy his cardinalatial robes.

[13] *Acta Pio X, Positio*, p. 116.

[14] ASV, SdS, Spoglio di Pio X, fasc. 10, receipt for 200,000 lire dated 14 Aug. 1907, signed by Marzolini, two others for 150,000 lire each dated 14 and 28 Sept. 1914 respectively.

[15] ASV, SdS, Spoglio di Pio X, fasc. 14, Studio, per l'Unificazione delle diocesi in Italia, 3 Nov. 1905, G. De Lai.

and what at best could only be described as old-fashioned working practices and perks, and at worst systematic plunder of the Holy See's limited
resources.[16] A further scandal was the presence in Rome of thousands of
'nomadic' priests, especially from the south of Italy, who had cast loose
from their dioceses and gone to the Eternal City in search of more lucrative employment and who subsisted on mass offerings and charities. As
far as the financial organisation of the Roman curia was concerned, there
were far too many congregations with autonomous powers to raise and
spend money, and too little control over their operations.

By the terms of the *motu proprio Sapienti Consiglio* of June 1908, a
total of twelve curial congregations were suppressed, their functions being
absorbed by others, but this still left some further work of rationalisation
to be completed in the field by Benedict XV between 1914 and 1922.[17]
Pius also introduced fixed salary scales for employees of the Roman curia
instead of the fee-farming system which had previously prevailed and even
considered trimming the staffing of the personnel of the Papal Court, with
the radical idea of reducing the papal armed corps to one, but resistance
from the members of the 'black' aristocracy thwarted this plan; it was
not until Paul VI came to the papal throne in 1963 that the plan would
be taken out of the drawer and implemented, and even then it took Papa
Montini five years to push it through.[18]

Papa Sarto was almost entirely unsuccessful in his efforts to rationalise
the financial affairs of the curia. The various congregations were tenacious
in their determination to retain control of their finances, especially Propaganda and the Congregation of the Council (of Trent), thus the pope's
aim of consolidating all accounts into a single, central fund, under the
aegis of the ABSS, was frustrated. Similarly, the Opera per Pias Causas
also remained autonomous. Pius did manage to separate the administration of the Apostolic Palace from the ABSS, and place it under the
control of the Cardinal Secretary of State.[19] Inasmuch as the Secretary
of State was also the president of the ABSS, this was probably not such
a major change as it looked on paper. Again, while formally deferring
to the cardinalatial commission which in theory ran the ABSS, Pius was
quite interventionist in its affairs and worked more and more closely and
directly through Marzolini, by-passing Mocenni and his colleagues.[20] As
will be seen later, like his predecessor, Pius also worked closely with
Ernesto Pacelli (see below, pp. 97–101).

Though he started his reign under a financial cloud, Pius did not in
fact face serious or enduring financial problems during his years of rule.

[16] Majoloni, *Il Giornale d'Italia*, 19 June 1925.
[17] *Acta Apostolicae Sedis*, 1 (1900), pp. 7–19.   [18] Rees, *Inside the Vatican*, p. 18.
[19] Lai, *Finanze e finanzieri vaticani*, p. 222.   [20] Ibid.

His natural pessimism and almost neurotic concern to be economical with resources did, however, sometimes create the impression that the Vatican was short of money. In 1904, Pius urged economies (including the axing of the little zoo which Leo had kept in the Vatican gardens) to surmount what appears to have been a short-term cash-flow crisis,[21] and a year later he refused money to a lawyer in Venice because 'in the present financial situation, it is impossible to offer even the smallest assistance'.[22] This was no bad thing from the point of view of income, as it seems to have stimulated the faithful into giving more generously, and his open disputes with secular governments, such as those with France, Spain and Portugal, were followed by especially significant increases in the revenue from Peter's Pence. In September 1904, following the usual Italian celebration of the breach of Porta Pia and the decision to hold an international conference of free thinkers in Rome, the Vatican was inundated with literally thousands of letters of sympathy from lay people, as a result of careful orchestration.[23] It is also significant that in 1907, following the publication of *Lamentabili* and *Pascendi* against 'modernism', there was a sudden and massive increase in contributions to Peter's Pence from dioceses and individuals alike, and from quite different geographical areas.[24] Three years later, after a particularly insulting speech on 20 September by the mayor of Rome, Ernesto Nathan, who was a leading freemason, Cardinal Fischer, archbishop of Cologne wrote to the pope explaining that he had sent a pastoral letter to the faithful of the diocese announcing that he would be coming to the Vatican to express his solidarity with the pope. He also informed him that he had called for a special collection of Peter's Pence in view of what had happened:

I think that the sad events which have recently occurred in Rome provide an opportunity for a special and generous collection and that we Rhineland Catholics must think with [the pope] and work with Him and that the attacks upon his Sacred Person will do nothing except increase our love of Him.[25]

Similarly, Pius's toughness in disputes with the Czar's government in 1907 and his refusal to give an audience to ex-president Theodore Roosevelt, because of the latter's desire to visit Masonic and Methodist organisations

---

[21] Ibid., p. 235.
[22] ASV, SdS, Spoglio di Pio X, fasc. 1, letter of 2 Apr. 1905.   [23] Ibid., fasc. 12.
[24] See Zambarbieri, 'La devozione al Papa', pp. 70–4; these contain graphs showing the rise and fall in receipts for Peter's Pence in the period 1903–29 according to dioceses, individuals and countries as recorded in *La Civiltà Cattolica*. They necessarily cover only a fraction of all of the offerings received by the pope in this period.
[25] ASV, SdS, Spoglio di Pio X, fasc. 1, 'Colletta straordinaria per il Santo Padre Sunday 16 October'. See the reference on page 2 of this document to Nathan, 'who characteristically in the city of the popes is not a Catholic but a Jew'.

in Rome, brought financial benefits.[26] This followed a pattern set in previous reigns; the more intransigent the popes were in asserting the rights of the Holy See and the Church in general, the more generous were the faithful in their contributions to sustaining the expenses of the curia and Papal Court; conversely, when Leo XIII had sought to impose the *Ralliement* upon unconvinced French Catholics, the income from Peter's Pence in France had fallen noticeably.[27]

With a handsome appearance, Pius X had as much charismatic appeal as his namesake Pius IX, with the result that both laity and clergy made extra efforts to come to his aid, as is testified by the beautifully hand-written lists of contributors, great and small, preserved in Pius X's papers.[28] After the 1908 earthquake in Calabria and Sicily, his appeal for relief funds quickly raised 6 million lire.[29] Such was the strength of his appeal among the Catholic clergy that the 'canonical prebend', which had been established in 1879, as a fund for the pope's personal use to be subscribed as a special act of devotion by the parochial clergy of the Catholic world, brought in much financial support from the members of cathedral chapters in particular.[30] Lai says that it was alien to Pius's nature actively 'to seek offerings in any form',[31] yet early on in his reign he engaged in precisely such an initiative which ultimately rebounded against him. In 1904 he and Cardinal Merry Del Val commissioned an American prelate, Bishop Bonaventure Broderick, formerly auxiliary to the archbishop of Havana, to act as a sort of semi-official papal *legatus a latere*, a roving representative in the USA, 'to organise and promote in each of the dioceses of his mother country the collection of Peter's Pence'.[32] Not unnaturally, the American bishops, who were shouldering an increasing financial burden for the Vatican, resented this apparent lack of confidence in their fundraising abilities and intrusion into their legitimate relationship with the faithful. No less a person than Cardinal Gibbons of Baltimore ordered Broderick to cease his activities.[33] It all ended in tears for Bishop Broderick. When he reported to the Vatican on the unfortunate way in which his efforts on behalf of the pope had

[26] Lai, *Finanze e finanzieri vaticani*, p. 262.   [27] Ibid.
[28] See, for example, ASV, SdS, Spoglio di Pio X, fasc. 4, Obulus S. Petri, letter from apostolic vicar of Hu-Nan, southern China, 1911. 4,000 lire, and fasc. 9, Obolo dei Bambini Polacchi, I centesimo of a rouble each. 23 Apr. 1908, and, ibid., Spoglio di Cardinale Merry Del Val, letter of 7 July 1913, in which the nuncio in Madrid relates that a pious Spanish layman had left the pope 25,000 pesetas in his will.
[29] Lai, *Finanze e finanzieri vaticani*, pp. 262–3.
[30] ASV, Spoglio di Pio X, fasc. 5, La Prebenda Canonicale di Sua Santità Pio X, Sarno, 1904.
[31] Lai, *Finanze e finanzieri vaticani*, p. 239.
[32] As quoted in R. I. Gannon, SJ, *The Cardinal Spellman Story* (New York, 1963), p. 148.
[33] Ibid.

been received by his fellow bishops in America, Pius misunderstood his request for an alternative posting as a bishop and accused him of trying to blackmail him. The poor man ended up effectively in disgrace, with a pension from the Secretariat of State of $100 a year.[34] Nearly thirty years were to pass until he was rescued by Archbishop Spellman of New York, in whose diocese he resided.[35] All this suggests a remarkable lack of understanding of the American Catholic world on the part of Pius X and his Secretary of State, all the more remarkable given Merry Del Val's very close and cordial relationship with William O'Connell, bishop of Portland, Maine, and later cardinal archbishop of Boston.[36]

Papal spending

If Pius had a near-obsession with economies, he was not entirely unwilling to spend money, except on himself, which stemmed from a life-time of frugality and of self-denial. Thus, when it became apparent that his apartments (private and public – the latter the so-called *appartamento nobile*) desperately needed re-furbishing after years of neglect, he was horrified by the projected cost. He only agreed to the expenditure when Merry Del Val managed to raise the funds from an enterprising Spanish religious.[37] Clearly, unlike either of his predecessors, or his successor, Pius had little concern over the externals, the trappings of papal power, the adulatory protocol and loathed being carried in the *sedia gestatoria* and was shocked when the congregation clapped on his entry into St Peter's.[38] But when it was really necessary, he was ready to spend. In 1909, he embarked upon the purchase of a building to house the new Pontifical Biblical Institute, to bring the study of exegesis more closely under papal control, and this cost him 400,000 lire.[39]

Another matter of importance to him, as it had been to his predecessors, was finding the money to extend the confines of his little domain, the Vatican. In 1917 Cardinal Pietro Gasparri, Secretary of State to two popes, Benedict XV and Pius XI, said that 'The Vatican, even with its gardens, is merely a palace not a state.'[40] It was small and, moreover, claustrophobic and lacking in privacy; the public had access to the Basilica, the museums, the gardens and even parts of the Vatican Palace. So in many

34 ASV, Delegation to the United States (DAUS), II, 70, Pensione mensile per SER Msgr Broderick Bonaventure, 1905–19.
35 Gannon, *The Cardinal Spellman Story*, pp. 146–51.
36 Fogarty, *The Vatican and the American Hierarchy*, pp. 218–19.
37 Snider, *L'Episcopato di Cardinale Andrea Ferrari*, II, pp. 107–8.
38 Chadwick, *A History of the Popes*, p. 354.
39 Lai, *Finanze e finanzieri vaticani*, p. 207.   40 Ibid., pp. 210–12.

ways, the Vatican really was a 'prison' and not a very convenient one at
that (see the map on p. 40). One building of uncomfortable proximity to
the Apostolic Palace which was in the possession of the Italian state was
the Zecca, the old pontifical mint which the Italians naturally took over
in September 1870 and continued to use for the making of Italian coins.
Thus right below the walls of the apartments near the Sistine Chapel
were Italian soldiers guarding their State Mint, so that in order to achieve
private access to the Vatican gardens by wheeled transport, it was necessary to construct a tunnel beneath the Apostolic Palace. In 1901, the
government announced its intention of building a new, and larger, mint
elsewhere. Leo immediately became concerned that if the building was
sold it might be purchased by a group inimical to the Church, for instance
an anti-clerical organisation like the Giordano Bruno Society which could
then use it to harass the pope and his court, a perfectly likely eventuality
given previous anti-clerical incidents in and around the Vatican.[41] After a
long wrangle, and some fancy parliamentary footwork designed to avoid
too much public knowledge and discussion, the Giolitti government in
power in 1904 sold the Zecca to the Vatican via Ernesto Pacelli.[42] Further properties around the Vatican were bought in the following years and
one purchase at least was to cause Pius's successor, Benedict XV, acute
embarrassment. At the height of the First World War, while Benedict and
his Secretary of State were pursuing a Vatican diplomatic policy of strict
impartiality and neutrality, it was discovered that one of the Holy See's
tenants was using the premises to manufacture munitions for the Italian
army![43]

The needs of the Roman curia also demanded considerable extra capital expenditure; thus in 1906 Leo paid 700,000 lire for the purchase of two
Roman palaces – the Palazzo Massimo and the Palazzo Folchi – in order
to provide more office accommodation for the Roman congregations, and
three years later he paid 800,000 lire for Palazzo Maresciotti to house the
offices of the Vicariato di Roma, the city's diocesan administration which
is now located, more appropriately, in the Lateran Palace adjacent to the
cathedral of Rome.[44] As in other major Italian cities in the first decade of
the twentieth century, so in the Eternal City urban expansion left large
numbers of 'unchurched', immigrant Romans to be provided for, and
in consequence during the course of his reign Pius was forced to spend

[41] As quoted in G. Spadolini (ed.), *Il Cardinale Gasparri e la Questione Romana. Con brani
delle memorie inedite* (Florence, 1972), p. 234.
[42] Ibid., p. 212.
[43] ACS, General Directorate of Public Security (DGPS), H4, Vaticano, Notizie, Commis-
sarato del Borgo, 1915, 22 Oct. 1915.
[44] Lai, *Finanze e finanzieri vaticani*, pp. 259–60.

12 million lire alone in order to buy land on which to build new parish churches in the burgeoning suburbs,[45] with further sums being spent on actual construction. In 1912, for example, Pius contributed 185,000 out of a total of 470,902 lire for the construction of the parochial plant of the new church of San Giuseppe, Quartiere Trionfale, not far from the walls of the Vatican.[46]

Italy's growing, and often troubled, Catholic movement was also a cause of considerable papal expenditure, in particular the Catholic press. When Pius came to the papal throne in 1903, the umbrella organisation of the movement, the Opera dei Congressi, was in crisis. The tensions between the old guard conservatives like Paganuzzi and Medolago-Albani and the radical, reforming Christian Democrats led by Don Romolo Murri and Don Luigi Sturzo had provoked a change in leadership, with Count Grosoli, a compromise candidate and a leading clerico-moderate banker, being appointed president in Paganuzzi's stead.[47] But the tensions continued and in 1904 Pius decided to sack Grosoli. Finding a replacement was no easy task. Apart from any other consideration there was a financial one: the president had tended, with an appropriate sense of *noblesse oblige*, not only to give immense amounts of time to the job, thus rendering the earning of his own living difficult, but was also expected to contribute towards the expenses of the office. Pius's instinct was to go back to a reliable and obedient conservative like Paganuzzi, or Rezzara or Medolago-Albani, but they could not do the job because they lacked sufficient private means.[48] The financial problem was a major factor in his decision to dissolve the Opera altogether and re-constitute its various activities in separate organisations more directly under the control of diocesan bishops – the Unione Economico-sociale to direct the Catholic banks, co-operatives, embryonic Catholic trade unions and mutual insurance societies, the Unione Popolare as an umbrella for all the others as well as their propaganda arm and the Unione Elettorale Cattolica in order to superintend the mobilisation of Catholic voters in local elections and in those parliamentary constituencies where they were allowed to vote in general elections.[49] And all of these activities were now brought more firmly under the control of the ecclesiastical hierarchy at every level, especially of the bishops.

[45] Ibid., p. 210.
[46] ASV, SdS, Spoglio di Pio X, fasc. 1, letter from Pius of 28 Sept. 1912 to the parish priest.
[47] Webster, *The Cross and the Fasces*, ch. 1.
[48] G. Aubert, 'Documents relatifs au movement catholique italien sous le pontificat de S. Pie', *Rivista di Storia della Chiesa*, 31 (1958), p. 223.
[49] Webster, *The Cross and the Fasces*, pp. 36–7.

Even in its re-constituted form, the Italian Catholic movement was a drain on the Vatican's finances. Regular subsidies were required for the Opera itself, for GIAC, the youth branch, and for FUCI, the Catholic students' organisation.[50] Other Catholic associations, like FASC, the Catholic sports federation, also needed help.[51] The Catholic press was even more of a problem. Running daily or even weekly broadsheets for the edification of the faithful as a part of the *buona stampa* (literally 'good press') campaign to insulate them from the blasphemies of the anti-clerical, liberal press was an expensive business. High levels of illiteracy, especially in the south, made readerships small and a fierce battle for advertising, plus a desire to keep prices down, made Catholic newspapers an extremely unprofitable undertaking. Editors had begun to direct their begging bowls at the Vatican even before Pius was elected: in 1895 the editor of *La Frusta*, a particularly intransigent Catholic paper in Rome, asked for a relatively small subsidy, 4,000 lire,[52] and in 1902 the editor of *La Sicilia Cattolica* wrote a letter to the Secretariat of State explaining that though the paper had kept going for thirty-five years, it could not continue without a generous and immediate subsidy.[53] *L'Unità Cattolica*, the rabidly intransigent paper of Florence, asked for 10,000 lire just in order to keep going in 1911.[54] As Ernesto Pacelli stated in a letter to the pope in 1907, 'The financial sacrifices which the Holy See has made for the [Catholic] press are only too well known: to date they have had almost entirely negative results.'[55]

By the middle of Pius's reign, *L'Osservatore Romano* was also in receipt of a regular subsidy, but the biggest financial headache for the Vatican was caused by the other Catholic newspapers in the city of Rome. In September 1907, directors of the Banco di Roma set up the Società Editrice Romana (SER), with a paid up capital of 150,000 lire, provided by the bank, to bail out the Catholic daily *Il Corriere d'Italia*.[56] Pacelli was not doing this entirely out of charity: the *Corriere* would later play an important role in the propaganda war over Libya (see below, p. 105) Over the years, other Catholic dailies would come under the aegis of the SER, including *L'Avvenire d'Italia* of Bologna, *L'Italia* of Milan, *Il Momento* of Turin, *Il Messaggero Toscano* of Pisa and *La Sicilia Cattolica* of Palermo. All of these papers followed an essentially clerico-moderate line, that is

---

[50] ASV, SdS, Rubricella, 1898–1922, 1903, O–Z, 1914, A–C, and 1907, D–K respectively.
[51] Ibid., Spoglio di Pio X, fasc. 12, letter from the president of FASC to the pope, no date.
[52] ASV, SdS, Spoglio di Cardinale Giacomo Della Chiesa, II, suppliche di denaro.
[53] Ibid., letter of 6 Feb. 1902.
[54] Ibid., Spoglio di Pio X, fasc. 10, letter from editor of 3 Apr. 1911; and C. Bertini, *Ai tempi delle guaranteggie. Ricordi di un funzionario di polizia, 1913–1918* (Rome, 1932), p. 20; Bertini was Manfroni's successor as Commissario del Borgo.
[55] As quoted in Lai, *Finanze e finanzieri vaticani*, p. 248.   [56] Ibid., p. 245.

offering the general support of the Catholic middle and upper class for the Liberal state, as opposed to the continuing intransigent hostility of Catholic organs like *L'Unità Cattolica* of Florence and *La Vera Roma* of the capital, which were the preferred newspapers of the Roman curia under Papa Sarto.

Two months after the establishment of the SER, Pacelli founded another company, the Società Tipografica Editrice Romana, again with a paid-up capital of 150,000 lire, but this time the Vatican subscribed two-thirds and officials of the ABSS, including its lawyer Carlo Patriarca, received places on the board of directors.[57] As usual, the Catholic newspapers of the capital were in financial trouble, but with the rise to power in the city of the *Estrema*, and the election of their leader, the notorious freemason Ernesto Nathan, as mayor of Rome, there was more need than ever for a strong Catholic, journalistic voice in the city. Pacelli was asked by the pope and his Secretary of State to consider a broader plan of action for establishing the Catholic press of the capital on a sound financial basis. His proposals were radical: he suggested that in order to reduce the losses of both *L'Osservatore Romano* and the printing press of the Propaganda congregation, that all printing be concentrated at Propaganda with its state of the art equipment; that *Il Corriere d'Italia* also be printed there; that *La Vera Roma* and *Il Bastone* be merged and finally that a publicity agency should be set up to attract advertising for the newspapers.[58] It was a fairly realistic business plan, and Pacelli's expectation that the operation would require a five-year period in which to make a profit and a capital investment of 400,000 lire was equally realistic, but Pius said 'no' on financial grounds and the only part of the plan that was implemented was the transfer of the printing press of Propaganda into the Vatican.[59] *La Vera Roma* folded in August 1914.[60] *Il Bastone* struggled on until the First World War when its subsidies from Germany provoked an embarrassing spy scandal involving one of Benedict's papal chamberlains, Msgr Rudolph Gerlach.[61]

The dispensing of charity was one of the major activities of all popes who reigned between 1870 and 1950. There was a special papal office, the *elemosineria*, which was usually run by a high-ranking ecclesiastic, and charitable works took up a large proportion of the budget of the Holy See – according to Cardinal Gasparri, in 1919 the Vatican was

---

[57] Ibid., p. 246.   [58] Ibid.   [59] Ibid.
[60] ASV, SdS, Spoglio di Pio X, fasc. 4, letter from editor of 17 July 1914 saying that he had been forced to suspend publication and that he needed an immediate, special subsidy and an assurance of a regular monthly subsidy; in a further letter of 7 August 1914 he informed the pope that he had been forced to close.
[61] Pollard, *The Unknown Pope*, pp. 103–7.

dispensing 800,000 lire, close to a fifth of its budget in charity of various kinds in the city of Rome.[62] Pius was a great believer in charity and practised it regularly, making donations to good causes on a personal basis and contributing to good works in Rome, such as schools for the 'ragged poor' and other charitable initiatives. He was also closely involved in the raising of money for the victims of the earthquake of December 1908 which destroyed the towns of Reggio-Calabria and Messina and cost 77,000 lives.[63] In addition, Pius contributed generously to the fund for the reconstruction of churches, presbyteries, convents and schools and the premises of Catholic associations in the stricken areas, plus some charity to private persons, a total of 3,790,651 lire being spent for these purposes in the dioceses of Reggio, Gerace, Oppido, Mileto, Tropea, Bova, Catanzaro and Messina, with further contributions to other church expenses and for other re-building.[64] In the never-ending battle with the anti-clericals, if not the secular Italian state itself, the Church and the Catholic 'party' had to show themselves as community-minded and patriotic as the 'enemy' when it came to natural and national disasters, and it is notable that Ernesto Pacelli was a prominent member of the non-party relief committee set up in the city of Rome after the 1908 earthquake.[65]

Anti-clericalism and financial threats to the Church

While there were definitely both ups and downs in the relationship between the Church and the Italian state during Pius X's reign, there were very few of those crises which had marked the pontificate of his predecessor and obliged Leo seriously to think of leaving Rome. Papa Sarto's reign coincided almost exactly with the *età giolittiana*, the eleven-year period from 1903 to 1914 when Italian politics was dominated by one man, the Piedmontese liberal conservative politician, Giovanni Giolitti.[66] According to Giolitti, Church and State were 'two parallels that should never meet',[67] and when he was in power as prime minister, which was most of this period, he consciously sought better relations with the Vatican. In fact, Pius, by virtue of various of his policies, also contributed to a

---

[62] Spadolini (ed.), *Il Cardinale Gasparri*, pp. 376–8, Document 59, Gasparri to Nitti, 18 Oct. 1919.
[63] Seton-Watson, *Italy from Liberalism to Fascism*, p. 323.
[64] ASV, SdS, Spoglio di Pio X, fasc. 9, report of 25 Nov. 1911, report from Emilio Cottafava.
[65] O. Logan, 'The Clericals and Disaster: Polemic and Solidarism in Liberal Italy', in J. Dickie, J. Foot and Frank M. Snowden (eds.), *Disastro! Disasters in Italy since 1860: Culture, Politics and Society* (New York, 2002), pp. 98–111.
[66] For the policies of Giolitti, see Seton-Watson, *Italy from Liberalism to Fascism*, chs. 7 and 8; and G. Spadolini, *Giolitti e I Cattolici* (Florence, 1960).
[67] Jemolo, *Church and State*, p. 150.

definite thawing in relations between the two Romes: he continued to employ the services of Ernesto Pacelli in various negotiations with the Italian government; he had cordial relations with members of the royal house, including King Umberto's widow, Queen Margherita who, unlike her husband, was a devout Catholic and he was less than attentive to either the needs or the advice of members of the 'black' aristocracy. By the beginning of the twentieth century, a well-organised working-class movement had appeared in Italy – the Italian Socialist Party with allied co-operatives, trade unions, peasant leagues and other institutions. The dominant faction in the movement was Marxian Socialist in inspiration, the Maximalists being more extreme than their Reformist allies, but there were also even more extreme elements, the Anarchists and Revolutionary Syndicalists. To meet this growing threat, Pius X issued instructions that the *Non Expedit* should be relaxed and Catholics allowed to vote, and in some cases even stand as candidates, in general elections in those parliamentary constituencies where there was a serious danger of Socialists being elected.[68] As a result, Catholics were elected to Parliament in the 1904, 1909 and 1913 general elections; indeed, in the 1913 elections, the so-called 'Giolitti–Gentiloni Pact', between the prime minister and the president of the Catholic Electoral Union, Count Ottorino Gentiloni, ensured that twenty-nine Catholic deputies (MPs) were elected and Giolitti's parliamentary majority was not swept away by a Socialist tide following the introduction of virtually universal adult male suffrage.[69] And these political developments were matched by an increasing display of confidence on the part of Catholic bankers, financiers and businessmen, who were also often these same deputies.[70] By the end of Pius's reign, Italian Catholics were much more in the mainstream of national life than they had been since unification.[71]

Yet Pius seems to have possessed a deep vein of pessimism, even fatalism, as far as Church–State relations in Italy were concerned, which got worse as he grew older, and perhaps his unhappy experiences with anticlerical governments in France, Portugal and Spain reinforced this.[72] He seems to have lived in a constant fear and expectation of clashes with the anti-clerical elements in the Italian political class, especially the

---

[68] Webster, *The Cross and the Fasces*, pp. 14–15.

[69] Seton-Watson, *Italy from Liberalism to Fascism*, pp. 388–9.

[70] J. F. Pollard, 'Conservative Catholics and Italian Fascism: The Clerico-Fascists', in M. Blinkhorn (ed.), *Fascists and Conservatives: The Radical Right and the Establishment in Twentieth Century Europe* (London, 1990), pp. 32–3.

[71] For a study of the new role of the 'Catholic' contingent in the Italian Parliament, see G. Formigoni, *I cattolici deputati (1904–1918)* (Rome, 1989).

[72] F. Crispolti, *Corone e porpore* (Rome, 1936), p. 112.

Estrema, re-inforced as it now was by a not insignificant presence of thirty-three Socialists in the Chamber of Deputies and the consequent danger of the introduction of further anti-Church legislation. There were some moments of acute tension, like the period following the revelations about abuse of their infant charges by male and female religious in 1907,[73] the attack on Church charities in Rome following Nathan's election as mayor (yet even disputes with Nathan were smoothed out by Pacelli's intervention), the refusal of the government *exequatur* (approval) for the appointment of Msgr Caron as archbishop of Genoa in 1914 and Giolitti's repeated tactic of introducing a bill on civil marriage or even divorce, only quietly to drop it at a later date.[74] Ironically, this manouevre was necessitated precisely by the fact that relations between the Church and the Italian government were so good, and Giolitti needed to employ a diversionary tactic in order to reassure his more anti-clerical supporters that he was not selling the pass.

The real problems were essentially legal. In the first place, there was a number of court cases in which the wills of the heads of religious houses were overturned on the grounds that their passing on of property from themselves to their surviving brethren was a 'pious fraud', since it was an evasion of the law forbidding the religious orders to acquire property, which is precisely what it was intended to be. Other stratagems were employed by the religious orders to get around the law, which, it has to be said, was a little ambiguous. In 1908, the Corte di Cassazione, Italy's supreme court, declared that lay people could not hold property on behalf of religious orders either.[75] To get round these difficulties, Pacelli was instructed to set up a company, the Società Proprietà Fondiaria, whose purpose it was to own the property of religious orders, especially landed property, for which the orders would benefit by means of dividends.[76] As late as 1912, Pacelli was receiving letters from the heads of religious houses offering to sell their property to the Società Proprietà Fondiaria as they feared another round of confiscations of the property of the religious orders.[77]

Another major worry emerged in 1912, the possibility of governmental interference in the Italian *casse diocesane*, the little diocesan 'banks' which handled legacies and other donations to the Church at this level, and sometimes provided clergy pensions. To avoid providing any pretext for government meddling in the financial affairs of the dioceses, the Congregation of the Council issued a long list of instructions labelled 'TOP SECRET' to the Italian bishops and ordered them to return the letter.[78] In

---

[73] Lai, *Finanze e finanzieri vaticani*, p. 242 fn. 1.
[74] Jemolo, *Church and State*, pp. 150–1.   [75] Lai, *Finanze e finanzieri vaticani*, p. 242.
[76] Ibid., p. 243 fn. 3.   [77] Ibid., p. 275.   [78] Ibid., pp. 274–5.

particular, the bishops were instructed to accept and transform cash and even shares in the Catholic *casse di risparmio* into bonds and to accept as gifts only loan stock of Italian and foreign governments, and the shares of property and manufacturing companies which were accompanied by 'real and valid guarantees, as adjudged by competent persons'.[79] In this the congregation was reflecting Pius X's distrust of taking risks with industrial companies.

One major financial dispute with the Italian government was, however, eventually solved in the Vatican's favour. The law of 1873 on the suppression of religious houses and the 'nationalisation' of the property which remained had failed to take account of the fact that in Rome, capital of the Catholic world, there were literally dozens of religious houses which were there solely because they housed the representatives, often the heads, of religious orders based abroad – the *case generalizie*. The government's attempt to give these houses exemption from the law had been frustrated by the opposition of the Left.[80] In 1902, the Holy See, exploiting the thaw in its relations with the Italian government, sought a settlement of the long-standing dispute over the income derived from the confiscation of the property of these houses, appointing the pope's Vicar-General of the diocese of Rome, Cardinal Respighi, to seek from the Minster of Justice, Cocco-Ortu, a final settlement consisting of 400,000 lire per annum, plus fifteen years arrears.[81] The negotiations, conducted by the Roman lawyer Andrea Chiari, languished until 1906, when an agreement was finally made.[82] Chiari tried two major tacks: the first was to ask for the hand-over of a capital of 10 million lire, which he eventually reduced to 7.5 million, plus unpaid back payments of 3.7 million.[83] The government held out, and the Vatican agreed in 1906 to accept 200,00 lire per annum and a further annual payment of 105,000 lire, being a return of 3.5 per cent on an endowment in government consolidated stock of 3 million lire.[84] Even then, it had to agree that the diocese of Rome would accept a reduction of 75,000 lire on the annual income it received from the Fondo per la Beneficenza di Roma, the state body which subsidised the collegiate chapters and the parishes of the city.[85] This was not exactly the best outcome in the circumstances for the Church, but to make matters worse Chiari, who with his dense network of governmental contacts had almost made a profession out of acting as an intermediary between the Vatican and the Italian state, demanded the enormous sum of 425,925 lire for his

---

[79] Ibid.   [80] Manfroni, *Sulla soglia del Vaticano*, I, p. 106.
[81] ASV, SdS, Spoglio di Pio X, fasc. 3, Relazione Storico-documentata della Transazione Stipulata tra la Santa Sede e il Governo Italiano.
[82] Ibid.   [83] Ibid.   [84] Lai, *Finanze e finanzieri vaticani*, p. 220.
[85] ASV, SdS, Spoglio di Pio X, Relazione.

services.[86] It is not clear whether he received all of this, but the enabling legislation had a slow passage through Parliament, where the chair of the Budget Committee, Bianchi, proposed acceptance of the transaction in November of 1906; it was finally approved just before Christmas of that year.[87]

The legal status of the Holy See and its financial implications

One of the matters of greatest concern to Pius for a large part of his reign was the still disputed legal status of the Holy See and therefore of himself, in the eyes of Italian courts, and the dangers which this posed to financial transactions in which the Vatican was involved. Ever since the passing of the Law of Guarantees, considerable uncertainty had surrounded the Holy See's position in Italian law; indeed, in 1904, much comment in the Italian secular press was excited by Merry Del Val's decision to move into the Borgia apartment of the Apostolic Palace while the Secretary of State's apartment was being refurbished. Some newspapers actually suggested that, strictly speaking, the Vatican was Italian property and a national monument, so its occupants had no right to make changes.[88] On the other hand, the ruling in the case brought by the Mastai-Ferreti family over the ownership of the unpaid arrears of the *dotazione annua* (subsidy) laid down by the Law of Guarantees, which they claimed as the popes' legal heirs, seemed to suggest that Pius IX was not entitled to this as an individual, but only in so far as he was the occupant *pro tempore* of the papal throne (see above, Chapter 2, pp. 53–4). That, indirectly, was a recognition of the Holy See's institutional existence in Italian law.

Apart from the Holy See's refusal to recognise the jurisdiction of the Italian government over the former Papal States, there was the problem that any recognition of the Italian courts would imply that the sovereign pontiff was subject to them, which he emphatically denied that he was.[89] Thus, whenever a third party sought to cite the pope before such a court, the pope's legal representative simply appeared in order to assert that the court held no jurisdiction over him, and then withdrew. Usually, before such cases reached judgement, the lawyers of the Holy See settled out of court, which obviously suggested weakness, invited exploitation and could be expensive.[90]

---

[86] Ibid., telegram to Chiari from Zincone, Director General of the Treasury, 21 Dec. 1906.
[87] *La Tribuna*, 3 Nov. 1903.
[88] AAES, Italia e Principato di Monaco, 826–298, Roma, 1910, Sulla condizione giuridico-patrimoniale del Sommo Pontefice e della Santa Sede in Italia, p. 4.
[89] Ibid.   [90] Ibid, p. 2.

Even if the Holy See was a legal entity (*ente morale*) in Italian law this was not an unalloyed blessing because Piedmontese ecclesiastical legislation of 1853, which was subsequently applied to the rest of Italy after unification, laid down that the permission of the civil authorities was necessary for ecclesiastical entities – like cathedral chapters, etc. – to acquire and inherit property and other assets, as part of a policy of discouraging the accumulation of wealth by the clergy and thus containing their economic and political influence.[91] Even the plea that the Holy See was a legal entity *sui generis*, and that the pope was in some sense like a foreign sovereign resident 'extra-territorially' in Italy, did not exempt him from the provisions of this law.[92] So, as far as the acquisition and inheritance of real estate and other assets was concerned, the Vatican had long practised a policy whereby such acquisitions were made in the name of a friendly third party, usually a curial official or a member of the 'black' aristocracy. The money-lending operations of the ABSS and other financial agencies of the Vatican were also conducted in a similar manner. Increasingly after his arrival in the Vatican, Ernesto Pacelli, with his useful legal and financial connections, performed this function.[93]

This policy of basically allowing sleeping dogs to lie, and carrying out financial and legal transactions by subterfuge, lasted until 1909, when the fact that over a half a dozen rather sensitive cases involving disputes between the ABSS or the pope and private individuals were before the Italian courts,[94] induced the ABSS to commission a thorough study of the Holy See's legal position in Italy and the policies that should consequently be followed from its legal adviser, Carlo Patriarca. The most serious case was one in which someone who had leased a property from the Holy See was unable to collect rents from the sub-tenants because they had challenged the Holy See's right to enter into leases without government authorisation: the lease-holder then sued the Vatican for his losses.[95]

Patriarca's carefully considered conclusion was that the Holy See did have institutional standing in Italian law and therefore could inherit and otherwise acquire property, as well as being at liberty to sell property that it had acquired since the Law of Guarantees. But the real problem was a *political* one, that even if the courts admitted that the Holy See was an ecclesiastical institution *sui generis*, public opinion and Parliament would not permit the Vatican to buy and sell property and other assets at will for fear that other religious bodies could do so as well.[96] Patriarca

[91] Jemolo, *Church and State*, pp. 11–12.
[92] AAES, Italia e Principato di Monaco, pp. 64–5.
[93] See Lai, *Finanze e finanzieri vaticani*, pp. 153–6.
[94] AAES, Italia e Principato di Monaco, pp. 80–4.
[95] Ibid., p. 43.   [96] Ibid., pp. 58–9.

advised that the Holy See should continue to proceed with caution, but nevertheless that it should register new acquisitions of property, especially real estate, in its/the pope's name unless and until it was challenged.[97] Lai confirms that this was indeed the policy which the Vatican followed from 1910 onwards.[98]

Pius X, Pacelli and the Banco di Roma

There were strong rumours during the 1903 conclave that Ernesto Pacelli had lobbied in favour of the candidature of Cardinal Girolamo Gotti and that the Austro-Hungarian and German cardinals, who tended to vote as a block, had abandoned Gotti for precisely this reason.[99] If true, Pius does not appear to have held this against Pacelli; indeed, in view of his extreme reluctance to take the papal throne, Pius may have regarded Pacelli's action as in some way benevolent, and he was to entrust the financial affairs of the Vatican to Pacelli with as much confidence as his predecessor. In fact, Pius seems to have trusted Pacelli's financial judgement absolutely. No doubt his confidence was re-inforced by the fact that Marzolini, who was by now a close confidant of the president of the Banco di Roma, was regarded by Pius X as totally trustworthy as far as the financial matters of the Vatican were concerned. The curial 'Triad' – Cardinals Merry Del Val (Secretary of State), De Lai (prefect of the powerful Congregation of the Consistory) and Vives y Tutto (Secretary of the Inquisition) – who enjoyed ultimate power during the pontificate of Pius also reposed their confidence in Pacelli.[100] In fact, Marzolini had by now become effectively the financial *factotum* and civil administrator or 'governor' of the Vatican: in 1913 he was writing to the apostolic delegate in Washington asking him to procure US-made typewriters for the various Vatican offices.[101] He was also charged with oversight of all major building and engineering projects carried on by the Vatican, including the re-building churches after the 1908 earthquake.[102] But Pacelli's influence over the pope was also a result of the important role which the banker continued to perform as intermediary between the Vatican and the Italian government. As the

---

[97] Ibid., p. 89.   [98] Lai, *Finanze e finanzieri vaticani*, p. 222.   [99] Ibid., pp. 201–3.
[100] For the role of the 'Triad', see Pollard, *The Unknown Pope*, pp. 24–5.
[101] ASV, SPA, Amm., fasc. 96, letter of Marzolini, 9 Apr. 1913, to Msgr Bonzano, apostolic delegate. See ASV, SoS, Spoglio di Pio X, fasc. 2, 'Seminario Regionale Calabrese', report from the architect Cav. G. B. Marina of 20 June 1913 in which he describes Marzolini, who accompanied Cardinal De Lai, prefect of the Congregation for Seminaries, on a visit of inspection to the new Calabrian regional seminary as having 'the special responsibility for the supervision of administrative and financial aspects of the works in progress'.
[102] Lai, *Finanze e finanzieri vaticani*, pp. 153–5.

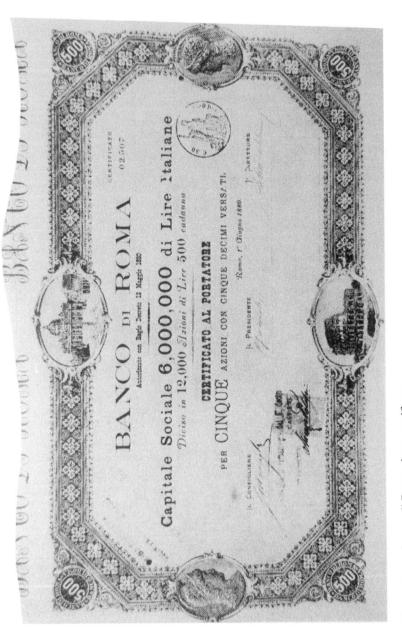

Illustration 7 Banco di Roma share certificate

president of the Banco di Roma, among whose directors was Romolo Tittoni, the brother of Tommaso who was Italian foreign minister for all but six months of the period November 1903 to December 1909, as a leading member of the Unione Romana and as a Rome city councillor from 1896 to 1905, not to mention his membership of the boards of other leading Italian banks and Roman utility companies, Pacelli was at the centre of powerful and interlocking economic and political networks. In the reign of Leo XIII he had, among other things, succeeded in extracting the government's agreement to the appointment of a new bishop of Perugia, a city dear to the heart of the pope, and in brokering a solution to the very delicate problems surrounding the wedding of Prince (later King) Victor Emmanuel to a Montenegrin, and therefore Orthodox, princess.[103] If anything, Pacelli's influence in Rome in the reign of Pius X was stronger than that which he had enjoyed in the reign of his predecessor. For example, despite Nathan's ferocious reputation as a *mangia-prete*, literally 'priest-eater', Pacelli succeeded in persuading the mayor of Rome to resolve three matters affecting the city council and the Vatican, to the satisfaction of both sides.[104]

The evidence of Pius X's trust in Pacelli and the Banco di Roma is remarkable; twice during the course of his reign he invested more funds in the Roma at Pacelli's request. In 1905, in order to finance the opening of the bank's new branch in Alexandria, a city with a very large Italian colony, and in an operation which was intended to be only the first of a series of initiatives involved in the penetration of the potentially lucrative Egyptian economy, the Roma made another share issue of 100,000 shares at 100 lire each, raising its capital from 10 to 20 million lire.[105] Through Marzolini and the ABSS, the Vatican acquired 31,447 new shares.[106] By the autumn of 1910, the ABSS already had a share-holding of 100,000 Banco di Roma shares as a guarantee for loans to the bank of 10,700,000 lire; when the loans expired in 1.5.1911, they were renewed to the tune of 10.2 million lire.[107] When Pius was again requested by Pacelli to invest in a new share issue in 1911, he was short of ready cash and offered Italian government loan stock in return for 9.5 million lire worth of new shares instead.[108] These new investments brought safe, if limited, returns to the Vatican; by 1912, interest on the ABSS's accounts at the Roma were bringing in roughly 400,000 lire a year and a year later nearer 330,000 lire, the largest

[103] Ibid., pp. 259–60.   [104] De Rosa, *Storia del Banco di Roma*, I, p. 219.
[105] Lai, *Finanze e finanzieri vaticani*, p. 236 fn. 1.   [106] Ibid., p. 266.
[107] De Rosa, *Storia del Banco di Roma*, I, p. 268.
[108] Calculated from the accounts in ASV, SdS, Spoglio di Pio X, fasc. 7, Rendiconto per il primo Trimestre del 1912, and Rendiconto del secondo Trimestre del 1913.

single source of regular income.[109] But there were limits to even Pius X's loyalty to Pacelli and the Roma. The income accounts of the ABSS in 1912 and 1913 clearly show that the Vatican had spread its capital investments fairly wide; Pius was suspicious of shares in commercial, especially manufacturing, companies, preferring guaranteed investments, so most of the ABSS's money was invested in foreign government stocks and utility companies. The accounts for the first quarter of 1912 list interest from Blount's Bank, the Bank of Italy and the Bank of France, Austrian loan stock and dividends from Acqua Pia Marcia (water company) and Molini Pantanelli (flour and milling). Those for the second quarter of 1913 list income from Bavarian, Italian and Spanish loan stock, interest from the Banco di Roma and dividends from gas, electricity and tramway companies, as well as Swiss Railways – about half came from the Banco di Roma.[110] When the Marchese Alberto Theodoli, a member of the 'black' aristocracy and of the board of directors of the Roma, at the instigation of the Italian government, sought to persuade Pius to consolidate his business by transferring the money in accounts with Rothschilds to the Roma, the pontiff replied in colourful Venetian dialect that when the popes had transferred their money from the safekeeping of Jews to that of Christians it had always ended in disaster![111]

The investment of the Vatican's capital, and the link with the bank generally, was of enormous benefit to the Roma. Pacelli made use of Vatican money to increase the bank's share-holding in a number of companies, like the sulphur, coal and antimony mines and new ventures like the Società Automobile La Roma (cars) and Cines (a film-production company).[112] Ironically, while Catholic financiers in Rome like Pacelli, Theodoli and Prince Prospero Colonna had invested heavily in Cines, and with 150 films being produced a year were making a handsome profit, the Church in Rome remained extremely suspicious of the new medium and in a series of decrees forbade priests from going to the pictures, even to see 'sacred' films.[113] The link with the Vatican also made it easier for the Banco di Roma to tap into sources of capital through Catholic banks, in this way making it possible to mobilise the savings of hundreds of thousands of small Catholic savers, often peasants, in the countryside and small towns of northern and central Italy.[114] This was

[109] Ibid., Rendiconto per il primo Trimestre di 1912, and Rendiconto per il secondo Trimestre di 1913.

[110] A. Theodoli, *A Cavallo di due secoli* (Roma, 1950), p. 49.

[111] Lai, *Finanze e finanzieri vaticani*, p. 259.

[112] F. Traniello and G. Campanini (eds.), *Dizionario storico del movimento cattolico in Italia (1860–1980)* (3 vols., Turin, 1981).

[113] Caroleo, *Le banche cattoliche*, p. 30.

[114] Lai, *Finanze e finanzieri vaticani*, pp. 194–5 and 259.

extremely important to Pacelli because, despite his well-known close links with the Vatican, and the Catholic world in Rome generally, the Roma was never, strictly speaking, a 'Catholic bank' and Pacelli, given his need to transact business in a number of different political spheres in Italy, including a secular-masonic one, had carefully avoided being identified with the 'clerical' banks in Italy. This also worked in the Vatican's favour, for when Catholic banks got into trouble, which they did from time to time, Pacelli, as an outsider, was induced to help out like the Banca Cattolica Vicentina in 1892 and the Cassa del Clero di Firenze (basically an ecclesiastical pension fund) in 1912, though here, it has to be said, most of the money which Pacelli used to liquidate the bank and pay off its creditors came from the Vatican's coffers.[115]

Pacelli very successfully used his role as mediator between Church and State to ensure the appointment of the Marchese Theodoli as Italian representative on the Board of the Ottoman Public Debt in 1905, the organisation which existed to protect the interests of the numerous foreign creditors of the Sultan's government. Given the increasing penetration of the Balkans and the Ottoman Empire by the Banca Commerciale, the Roma's rival, this was a rather cheeky coup, and marked the high point of the influence of Pacelli and the Banco di Roma in political and economic circles in Italy.[116] It also demonstrated the warmth of Church–State relations in Italy, which were effectively mediated by Ernesto Pacelli and his brother-in-law Romolo Tittoni, whose own brother, Tommaso, was, as has been seen, a leading Italian politician. The Vatican 'connection' was also exploited very successfully by Pacelli in his efforts to expand in the Roma's more usual area of commercial operations, the Mediterranean, with the opening in 1906 of a branch in Malta which, though it was a British colonial possession, was also a country in which the Church had an overwhelming influence on the population.[117]

The Banco di Roma, the Libyan War and the Vatican

By the middle of the 1900s the Banco di Roma was recognised as one of the 'big four' Italian banks, the others being the Banca Commerciale, the Credito Italiano and the Società Bancaria Italiana. But the Roma was having difficulty competing with its rivals. Based in Milan, the Commerciale and the Credito were able to benefit from the advantages of their geographical location. Their proximity to the economically developed

---

[115] Theodoli, *A Cavallo di due secoli*, p. 38.
[116] De Rosa, *Storia del Banco di Roma*, I, p. 221.
[117] Lai, *Finanze e finanzieri vaticani*, pp. 225–6.

Table 4 *Capital share-holding of the four biggest Italian banks (in millions of lire at 31 December)*

	1910	1911	1912
Banco di Roma	100	150	200
Banca Commerciale	105	130	130
Credito Italiano	75	75	75
Società Bancaria Italiana	40	40	40

Source: De Rosa, *Storia del Banco di Roma*, I, p. 228.

countries of north-western and central Europe, France, Switzerland and Germany, offered important commercial opportunities and sources of capital. In addition, the proximity of the so-called 'industrial triangle' of Milan, Turin and Genoa made accessible to these banks profitable invest-ments in the manufacturing industries of these areas, which underwent massive growth in the 'big spurt' of Italian economic growth between the 1890s and early 1900. As a result, the Commerciale now dominated steel, electrical, chemical and mechanical sectors.[118] The Roma, on the other hand, being situated in the capital could find few such opportunities in the contiguous areas of central and southern Italy and the islands of Sicily and Sardinia, which were way behind the north in terms of commercial and industrial development, and consequently also enjoyed much lower levels of personal income, hence the importance of being able to tap into the pennies of Catholic small savers from the north and centre.

The only alternative was to channel the energies and capital of the bank into initiatives abroad, two areas presenting themselves as offering seri-ous possibilities of commercial expansion from virtually the beginning of the new century, France and the Americas. With the considerable Catholic presence in 'the eldest daughter of the Church', it was hoped that lucrative business could be developed through a network of contacts, beginning with the apostolic nuncio and the archbishop of Paris and in 1902 Pacelli took over a local bank, the Caisses des Dépôts, in Paris.[119] But the hopes of the Roma took some time to realise, as relations between France and the Vatican deteriorated following President Loubet's con-troversial visit to the Quirinale in 1905 and the implementation of laws against the Church, culminating in the rupture of diplomatic relations

---

[118] R. Di Quirico, *Le Banche Italiane all'Estero, 1900–1950: espansione bancario all'estero e integrazione finanziaria nell'Italia degli anni tra le due guerre* (Fucecchio (FI), 2000), p. 30.

[119] De Rosa, *Storia del Banco di Roma*, II, p. 240.

in 1906. In this situation the desperate need of French religious orders and other religious organisations for banking and other services offset the effective boycott of the 'Vatican bank' by other important sections of French society and by 1912 the Roma's directors were able to claim that their business in France was making a handsome profit.[120]

Both North and South America offered interesting prospects in the early 1900s, in particular the banking needs of Italian immigrants, who by 1900 were leaving Italy at the rate of 600,000 per year. Yet, Pacelli seems to have dismissed the commercial prospects available in the USA. Perhaps he believed that being a Protestant nation, the Americans would not have judged a Roman venture favourably. He seems to have believed that American Catholics were economically and politically weak, despite the visit there by the Marchese Theodoli to negotiate a financial settlement of the affairs of the Philippine Church following the archipelago's annexation by the USA during the Spanish-American War.[121] Nor did the glowing picture of the vitality of the American Catholic community and its growing contribution to Peter's Pence painted by Marzolini, who accompanied Cardinal Vannutelli on a visit to the USA in 1910, in a letter to Pacelli, alter the banker's mind; he remained impervious to the prospects for financial success afforded by American markets.[122] In this respect, Pacelli seems to have been rather behind the ecclesiastical world in recognising the economic importance of America. The Banco di Napoli, located in the main port of exit for many of these emigrants, established a very profitable business in North America on this basis. Again, the various South American countries affected by substantial Italian immigration offered considerable scope for the establishment of banking facilities by Italian institutions. But in the end, it was the Banca Commerciale which reaped the harvest, when it bought the Banca Commerciale di San Paolo in 1905,[123] and five years later, in conjunction with its French partner, Paribas, it established Sudameris, with branches in Argentina, Brazil and Uruguay, both to exploit local commercial opportunities in developing economies and to regulate the flow of immigrant remittances to the folks back home in Italy.[124]

Nearer to home were three areas offering prospects of commercial growth, the Balkans, the Anatolian heartland of the Ottoman Empire and North Africa, and these possibilities were seized upon by Pacelli. These were also areas which the Italian Foreign Office regarded as important potential spheres of Italian influence, since Italian colonial expansion

---

[120] Lai, *Finanze e finanzieri vaticani*, p. 242 fn. 2.
[121] Ibid, p. 225 fn. 5.   [122] Di Quirico, *Le Banche Italiane*, p. 30.
[123] Ibid., p. 31.   [124] De Rosa, *Storia del Banco di Roma*, I, p. 243.

into the Red Sea and East Africa had been effectively blocked by the British presence but also by the defeat of Italian armies at Dogali in 1887 and Adowa in 1896 at the hands of the Abyssinians (present-day Ethiopians). So in theory at least, the Roma would have the backing of Italian diplomacy which, for several years was in the hands of Tommaso Tittoni, though De Rosa makes the point that the Italians believed that the rupture of diplomatic relations between the Vatican and France could be exploited to further efforts to undermine the French 'protectorate' of Catholics inside the Ottoman Empire.[125] In fact, the field was not entirely free in these areas for Italian initiative. In the Balkans, and at Istanbul in particular, British, French, German and Viennese banks were already vying for influence.[126] In Istanbul, the Roma quickly came into competition with the Banca Commerciale, and Bernardino Nogara, who was to preside over the Vatican's finances from 1929 onwards (see below, Chapter 5 *et seq.*) and who ran the Commerciale's eastern arm, the Società Commerciale d'Orientale.[127] But the area of greatest competition with the Commerciale, and the one in which Pacelli was to deploy the bulk of the Roma's resources, was North Africa.

All the way along the coast of North Africa, nominally under the sovereignty of the Ottoman Empire, from Tunis in the west to Alexandria in the east, were significant communities of Italian merchants and other settlers. Though Tunisia had been snaffled from under the noses of the Italians by the French, and its ruler, the *Bey*, had been induced to accept the protection of the French Empire by the terms of the Treaty of Bardo of 1881, a sizeable Italian community remained, and in 1900 the Commerciale sought to meet their needs by the creation of the Banca Commerciale Italo-Tunisina, but with an especial eye to the exploitation of phosphate deposits as well.[128] Pacelli was rather slower off the mark, and it was not until 1905 that he founded a branch of the Roma at Alexandria, with another in Cairo three years later.[129] In Libya, expansion was more rapid. In 1907 the first branch was founded at Tripoli and by the outbreak of the Libyan War in 1911, a total of eighteen branches had been established, divided more or less equally between the two provinces of Tripolitania and Cyrenica, with increasing attempts on Pacelli's part to exploit the possibilities for the development of infrastructure and the mining of minerals.[130] Soon, Pacelli joined in the demands of the new Italian Nationalist movement led by Enrico Corradini, Luigi Federzoni

[125] Di Quirico, *Le Banche Italiane*, p. 35.   [126] Ibid., p. 35.   [127] Ibid., p. 30.
[128] De Rosa, *Storia del Banco di Roma*, I, p. 224.
[129] Di Quirico, *Le Banche Italiane*, pp. 30–1.
[130] Seton-Watson, *Italy from Liberalism to Fascism*, p. 370.

and Alfredo Rocco that Italy's imperial progress should recommence with the annexation of Libya, her 'fourth shore'.[131] In his efforts to pressurise the Italian political class, Pacelli brought into play the propaganda broadsides of the 'Trust' Catholic newspapers, *Il Corriere d'Italia*, *L'Avvenire d'Italia*, *Il Momento* and *L'Italia*, all located in key cities as far as middle-class public opinion was concerned – Rome, Bologna, Turin and Milan respectively.[132]

The attitude of the Vatican to the Libyan adventure was very much more reserved. *L'Osservatore Romano* approved of 'peaceful' economic penetration of the Turkish provinces and Merry Del Val and Pius supported 'the investment of the capital of the Banco di Roma in the Italian colonial venture',[133] but war evoked a different response. While Cardinal Vannutelli responded to a deep vein of Italian Catholic patriotism by declaring Italy's invasion to be an enterprise of the 'civilisation of the Cross in lands subjected to ignominious yoke of the half-moon',[134] Pius was deeply disturbed. The terms of the ultimatum handed to the Turks implied that the war was being carried out in order to defend the interests of the Banco di Roma, which everyone knew was *his* bank, and so he insisted that the cardinal's declaration be disowned by the Vatican organ.[135] Paradoxically, despite Pius's justifiable fears for the diplomatic neutrality of the Holy See, the war appears to have had a beneficial effect on its finances; in the wake of the war, Italian contributions to Peter's Pence tripled, suggesting that the war had ignited the patriotism of Italian Catholics.[136]

So Pacelli had finally fallen out with the Vatican; indeed, he was refused access to the pope's deathbed in August 1914, which negated his efforts to gain papal assistance to resolve the dangerous cash crisis provoked for the bank by the outbreak of the First World War. He also fell out with the Italian government – there was much criticism of the Banco di Roma's monopoly of provisioning the troops, and the inadequacy of that provision.[137] On the other hand, the bank had made great sacrifices which the government seemed unwilling to recognise; it had taken its share of the government debt issues of 1913,[138] and when it demanded 20 million lire in damages from the government to cover the losses in real

[131] Lai, *Finanze e finanzieri vaticani*, p. 265.
[132] Ibid.   [133] *L'Avvenire d'Italia*, 19 Oct. 1911.
[134] M. Petriccioli, *L'Italia in Asia Minore: equilibrio mediterraneo e ambizioni imperialiste alla vigilia della prima guerra mondiale* (Florence, 1983), p. 24 fn. 16.
[135] Lai, *Finanze e finanzieri vaticani*, p. 278.
[136] Zambarbieri, 'La devozione al Papa', p. 71.
[137] De Rosa, *Storia del Banco di Roma*, I, p. 242.   [138] Ibid.

estate and business which it had suffered in the Ottoman Empire during the war, it was bluntly refused.[139] To add insult to injury, the Banca Commerciale profited hugely from this situation: Volpi (a member of the Banca Commerciale board) and Nogara were involved in the peace negotiations which brought the conflict to an end at Ouchy (Lausanne), Switzerland, in 1912, and Nogara then replaced Theodoli as Italian representative on the Board of the Ottoman Public Debt in 1913.

But Nogara was a Catholic who already had connections with the Vatican and his appointment was a sign that the government did not intend to alienate itself from the Catholic world and regarded good relations with the Vatican as being of prime importance.[140] Italo-Vatican relations had come a long way since 1870. Though there were no formal diplomatic links, and there were spats between Catholic and anti-clerical papers from time to time, the two Romes had learned to live together in comparative harmony by the outbreak of the First World War. Much of that progress was due to *economic* developments. In general terms, the Catholic and liberal-conservative capitalist forces had vital common interests, and nowhere more so than in Rome. And here the key, controlling element in the Catholic economic bloc in Rome was the Vatican and the capital which it supplied for investment in the economy of the city from Peter's Pence and the accumulated resources of the ABSS. The Catholic aristocracy and bourgeoisie, together with the Church, now had a massive stake in the Italian economy which accordingly necessitated a close working relationship with the Italian political class, both outside and inside of Parliament.

Conclusion

There can be no doubt that according to his own lights, Pius X was a prudent and careful administrator of the Vatican's money. He certainly knew how to take care of the pennies but, unfortunately, the pounds did not always, in consequence, necessarily take care of themselves, at least not in the longer term. The delegation of so much of the ultimate control over the Vatican's capital to Marzolini and Pacelli, the consequent disproportionate investment of so much of that capital in the Banco di Roma – by 1914 the Holy See owned a quarter of the total share-holding of the bank and had large deposits there, which was a very substantial part of its investment portfolio – despite his other efforts to avoid putting too many eggs in one basket, would have serious consequences later. A further

---

[139] Ibid.
[140] R. A. Webster, *Industrial Imperialism in Italy, 1908–1915* (Berkley, Calif., 1974), p. 453.

problem lay in the hostages to fortune which Pius left behind in the form of a sustained and developed policy to underwrite the financial liabilities of various elements of the Italian Catholic movement, and above all the Catholic press. This was to prove to be a grave, costly mistake. These two time bombs ticked away until they exploded in the reigns of Pius X's two successors.

5 'The great charitable lord'?: Vatican finances under Benedict XV (1914–1922)

Introduction

Benedict XV was born Giacomo Della Chiesa of a noble Genoese family in 1854. After graduating from a secular university with a law degree (*dottorato di legge*) his ecclesiastical education was at the Capranica College and the Gregorian University in Rome and at the prestigious Accademia dei Nobili Ecclesiastici, the training ground of Vatican diplomats and curial bureaucrats. Catching the eye of Cardinal Rampolla del Tindaro, he served first in the Madrid nunciature and then as *minutante* to that great Secretary of State.[1] In 1901 he became Substitute Secretary of State (*Sostituto*), and thus one of the most powerful men in the Vatican, and as such would have learnt a great deal about the rather shaky finances of the Vatican at the end of Leo XIII's reign and the beginning of Pius X's.[2] But the election of the latter in 1903 spelled the beginning of the end of Della Chiesa's influence in the Vatican as he found himself increasingly at odds with the policies of Papa Sarto and his very young Secretary of State, Cardinal Rafael Merry del Val, particularly on the questions of France and 'modernism'. Indeed, there seems to have been something of a personality clash between the *Sostituto* and his new boss.[3] Eventually, in 1907, Merry Del Val managed to get him out of the way by sending him to be archbishop of Bologna. Made a cardinal, rather tardily, in May 1914, four months later Della Chiesa was elected pope after a three-day conclave, despite the opposition of Merry Del Val and the more intransigent cardinals.[4] Partly because of the shortness of his reign, but also because of the lack of success of his peace diplomacy during the First World War, and the opposition it aroused in both camps, Benedict is little known, indeed Peter Hebblethwaite said of him that he was 'the most unappreciated and least visible pope this century'.[5] Despite being largely unknown, Benedict's pontificate was an important one in the history of the modern

---

[1] The most up-to-date biography is Pollard, *The Unknown Pope*.
[2] Lai, *Finanze e finanzieri vaticani*, p. 285.   [3] Pollard, *The Unknown Pope*, pp. 20–7.
[4] Ibid., pp. 60–5.   [5] Hebblethwaite, *John XXIII*, p. 105.

Illustration 8 Pope Benedict XV

papacy: though he failed to bring peace to Europe, he brought peace to the Church after the terrible 'anti-modernist' persecutions of his predecessor; he promulgated the Code of Canon Law in 1917, he began the policy of concordats with states based on that Code; he revitalised papal diplomacy and consequently the international influence of the papacy, and renewed the Roman Catholic Church's missionary outreach and its relations with the Eastern Churches in communion with Rome. It is a tribute to the soundness and importance of his policies that they were all continued by his successor, even to the extent that Pius XI kept on Benedict's Secretary of State, Cardinal Pietro Gasparri.

Benedict as financial manager

Historians and journalists alike have been extremely critical of Benedict XV's financial capabilities and tend to write in apocalyptic terms about the state of the Vatican's finances during his pontificate. The American journalist Seldes, for example, wrote in 1935 of 'the financial management, or almost lack of management, of Pope Benedict XV, which however, showed him to be the great charitable lord rather than the economic and prudent bourgeois'.[6] In the light of what Seldes says elsewhere, we can take it that by 'economic and prudent bourgeois', Seldes means Benedict's successor, the Milanese pope Pius XI. This story is repeated by later writers, such as the Australian historian Molony who, in his book on the Italian People's Party of 1977, talks about 'the state of chaos into which the Vatican finances were reduced' by the end of the war and who claims that this was a major reason for 'Benedict XV's anxiety to get a solution of the Roman Question',[7] and by the French historian Uginet, in the very authoritative *Dictionnaire de la papauté* of 1997, who even claims that Benedict 'did not like savings'.[8] Lo Bello claims that Benedict was so hard up in 1919 that he 'tried, unsuccessfully, to get a loan of one million dollars via Cardinal Mundelein, archbishop of Chicago using the wealth of that great archdiocese as collateral', and even goes so far as to say that, 'the Vatican was virtually bankrupt on Benedict's death, and the Secretary of State, Cardinal Gasparri, was forced to obtain a loan from Rothschilds in order to cover the costs of the 1922 Conclave'.[9] We shall come back to

---

[6] Seldes, *The Vatican*, p. 246.
[7] J. N. Molony, *The Emergence of Political Catholicism in Italy: Partito Popolare, 1919–1926* (London, 1977), p. 59.
[8] F.-C. Uginet, 'Les finances papales', in P. Levillain (ed.), *Dictionnaire de la papauté* (Paris, 1997), p. 600.
[9] N. Lo Bello, *L'oro del Vaticano* (Milan, 1971), p. 62; see also Gollin, *Worldly Goods*, p. 437, where he says Benedict 'seriously endangered the whole papal economy'.

these individual claims later, but it is indicative of the persistence of the legend of Benedict's financial fecklessness that it is even celebrated in a fictional work. In his novel *Earthly Powers*, Anthony Burgess wrote: 'Pope Benedict XV, that great pacifist prelate to whom neither the Germans nor the allies would listen, Giacomo Della Chiesa, James of the Church, lawyer and diplomat, hopeless with money, his prodigality of aid to the needy having put the Vatican in debt, he had died and been succeeded by Pius XI.'[10] The essence of these various criticisms is that Benedict was a bad financial manager and that, in consequence, the finances of the Vatican were a shambles at the end of his reign. But as the sad history of the Società Editoriale Romana will demonstrate (see pp. 119–21), Benedict was far from being naive in financial matters, and other evidence suggests that he was a good financial manager, as well as being a good judge of men, rather than being financially incompetent and a careless spendthrift. In the papers preserved by his family are his private accounts which he kept in meticulous order from the age of eleven,[11] and he did not waste anything; until his death in 1922, he continued to use the headed notepaper which had been made for him on his appointment as cardinal in May 1914.[12] And as the archives of the state-run Fondo per il Culto (the office responsible for Church–State relations) show, he ran a very tight ship as archbishop of Bologna between 1907 and 1914.[13] In particular, Benedict battled persuasively, though ultimately unsuccessfully, with the local office of the Fondo to obtain a larger annual income from the state on account of the fact that his diocese was, as he pointed out, the fourth largest in Italy.[14] Benedict made few changes to the organisation of the Roman curia during the course of his pontificate, but they included a reform at the Congregation of the Clergy which was certainly prompted by financial considerations. According to Corrado Pallenberg: 'The important and technical character of the business dealt with by the Congregation required a specialised staff. In 1919, Benedict XV attached to the finance office a school attended by young priests who took a three-year course.'[15]

The impact of the war

The financial situation which Benedict inherited from his predecessor was not, on the surface, at any rate a bad one. Two sources claim that

---

[10] A. Burgess, *Earthly Powers* (Harmondsworth, 1980), p. 199.
[11] Pollard, *The Unknown Pope*, p. 3.   [12] Ibid., p. 83 n. 67.   [13] Ibid., pp. 39–40.
[14] ACS, Ministero della Giustizia, Direzione Generale per gli Affari di Culto, Placet et Exequatur, Bologna, letters of 24 Feb. and 29 Mar. 1908.
[15] Pallenberg, *Vatican Finances*, p. 98.

Pius X actually left the Vatican's finances in good shape, one being Lo Bello, the other the Italian journalist Benny Lai.[16] According to Lai, at the beginning of his reign, the new pope asked to see the accounts, and from the balance sheet presented by Marzolini, and the annual summaries compiled by Pius X, it was clear that Papa Sarto had administered the Vatican's finances with great care; indeed, Msgr Nicola Canali, right-hand man of Secretary of State Merry Del Val, testified at the beatification process for Pius X that he had left a cash reserve of 6 million lire.[17] But as a result of the Great War, which had broken out only a few weeks before his election, Benedict soon faced pressing financial problems. Most of the authors cited above, however, take little account of these problems. The war was to engage Benedict's greatest energies, in his attempts to bring about peace between the warring powers, culminating in his Peace Note of August 1917. On the one hand, the war caused the Vatican's income to fall drastically, particularly after the publication of the Note.[18] Neither French nor Belgian Catholics were able to send much in the way of Peter's Pence, after August 1914; according to Carlo Monti, the pope's friend and go-between with the Italian government, Benedict told him in January 1917 that 'France and Belgium have sent virtually nothing since the outbreak of war',[19] and Gasparri confirmed that 'In fact, Germany is the only one of the belligerent states from which money reaches the Obolo [Peter's Pence].'[20] It is understandable, therefore, that Benedict feared that Peter's Pence income from the Central Powers would be interrupted when Italy joined in the war on the side of the Entente powers in May 1915.[21] In the event, this did not happen: Benedict used his German chaplain, Msgr Gerlach, later to be involved in a spy scandal, to organise the continued flow of money from Germany and according to documents in the file on Gerlach in the Vatican archives, between July 1915 and July 1916 alone, the Vatican received nearly 2.4 million lire in mass offerings from Germany.[22]

Molony is almost certainly correct when he suggests that one of the reasons why Peter's Pence dried up in France was because 'the anti-war politics of Benedict were unwelcome'.[23] The French tended to see the

---

[16] Lo Bello, *L'oro del Vaticano*, p. 63; and Lai, *Finanze e finanzieri vaticani*, p. 286.

[17] Lo Bello, *L'oro del Vaticano*, p. 83 fn. 67.

[18] The graphs showing receipts for the Peter's Pence from Germany, France, the USA and Italy, as recorded by *La Civiltà Cattolica* and shown in Zambarbieri, 'La devozione al Papa', pp. 71–3, are less clear for the early part of the war, though they are uniform in suggesting a massive fall in 1917.

[19] Scottà (ed.), *La Conciliazione Ufficiosa*, p. 3, II, Jan. 1917.

[20] Ibid.   [21] Hachey (ed.), *Anglo-Vatican Relations*, p. xvii.

[22] ASV, SdS, Guerra, 1914–18, busta 99, memorandum of 25 Apr. 1917.

[23] Molony, *The Emergence of Political Catholicism*, p. 59.

Vatican as pro-German: in many circles Benedict was described as 'Le Pape Boche' and in August 1917, following the publication of his 'Peace Note', a preacher in the church of La Madaleine, Paris, exclaimed: 'Holy Father we do not want your peace.'[24] The Peace Note is likely to have affected the inflow of Peter's Pence from France, and also from Italy after its disastrous defeat at Caporetto in November 1917 when the pope was blamed for spreading 'defeatism'.[25] The decline in the number of bishops making their regulation five- or ten-yearly *ad limina* visits to report to the pope, and virtual absence of large-scale papal audiences in the Vatican after Italy's declaration of war in May 1915, also reduced the inflow of funds, for frequently those same bishops and other pilgrims had been the bearers of Peter's Pence. In particular, submarine warfare in the Atlantic kept away American pilgrims. The Rome correspondent of *The Tablet* described the effects which the First World War, and especially Italy's entry into it in May 1915, had upon the Vatican:

the devout crowds of pilgrims entering by the Bronze Gates, the long stream of sightseers on their way to the galleries and museums, the carriages of foreign prelates who drove every morning to be received in audience by the Holy Father, the swarms of itinerant vendors that hung about the colonnade – they have all disappeared.[26]

The Serbo-American historian Dragan Zivojinovic, in his book *The United States and the Vatican Policies, 1914–1918*, implies that as a result of the fall in income from Belgium and France, the pope fell under German influences:

Although the Vatican pretended to be impartial and neutral [during the First World War], there is now evidence that its sympathies lay with the Central Powers, particularly Austria-Hungary. He [Benedict] was dependent on Erzberger, German Centre party leader, on account of his fund-raising activities on the Pope's behalf. This relieved the Pope's situation but made him, and the Curia, dependent upon Germany and on occasion ready to voice views that reflected Germany's desires and needs.[27]

Zivojinovic's allegations are based on evidence in the Erzberger papers, the so-called Bachem Memorandum, which claimed that 'The finances

---

[24] As quoted in Pollard, *The Unknown Pope*, p. 68.
[25] Ibid., p. 103; G. Salvemini, *Chiesa e stato in Italia* (Milan, 1969), p. 384, is of the opinion that French Catholics were not pleased with the pope's neutralist stand and the 'Peace Note'.
[26] *The Tablet*, 13 Jan. 1917, p. 49.
[27] D. Zivojinovic, *The United States and the Vatican Policies, 1914–1918* (Boulder, Colo., 1978), pp. 12 and 13; Salvemini, *Chiesa e stato*, p. 384, adds a variant to this argument by saying that the Vatican was so convinced that the Central Powers would win that it invested its own money and that of Italian religious orders heavily in Austrian loan stock and lost badly as a consequence.

of the Vatican were completely exhausted upon the death of Pius X, with the treasury being literally empty. Pius X had known nothing about the management of money. Benedict, in consequence, was not able to pay the salaries of his court officials during the first period of his pontificate.'[28] As has been seen, this claim is contradicted by at least two other sources which state that the 'peasant pope' had very cannily left a substantial reserve at his death. In any case, the question of the Vatican's impartiality and neutrality during the First World War is a complex one, and Zivojinovic fails to mention a reference in the same memorandum to Benedict succumbing to 'Entente influences, and especially French prelates' after the money which Erzberger had collected had run out.[29] Zivojinovic also overlooks, or was ignorant of, the major role by now played by American Catholics in financing the Vatican. Benedict told Monti in 1917 that 'the bulk of the offerings [Peter's Pence] come from the United States, and then from Germany', and this situation had consolidated itself by the end of the war.[30] Writing to the apostolic delegate in Washington in September 1919, Bishop McNicholas of Duluth informed him that he hoped that the annual contribution of the US Bishops Conference, of which he was the secretary, for that year 'would be a little larger than usual, that is $1,500,000'.[31] The logic of Zivojinovic's argument, then, would be that this inevitably meant that the American government had a great influence on Vatican diplomatic policy, but there is absolutely no evidence to suggest this. This was not the first occasion on which the question of the relationship between the sources of Vatican financing and its diplomatic policy was raised and it would not be the last.

While income from Peter's Pence fell, on the other hand, the war massively increased the expenditure of the Vatican, which was also affected by inflation of the lira – 300 per cent between 1914 and 1919 – which, even assuming that North America was now its main source of income, was only partially offset by a 90 per cent fall in the value of the lira against the US dollar in the same period.[32] Though extremely frugal in his own personal habits, within the walls of the Vatican, and in particular within

[28] K. Epstein, *Mathias Erzberger and the Dilemma of German Democracy* (Princeton, N.J., 1959), pp. 103–4.

[29] Ibid.

[30] Scottà (ed.), *La Conciliazione Ufficiosa*, II, p. 3, 3 Jan. 1917; Salvemini, *Chiesa e stato*, p. 384, claims that by the middle of the war half of the receipts from Peter's Pence came from the United States.

[31] ASV, DAUS, 284, letter of McNicholas to Bonzano, 27 Sep. 1919; see also Salvemini, *Chiesa e stato*, p. 384, where he says that half of the income from Peter's Pence during the war came from the United States.

[32] Zamagni, *The Economic History of Italy*, p. 213; and D. J. Forsyth, *The Crisis of Liberal Italy: Monetary and Financial Policy, 1914–1922* (Cambridge, 1993), p. 330.

the restricted circle of his court, Benedict XV maintained the traditional style and pomp of the papacy, reviving traditional ceremonies like the 'Mandatum', the washing of the feet on Maunday Thursday. After the comparative simplicity of his predecessor's reign, that of Benedict was a return to the Leonine pontificate in more than just policy.[33] But pomp, protocol and etiquette cost money. Benedict also felt obliged to parallel his peace diplomacy with sustained humanitarian relief efforts. In these endeavours he was prodigally generous: the author of the biographical essay in the *Dictionnaire de la papauté* calculates that he spent something in the region of 82 million lire on relief for soldiers, civilian and POWs during the First World War.[34] As well as providing an information bureau for missing persons in the Vatican, and assisting the repatriation of civilians and POWs to neutral Switzerland – by January 1917, 26,000 POWs and 3,800 civilian detainees had been given the opportunity to convalesce in hospitals or sanatoria in Switzerland[35] – Benedict organised massive efforts to re-victual famished populations. The Vatican was involved in a number of operations aimed at providing foodstuffs for populations in or behind the war zones: to quote a few examples, Lithuania, Montenegro in both 1916 and 1917, Poland in 1916, Russian refugees in 1916 and Syria and Lebanon from 1916 through to 1922.[36] Much of the funding came from special appeals, like the one in October 1916 which he addressed to the clergy and laity of the United States for money to help feed the children of Belgium,[37] but the Vatican's own resources were used as well. And as Monti and other sources testify, he also spent large sums on relieving famine and other disasters after the war was over, and was particularly concerned about the plight of children, such that he can be counted as one of the founders of the Save the Children Fund.[38] In 1919 and 1920 he made appeals for the relief of famine in Eastern and Central Europe, and in 1920 alone he raised 50 million lire for famine relief in Russia.[39]

The Vatican and Catholic banks

Another major financial problem facing Benedict during the course of his pontificate was the pressure put on him to bail out various Italian Catholic institutions, banks, including the Banco di Roma, and the most important part of the Catholic press. After Benedict's election, it soon became clear, for example, that the Banco di Roma, which was one of

---

[33] Pollard, *The Unknown Pope*, p. 115.
[34] K. Jankowiak, 'Benoit XV', in Levillain (ed.), *Dictionnaire de la papauté*, p. 221.
[35] Pollard, *The Unknown Pope*, pp. 112–15.   [36] Ibid., p. 15.   [37] Ibid., pp. 147–8.
[38] Scottà (ed.), *La Conciliazione Ufficiosa*, II, p. 531, 31 Jan. 1920.
[39] Molony, *The Emergence of Political Catholicism*, p. 103.

the Vatican's major investments (it owned a quarter of all the shares) but was at the same time its biggest potential liability, was once more in great difficulties.[40] The bank had never really recovered from the damage inflicted on it by the Libyan War, but the disturbed international financial position following the outbreak of the First World War in August 1914, and then the need to subscribe to massive public war loans following Italy's intervention, enormously aggravated matters. In January and February 1915 the public withdrew 12 million lire of deposits from the Bank, and in the first three weeks of March a further 6.3 million.[41] Benedict was by no means unsympathetic to the Bank's position, and especially that of its president, Ernesto Pacelli, but he sought to avoid a major loss of capital on the part of the Vatican.[42] A salvage package was worked out at the end of March 1915 whereby the new Credito Nazionale, the emanation of the Catholic Banking Federation, handed over 9 million lire to the Bank, with the Vatican's share-holding as a guarantee.[43] This was the end for Pacelli and his privileged relationship with the Vatican. By November 1915, Italian police informants in the Vatican were reporting that its 'ruling spheres' were also extremely concerned by the failure of various Banco di Roma-run enterprises in Tripoli and Salonika, and the collapse of the film company Cines, and that in consequence Benedict was planning to transform the bank into an essentially confessional or Catholic institution.[44] In 1916 Pacelli was replaced as president of the Bank by Count Carlo Santucci, a devoted lay servant of the Church who was also a legal adviser to the ABSS, and by other directors, all appointed by Credito Nazionale, who were more clearly representatives of the Italian Catholic movement.[45] In this way, Benedict XV effectively carried out the 'confessionalization' of the Bank referred to earlier, a fate which Pacelli had always sought to avoid. According to Lai, Pacelli had always kept 'well away from confessional credit institutions on the ideological as well as practical plane'.[46]

But even this rescue operation did not succeed. Shortly before his departure in September 1915, Pacelli had contracted a 15 million lire loan on the bank's behalf with the Banca d'Italia. This was not enough to restore confidence and there was a further haemorrhage of deposits which reached a total of 8 million lire in April 1916. Pacelli was deeply indebted to the bank on his own account, and Benedict authorised him to

40 De Rosa, *Storia del Banco di Roma*, II, p. 2.
41 Ibid., p. 75.   42 Ibid.   43 Ibid., p. 82.
44 ACS, Ministero del Interno (MdI), DGPS, 1917, b. 113, H4, Notizie vaticane, report of 12 June 1917.
45 De Rosa, *Storia del Banco di Roma*, II, p. 98.
46 Lai, *Finanze e finanzieri vaticani*, p. 289.

hand over 425,000 shares in the bank which he held on behalf of the ABSS and which had been used to guarantee the Credito Nazionale's loan. Nor did this suffice, because, as a result of the bank's difficulties, the Vatican's share-holding had been seriously devalued: whereas the shares had cost 42.5 million lire to buy, they were now worth less than 15 million.[47] In return for the proceeds of the sale of Pacelli's villa, Gasparri authorised the hand-over of a further 90,000 bank shares owned by the Holy See, worth over 3.15 million lire.[48] Lai says: 'With the handover of the shares administered by the banker and those officially belonging to the Vatican's endowment, the Holy See definitively ceased to be a participant in the management of the Banco di Roma.'[49] It seems likely that Lai is right, if only because as early as July 1916 Benedict had indicated that he wanted no further 'business entanglements between the Holy See and the Banco di Roma, indeed [he wished] to loosen the old links, except for leaving papal deposits with the bank'.[50] And the Vatican did, indeed, retain considerable deposit accounts, hence its continuing concern for the future of the bank.[51]

It is difficult to assess just how much more of the capital of the Vatican was used in order to pay the debts of other Italian Catholic banks in the war years, but we do know that in 1914 Benedict intervened to help the Florentine Cassa del Clero in order to protect the pensions of the diocesan clergy,[52] and that in 1916 the Holy See intervened to help a Catholic savings bank in central Italy, The Piccolo Credito of Ferrara.[53] In 1917 the Holy See was obliged to intervene again and hand over its share-holding in the Credito Centrale del Lazio, worth 500,000 million, to the Banco di Roma in order to bail out this local credit institution.[54] This was done in order, according to Gasparri, 'to save the local savings banks otherwise poor people would have been ruined'.[55] The problems of the Credito were largely the result of mismanagement on the part of one of the directors, Manfredini Derela, and fraud on the part of a major customer.[56] A venomous and anonymous report to the Commissario del Borgo blamed the disaster on incompetence, and reveals a highly incestuous relationship between Vatican lay advisers (like Santucci), the Banco di Roma,

[47] De Rosa, *Storia del Banco di Roma*, II, p. 101.
[48] Ibid.   [49] Lai, *Finanze e finanzieri vaticani*, p. 287.
[50] AAES, ASV, Italia, 1917–18, 833, Supplica al Santo Padre per sostentamento della Società Editrice Romana che si occupa dei giornali cattolici, letter of Filippo Crispolti, 12 July 1916.
[51] Ibid.
[52] AAES, ASV, Italia, 1914–18, 835, 1914, Cassa del Clero, letter of 13 Oct. 1914 from Cardinal Mistrangelo, archbishop of Florence, to Benedict.
[53] Lai, *Finanze e finanzieri vaticano*, p. 287.
[54] Scottà (ed.), *La Conciliazione Ufficiosa*, II, p. 80, 3 May 1917.
[55] Ibid.   [56] De Rosa, *Storia del Banco di Roma*, II, p. 151.

the Latium bank and the Società Editrice Romana, the largest Catholic newspaper company in Italy, which later in that same year Benedict was called upon to save by its desperate directors.[57]

Benedict and the Società Editoriale Romana

By the beginning of Benedict's reign, the Società Editoriale Romana controlled the five leading Catholic dailies in Italy – *Il Corriere d'Italia* (Rome), *Il Momento* (Turin), *L'Avvenire* (Bologna), *Il Messagero* (Pisa) and *L'Eco di Bergamo*. According to documents in the Vatican archives, the chairman of the SER, otherwise called the 'Trust', Count Giovanni Grosoli, wrote to Benedict shortly after he was elected in September 1914, to seek help for the ailing newspaper combine.[58] Grosoli explained that thanks to the help (presumably financial) given by the Holy See, 'the intrinsic conditions of the SER have improved since September 1914, including an increase in the number of subscribers', but that Italy's entry into the war had caused problems – in particular, loss of advertising and difficulties with the supply of paper, with the result that the papers had made a loss of 300,000 lire.[59] Even worse, the plans which had been drawn up to improve the longer-term financial performance of the 'Trust' and thus secure its future, had been blown off course by the war; it was now no longer possible to make another share issue due to the building crisis in Milan, and more generally the stasis in business affairs caused by the war.[60] And because of the stasis, the Trust's financial supporters were now asking for their money back; in order to meet these demands it would be necessary to raise 1.5 million lire in the medium term, but the situation was already so serious that 200,000 was required immediately.[61] Grosoli, inevitably, made the point that since the outbreak of the war in the summer of 1914, the papers of the Trust had maintained a scrupulously neutralist stance, in line with Holy See's own policy, and that they would continue to serve the Church 'at whatever cost'.[62]

Less than a year later, the Marquis Crispolto Crispolti, editor of *L'Avvenire* of Bologna, and therefore someone whom Benedict knew from his Bolognese 'exile', wrote another begging letter to the pope on behalf of the Trust.[63] Benedict gave a non-committal reply, but by December of that year both Crispolti and the Holy See were extremely worried about the future of the Trust, and in their desperation they turned to Uncle

---

[57] ACS, MdI, DGPS, 1917, b. 42, H4 Notizie vaticane, report of 12 June 1917.
[58] ASV, Seg. di Stato, Spoglio di Benedetto XV, letter from Grosoli of 18 Nov. 1914.
[59] Ibid., letter of 17 Aug. 1915.   [60] Ibid.   [61] Ibid.   [62] Ibid.
[63] AAES, Italia, 1914–18, 930, 335, Società Editrice Romana, unsigned memorandum of 12 July 1916.

Sam. According to Gasparri, Vicentini had asked Cardinals Gibbons of Baltimore and Farley of New York for a $500,000 loan, with guarantees from the Guarantee Trust or the Banca d'Italia, in order to preserve the newspapers.[64] Farley made short work of Vicentini, saying that he was quite naïve imagining that he could ask for a long-term loan with a very low rate of interest, and no guarantors: 'American financiers do not make loans without guarantees.'[65] The last word in this affair came from Bonzano, who baldly informed his superior, the Secretary of State, that he had no intention of talking to the American bishops about it because

They have always responded generously to my repeated appeals for Peter's Pence. But the fruits of their generosity have rarely exceeded more than $300,000 per year [underlined]. They have many Catholic good works to support, and since there is not a Catholic newspaper in the whole of the United States, they will not be easily convinced of the need to contribute or make appeals for offerings to support Italian Catholic newspapers. In addition, even if a financier were to be found who would be willing to concede such a loan, I have no guarantee to give, nor do I believe it wise to commit the Holy See, since I have no authorisation.[66]

He concluded his letter with a very telling statement: 'Italians think that the American Catholic [bishops] are made of money.'[67] Italians did think that, and their belief was to be strengthened by events later in Benedict's pontificate (see below, pp. 124–5). Gasparri clearly believed it, otherwise he would not have encouraged Crispolti and Vicentini to approach the American bishops.

In November 1916, the SER was replaced by the Unione Editoriale Italiana (UEI), which was founded on the basis of staff reductions and austerity and a substantial financial contribution from the Holy See, but by Christmas 1916, the financial situation of the press combine had deteriorated further and debts of 7,559,530 lire had accumulated, prompting the writer of an unsigned memorandum to the pope to declare that it was not possible to liquidate the company and that catastrophe was inevitable unless substantial help was forthcoming.[68] Benedict was now asked to make a further, longer-term contribution by the owners of the UEI, and the documentation in the Vatican archives testifies to Benedict's financial acumen when he was presented with the salvage plan for the newspapers, whose debts by December 1917 amounted to nearly 8 million lire. In a note of 4 January 1918, written in Benedict's own inimitable hand, he

---

[64] ASV, DAUS, b. 70, Prestito a favore dell'Unione Editoriale Romana (1915–16), letter of 21 Dec. 1915.
[65] Ibid., letter of Farley to Bonzano, 5 Jan. 1916.
[66] Ibid., letter of Bonzano to Gasparri, 10 Jan. 1916.   [67] Ibid.
[68] A. Majo, *La stampa quotidiana cattolica Milanese*, vol. II: *1912–1968 le vicende de l'Italia* (Milan, 1974), p. 24.

shrewdly identified all the flaws in the plan which proposed to save the newspapers by paying an increased rate of interest on the Vatican's current accounts in the Banco di Roma, which would then be given to the chief creditor of the Società, the local bank known as the Piccolo Credito di Ferrara. As Benedict pointed out, the plan was based on 'the false supposition that all the [Holy See's] accounts held at the Bank yielded only an interest of 3.5%; in fact, several already yielded 4% and others 5%, so the figures did not add up'.[69] Even worse, he was rightly afraid that when 'the shareholders learnt that the Bank's losses had grown because of increased payments to the Holy See, would they not have words of resentment against the Holy See as their dividend was accordingly reduced?'.[70] And he went on to say: 'In effect, the Holy See would not have received any greater amount, but in the Bank's [annual] Report it would appear that it had. Then the Bank of Rome could defend itself by saying "otherwise the Holy See would have withdrawn its deposits", in which case the Holy See would have appeared to be an extortionist.'[71] A further worry on Benedict's part was that as the proposal stood, the Holy See would be committed to paying out to the Piccolo Credito for fourteen years, which would leave it open to losing all its capital in the event of the Bank failing.[72] In the end, a compromise was reached: the Bank agreed to give some protection to the capital of the Holy See invested in the Bank in the event of collapse, and Gasparri instructed the Bank to pay 200,000 lire per year to the Piccolo Credito for fourteen years.[73] The Unione was dissolved and the financial management of the five newspapers was devolved to the local dioceses. In a letter to his successor as archbishop of Bologna Benedict wrote:

The Holy See is exhausted and indignant; exhausted because in 1916 it gave three million lire to these newspapers; indignant, because in September they extracted from me a further one million and two hundred thousand lire saying that with this sum the Banco di Roma would be able to mount a rescue operation for the trust . . . whereas the operation was not carried out.[74]

Benedict added that though he regretted the loss of the papers, 'the tributes to their supposed services to the Catholic cause should not be exaggerated'.[75] This latter was probably a reference to Pius X's suspicions about the orthodoxy of the Catholic newspapers. The future of

---

[69] AAES, Italia, 1914–18, 930, 335, Società Editrice Romana, unsigned memorandum of 22 Dec. 1916.
[70] Ibid., 833, Società Editrice Romana, pro-memoria di Benedetto XV, 2 Dec. 1917, pp. 42–3.
[71] Ibid.   [72] Ibid.   [73] Ibid.
[74] As quoted in Majo, *La stampa quotidiana cattolica Milanese*, p. 24.
[75] Ibid.

UEI was not sorted out until September 1918, when complicated plans to devolve them to the responsibility of the local dioceses were finally implemented; even then, the massive cost of clearing their debts took all of Count Grosoli's family fortune.[76]

The finances of the Vatican at the end of Benedict's reign

Clearly, as a result of all these operations, the Vatican must have lost a substantial part of its capital during the First World War; its identified losses on the Banco di Roma, the Trust newspapers and the Credito Centrale amount to roughly 56 million lire, and it may have lost more. The Vatican narrowly escaped further financial loss in late 1921 when the Banco Italiano di Sconto collapsed: Gasparri explained to Monti that he had withdrawn the Holy See's funds just in time.[77] In 1919, in a letter to Prime Minister Francesco Nitti, Gasparri provided a breakdown of the Vatican finances in an attempt, successfully as it turned out, to dissuade the Italian government from taxing the Vatican's income. In the letter he was at pains to stress that taxing the Vatican's investments would discourage the faithful from giving generously since they had been built up over the years precisely on savings from these offerings; he claimed that none of the property owned by the Holy See in Rome brought in any income, which, however, is contradicted by the accounts of the Administration of the Sacred Palaces (see Chapter 3, p. 47), and that the holdings of the Propaganda congregation were entirely separate.[78] Gasparri also stated that the total value of the Vatican's holdings of stocks and shares amounted to 86.4 million lire. Though he did not make it absolutely clear whether his figures included the value of accounts and investments held abroad, he implies it.[79] This means, at a conservative estimate, that the Vatican had lost nearly 40 per cent of its capital during the war. This must have had serious consequences for the Vatican's ordinary income: given a usual average return of 4 per cent, the Vatican's investment income must have dropped from roughly 5.7 million lire to an absolute maximum of 3.45 million per year. Yet in January 1917, when the bulk of the losses had already been sustained, Monti says that Benedict 'told me that 6 million lire are required to meet the expenses of the Holy See and that the income from the Holy See's investments amount to nearly 3 million, the difference being met by Peter's Pence, and that every month he hands over 300,000 lire (from Peter's Pence) to the Vatican administration'.[80]

---

[76] Ibid., p. 25.
[77] Scottà (ed.), *La Conciliazione Ufficiosa*, II, p. 569, 1 Jan. 1922.
[78] Spadolini (ed.), *Il Cardinale Gasparri*, pp. 376–7, document 59, Gasparri a Nitti.
[79] Ibid.   [80] Scottà (ed.), *La Conciliazione Ufficiosa*, II, p. 3, 3 Jan. 1917.

Providing a rare glimpse into the financial workings of the Vatican, Benedict went on to tell Monti that the income from Peter's Pence 'amply covered' the Vatican's remaining outgoings.[81] Gasparri, in the letter to Francesco Nitti, confirmed that the income from Peter's Pence made up the difference.[82] Simple arithmetic would suggest that, on the basis of these figures, the Vatican was accruing a surplus of roughly 600,000 lire a year, which was presumably invested. On the other hand, it is equally possible that Benedict was using the surplus for extraordinary expenditure, i.e. on his humanitarian efforts. Whichever was the case, this suggests that the Holy See was just about keeping its head above water until the end of the war, as does the fact that both during and after the war, under pressure from the Italian government via Monti, the Vatican subscribed several million lire to national loans.[83] In the case of the post-war 'peace' loan, the ABSS, the Amministrazione per le Opere di Religione (forerunner of the Vatican bank) and the Sanctuary of the Madonna of Pompei (under direct Vatican administration) subscribed 2 million lire between them.[84] This was part of a deliberate policy on the Vatican's part to improve relations with Italy; it also had the effect of starting a process whereby the finances of the Vatican would become closely linked to those of the Italian state (see Chapter 6).

After the end of the war, the financial situation almost certainly got worse: an impoverished and famished Germany meant that, as Molony states, 'German Catholics, who had previously contributed generously to papal finances, were now unable to do so.'[85] This is indeed what Gasparri claimed in a conversation with Monti in 1920, that those countries which had once been sources of financial support were now expecting help from the Holy See, the only bright spot in the picture being France, where offerings for Peter's Pence rose dramatically in 1919 and early 1920 in the run up to the canonisation of Joan of Arc.[86] Inflation had also increased apace since 1917. In addition, it is extremely probable that the Vatican lost out on Austrian loan stock at the end of the war. It would, therefore, seem likely that there is some truth in the numerous claims that the Vatican was obliged to seek a loan in 1919. Seldes claims that 'In 1919 Monsignor Cerretti made a trip to America for the reported purpose of floating a loan of a million, but this did not eventuate. It proved unnecessary, for in the same year the pilgrimage of the Knights of Columbus brought a

[81] Ibid.   [82] Spadolini (ed.), *Il Cardinale Gasparri*, p. 377.
[83] Scottà (ed.), *La Conciliazione Ufficiosa*, II, p. 532, 1 Feb. 1920.
[84] Ibid.   [85] Molony, *The Emergence of Political Catholicism*, p. 59.
[86] Zambarbieri, 'La devozione al Papa', p. 72. The other graphs on pp. 70–4 confirm that receipts from Peter's Pence reached an all time low at the end of the war and did not begin to pick up again until late in 1919.

gift estimated at a quarter of a million dollars.'[87] Lo Bello tells much the same story, presumably because he got it from Seldes, but his version states that the mission was a failure because 'the Vatican apparently went about it the wrong way'; he also says that the Knights of Columbus gave only $50,000.[88] Ultimately, the story seems to have derived from a spat between the Italian newspaper *Il Giornale* which claimed that Msgr Cerretti had been sent to America to seek a 1 million dollar loan[89] and *L'Osservatore Romano* which replied with the usual caustic venom that it employed when dealing with the Italian secular press. The Vatican organ complained that it was a pity that journalists could never get anything right when reporting on the Vatican, claiming that Cerretti had gone to collect the offerings of the faithful and the generous subsidies provided by loyal Catholics in the USA, and added that, of course, the Vatican did not need a loan because it met its expenses from the collections for Peter's Pence and the rest of the goodwill offerings. Furthermore, it argued that the Vatican did not have a big material patrimony to administer and that it always balanced its budget.[90] All this suggests that the Vatican's financial situation had deteriorated since Benedict's conversation about the Vatican finances with Monti. It was certainly not usual for a high-ranking Vatican official to go to the United States to collect Peter's Pence. But Cerretti may very well have been sent to America precisely in order to raise a big sum of money, either by means of further subsidies from the bishops or indeed in the form of a loan. The words of Bishop McNicholas, secretary of the US Bishops' Conference, in his letter to Bonzano in September of the same year that 'Many of the Bishops now I think begin to realise the position and needs of the Holy See', would make sense in the context of Cerretti's 'begging' mission.[91] Seldes's suggestion that the Knights of Columbus eventually saved the day for the Vatican would also make sense: by 1919 the Knights had become a very big organisation indeed among US Catholic men, and that more and more of their fundraising was targeted at the Vatican is proven by their involvement from 1920 onwards in supporting playgrounds for the children of Rome.[92]

On the other hand, Molony's claim that one of the main motivations of Benedict's attempts to solve the Roman Question was financial necessity is rather undercut by the great Italian ecclesiastical historian Carlo Jemolo, who says emphatically that the Vatican did not include a

---

[87] Seldes, *The Vatican*, p. 249.   [88] Lo Bello, *L'oro del Vaticano*, p. 59.
[89] AVS, DAUS, v (Foreign Policy), Scatola 97, press cutting from *Il Giornale d'Italia*, no. 253.
[90] Ibid., press cutting from *L'Osservatore Romano*.
[91] AVS, DAUS, 284, McNicholas to Bonzano 27 Sept. 1919.
[92] Gannon, *The Cardinal Spellman Story*, pp. 43–6.

financial element in the proposals for a solution which Msgr Cerretti negotiated with the Italian prime minister Vittorio Emanule Orlando at Versailles in 1919.[93] Nevertheless, it is inconceivable that the resolution of the Roman Question which Benedict and Gasparri sought would not have included some financial element, if only an acceptance of the annual payment of the indemnity established by the Law of Papal Guarantees. That alone would have enormously improved the Vatican's financial position.

This finally brings us to Lo Bello's allegation that the Vatican was bankrupt on Benedict's death in January 1922 and that Gasparri was forced to get a loan from Rothschild's in order to pay for the cost of the ensuing funeral, conclave and coronation. Seldes's variant on this story is that the Cardinal Camerlengo (Gasparri) was saved from having to get a loan by the discovery of 'a little unembellished box, the contents of which would pay the expenses of the conclave. The box contained a large cheque sent by an American.'[94] No evidence has been found to back up either story. The Rothschild archives in London and Paris have revealed nothing which would support Lo Bello's story about a loan; in fact, the last recorded Rothschild loan to the Vatican was in the 1860s.[95] Since the papers of the Rothschild branch in Vienna were seized by the Nazis in 1939 and never returned, it is just possible that Gasparri received funds from that quarter, but unlikely: Austria in 1922 was both a defeated power and bankrupt. So much so that it had to be bailed out by the League of Nations. Its private banking institutions were also badly affected. The evidence of both Gasparri's memoirs and the papers of the apostolic delegation in Washington suggests that Gasparri did not need a loan. Gasparri actually says that he found 75,000 lire in the pope's desk when he died, which was clearly inadequate to meet the extraordinary expenses of the funeral, conclave and coronation: 'what were 75,000 lire when it was estimated that several millions would be needed?'.[96] He went on to say that he did consider seeking a bank loan, but that he was able to avoid this by requesting the apostolic delegate in Washington, Archbishop Bonzano, to send him a cheque for the balance of the US Bishops' contribution which had built up between the usual quarterly payments which he sent

---

[93] Jemolo, *Church and State*, p. 166.

[94] Seldes, *The Vatican*, p. 246; Gollin, *Worldly Goods*, p. 437, offers another variant, saying that Gasparri was so hard-pressed for cash that he 'had to borrow $100,000 from a Rome bank to cover the expenses of Benedict's funeral and of the conclave of cardinals which elected his successor, Pius XI'. That seems unlikely in view of the size of the Vatican funds deposited with the Banco di Roma.

[95] Letter of the archivist of Rothschilds, London, Mr Victor Gray, to the author, 27 Nov. 1998.

[96] Spadolini (ed.), *Il Cardinale Gasparri*, p. 250.

to Rome.[97] This is confirmed by the archives of that Delegation which contain correspondence in which Gasparri asked for the usual cheque to be cancelled and another with additions to be sent instead: he also asked Bonzano to obtain extra money from the US cardinals to cover the 'substantial costs of the conclave'.[98] Bonzano replied that the 'usual cheque' had been for $210,400, from a variety of funds: this was stopped and presumably the replacement cheque eventually sent was somewhat in excess of that figure.[99] The money in Benedict's desk and the cheque from the USA would have fallen short of the 'several millions' that Gasparri anticipated, but as he himself made clear, by practising economies during the conclave, he says he made ends meet.[100] With the benefit of this information, it would seem that the situation confronting Gasparri in January 1922 was rather more of a short-term cash-flow problem occasioned by the unfortunate and immediate financial consequences of the pope's unexpected demise than the 'bankruptcy' described by Lo Bello and others.

Conclusion

While the evidence overwhelmingly proves that Benedict was not as financially incompetent or careless as some authors have claimed, it is clear that, unlike Pius X, he was faced by some very serious financial problems, most importantly the unexpected demands of war. This would account for the fact that Benedict did not leave the Vatican with a cash reserve at the end of his reign, though it is far from certain that he left it in the financial mess which so many of his detractors have claimed. One of the major problems he faced was the financial crisis of various Italian Catholic institutions which had been maturing in his predecessor's reign but was exacerbated by the war. Benedict showed a real concern for the future of Italian Catholic economic and social initiatives in particular, but it was clear that their problems had not been resolved by the end of his reign and that they would continue to turn to the Holy See for help in the future. What was also clear by the end of Benedict's reign was the degree to which the Vatican had become dependent upon the financial support of American Catholics to keep it afloat, as the situation which developed immediately after his death so sharply demonstrates. On the debit side, so to speak, what is perhaps most striking about Benedict's

---

[97] Ibid, p. 251.
[98] ASV, DAUS, I, 118, Malattia e Morte di Benedetto XV, telegram of Gasparri to Bonzano, 21 Jan. 1922.
[99] Ibid., telegram of Bonzano to Gasparri, same date.
[100] Spadolini (ed.), *Il Cardinale Gasparri*, pp. 251–2.

experience is how it revealed that the Vatican was trapped in a complex of financial relationships involving the Banco di Roma, other Catholic banks and institutions, all of them involving leading lay members of the Papal Court and administration, relationships which were unhealthily incestuous. Most seriously, as a result of these relationships, it possessed no truly independent financial advisers on whom it could rely in its dealings with banks, etc. Unless and until it could find such advisers, it would be at the mercy of poor and self-interested financial advice.

6　'Economical and prudent bourgeois'?: Pius XI (1922–1929)

Introduction

Whether Pius XI was the 'economical and prudent bourgeois' that Seldes implies (see Chapter 5, p. 110) is debatable, but that he was of bourgeois extraction there can be no doubt. Born the son of a silk worker who later became a mill manager in Desio (Milan province) in 1857, Achille Ratti studied at local schools, at the diocesan seminary in Milan and the Lombard seminary in Rome, and became librarian of the prestigious Ambrosian Library in the Lombard capital in 1907. Three years later, he was called to the Vatican Library of which he became the prefect in 1912. His career took a different turn when, in April 1918, Benedict XV took him away from his books, and sent him as apostolic visitor to newly emerging Poland and Lithuania. Eventually he was promoted to archbishop and nuncio to Poland in 1919. One of the key elements in his experience was to stare into the abyss, to witness the approach of the Red Army to within striking distance of Warsaw in the summer of 1920. But his mission was not entirely successful, the local hierarchy being dissatisfied with his attitude towards the Lithuanians and the Polish government for his involvement in the vexed Silesian question.[1] In May 1921, he was recalled to Italy, being made archbishop of Milan and a cardinal. He did not stay long in the chair of St Ambrose; on 6 February 1922 he was unexpectedly elected pope in the conclave which followed Benedict's death.[2] Pius XI continued many of the policies of his predecessor in the fields of missionary endeavour (consecrating six Chinese bishops in 1926), in respect of the Eastern Rite and Uniate Churches, and even in the field of diplomacy; in an unprecedented move he retained Benedict's Secretary of State, Cardinal Pietro Gasparri. With Gasparri, and his successor in 1930 Cardinal Eugenio Pacelli, later Pius XII, Pius pursued a vigorous

---

[1] While there is a large literature on various aspects of his pontificate, there are no good biographies of Pius XI, in English, but there are useful biographical sketches in Falconi, *The Popes in the Twentieth Century*, p. 178; and Levillain (ed.), *The Papacy*, I, pp. 1209–16.
[2] Falconi, *The Popes in the Twentieth Century*, pp. 151–234.

Lo storico colloquio dell' 11 febbraio tra Pio XI e Mussolini

(Disegno di A. Beltrame)

Illustration 9 Pope Pius XI

diplomacy which led to the conclusion of concordats with half a dozen states including Italy, Prussia and the Third Reich. Even more remarkably, for the first time since 1870, he insisted on giving his first blessing from the external loggia of St Peter's, as a token of his concern for reconciliation with Italy. Pius XI's pontificate will be remembered for a number of important initiatives in the teaching magisterium of the Church: his encyclicals on youth (*Rappresentanti in Terra*, 1929), on marriage (*Casti Connubi*, 1930) which re-iterated traditional Catholic teaching on the role of women and the ban on artificial birth control, and on Catholic social teaching (*Quadragesimo Anno*, 1931); and the rapprochements with both Italian Fascism and German National Socialism, which led to concordats with those regimes in 1929 and 1933 respectively.[3] As the 1930s wore on, Pius XI came into increasing conflict with both Fascist dictatorships and also, inevitably, the Soviet Union. The errors of the totalitarian states were castigated by him in a series of encyclicals, *Non Abbiamo Bisogno* against Fascism in 1931, *Mit Brennender Sorge* against National Socialism in 1937 and *Divini Redemptoris* against atheistic communism in the same year, culminating in the 'hidden', unpublished encyclical on racism, *Humani Generis Unitas* of 1939.[4]

The state of Vatican finances at the beginning of Pius XI's reign

Gasparri's prompt action may have resolved the financial difficulties surrounding the 1922 conclave, but there were still claims that Pius XI inherited a difficult financial situation, in particular, that there had been a fall in the income from Peter's Pence from various parts of the world, and especially Belgium, France, Great Britain and Germany.[5] And these difficulties would not have been helped by Papa Ratti's continuation of the policy of his predecessor of contributing to emergency aid to countries in distress – Austria, Germany and Russia – a contribution estimated at between 2 and 2.5 million lire.[6]

According to Seldes,

The (financial) reforms of Pius XI began even before the Lateran Accords. He had found about £11,000 in the Vatican treasury, and expenses of about £1,000 a day (which, however, were covered by income) and after re-organising the household

---

[3] See J. F. Pollard, 'Fascism', in Dwyer (ed.), *New Dictionary of Catholic Social Thought*, pp. 381–8.

[4] For the texts of Pius XI's major encyclicals see Carlen (ed.), *Papal Encyclicals*, III; for that of *Humani Generis Unitas*, see G. Passalecq and B. Suchecky, *The Hidden Encyclical of Pius XI* (New York, 1997).

[5] Binchy, *Church and State*, pp. 307–8.   [6] Ibid.

economy, he sent for Catholic accountants who made what is generally called the first audit in Church history. In 1928 strict measures were taken, which were reported in the Pontifical Annual of that year.[7]

Then followed a quotation, allegedly from the *Annuario Pontificio*:

His Holiness Pius XI beginning from 1927 has reformed the administration of the Vatican finances. The entire administration of the apostolic palace has been placed under the control of a commission of cardinals. The gifts of the faithful brought to Rome by the bishops are a sum kept apart, administered by the personal control of the pope, paid by a person of confidence who keeps a book in which are marked all receipts and expenses, and which is balanced each week. Expenses figure annually about 20,000,000 lire. The bookkeeping is carried out according to the most modern principles and is severely controlled.[8]

Lo Bello carries more or less the same version of this story, including the alleged quotation from the *Annuario Pontificio*, proving, if ever proof were needed, that much of his information was derived from Seldes, but he adds a twist by saying that the 'first audit in Church history' was in 1928, that Msgr Damaiani conducted it, and that 'to all intents and purposes the Vatican was down to its bottom dollar that year but that the audit did turn up a "lost" $55,000, which saved the day'.[9] It is fascinating how little 'windfalls' were always saving the day in the Vatican! It is not clear what either author means by the 'Vatican treasury': was this the box in the pope's desk or a safe in the ABSS? And no trace of a statement about the finances of the Vatican has been found in the *Annuario Pontificio* for 1928. In view of the evidence that the Vatican did face serious financial problems in the mid- and late 1920s (see below, p. 135), Lo Bello's more precise date of 1928 for the audit does seem to make some sense, otherwise, if Seldes was arguing that the audit took place upon Pius XI's accession, then it took a very long time – six years – for it to bear its fruits in terms of the reform of financial practices. It is also curious that Seldes should talk about 'Catholic accountants', since it would not have been easy to find accountants of any other kind in Italy at that time, unless they were Jews! The one kind of financial reform that we can be fairly sure that Pius XI introduced into the Vatican after his election was the 'household economy' referred to by Seldes. Of this he says: 'Pius XI, who having noticed that the chicken for lunch left no remnant for dinner, discharged the royal household which had reigned in the Vatican for centuries, enthroning in its place his mother's cook, Signora Linda, and five

---

[7] Seldes, *The Vatican*, pp. 253–4; Binchy, *Church and State*, p. 307, confirms that Pius XI carried out financial reforms.
[8] Seldes, *The Vatican*, p. 254.   [9] Lo Bello, *L'oro del Vaticano*, p. 61.

brave religious who undertook the services of *valets de chambre*.'[10] This is very plausible. Even allowing for a certain journalistic 'colouring', this story rings true. The thrifty Milanese 'bourgeois' was very likely to be outraged by Roman waste. More significantly, the good 'Signora Linda' was no mythical figure. On the contrary, Pius XI's faithful housekeeper for forty years, she became a legend in the Vatican, the first in a long line of *puissant virgins* to act as the papal housekeeper.[11] When Pius was told by his advisers that no pope had ever allowed a woman to take up service in the Vatican, he remarked: 'Then I shall be the first.'[12] Much to the scandal of the Romans, lay and clerical, she quickly established a powerful position for herself there after the election of Papa Ratti, with unlimited right of access to the papal private apartment. In fact, she had arrived ten years earlier when Ratti became head of the Vatican Library: by the time of his election, Teodolinda Banfi (her marital status is uncertain, but it seems likely that she was a spinster and that her title was, therefore, an honorary one, similar to that enjoyed by the housekeeper in English country houses) had been his housekeeper for thirty-three years.[13] By 1926 she was regarded by the Commissario del Borgo as exercising a powerful influence on Pius XI, and she was even accused of being a German spy.[14] Finally, in November 1926 she was dismissed, but not before she had made economies and reforms in the papal household.[15] One does not envy the poor Vatican official, almost certainly Cardinal Gasparri, who had to persuade the notoriously imperious and authoritarian Pius XI of the necessity of dispensing with the services of 'Signora Linda'.

The advent of Fascism and the salvage of the Banco di Roma

Whatever the truth of Seldes's story about the financial condition of the Vatican at the beginning of the new reign, the most pressing financial

---

[10] Seldes, *The Vatican*, p. 246.

[11] Mother Pasqualina Lehnert, who had been Eugenio Pacelli's housekeeper when he was nuncio in Germany from 1917 to 1930, moved with him to Rome when he became Secretary of State in 1930 and became a powerful figure in the Vatican after his election as Pius XII in 1939 (see P. Murphy, *La Popessa* (New York, 1983)). Sister Vincenza was housekeeper to Pope John Paul I and Sister Teodolina was housekeeper to John Paul II. See P. Hoffman, *Anatomy of the Vatican* (London, 1985), pp. 130–1.

[12] L. Lazzarini, *Pio XI* (Milan, 1937), p. 312.

[13] T. Natalini (ed.), *I diari del Cardinale Ermengildo Pellegrinetti (1916–1922)* (Vatican City, 1994), pp. 230–1.

[14] ACS, MI, DGPS, 1926, b. 113, H4 Notizie Vaticane, reports of 3 Oct. 1926 and 1 Nov. 1926.

[15] Ibid., report of 2 Nov. 1926.

problem which Pius XI discovered he faced was that of the Banco di Roma: during the course of 1922, the bank was once again in trouble, inevitably threatening the substantial deposits which the Vatican held there. The bank's position had improved in the later years of the war, after the salvage operation of 1916; indeed, there was bullish expansion until the spring of 1920. Thereafter, the Roma was affected both by difficulties in foreign operations, with especially heavy losses in the Middle East, and by the domestic post-war recession in general terms, and the difficulties of the Catholic co-operative movement in particular.[16] The collapse of the Banco Italiano di Sconto also had its repercussions for the Roma: by mid-1922 there were large deposit withdrawals and help was being sought from the Banca d'Italia.[17]

The salvage of the Banco di Roma has to be seen against the background of the critical Italian political situation in the early 1920s. Even as Benedict had lain on his deathbed in January 1922, he had not been spared Italy's political problems. Giolitti had sought the support of the Vatican in his efforts to form a new government with the powerful Catholic Party, the Partito Popolare Italiano.[18] In fact, Italy's system of parliamentary government was in deep crisis, undermined by Left-wing militancy, a split within the traditional liberal-conservative political elite, and the challenge from the violent, radical Right – Mussolini and Fascism. Indeed, one of the reasons for the problems of the Catholic co-operative movement, and consequently those of the Banco di Roma, were the violent attacks of the Fascists' paramilitary squads against Catholic economic and social institutions in northern and central Italy. The crisis worsened throughout 1922 and reached its climax in the so-called 'March on Rome' of October, after which Mussolini came to power. The election of Achille Ratti to the papal throne marked a change in the Vatican's official attitude towards Fascism, possibly prompted by the sympathy which Ratti had shown towards Fascism while archbishop of Milan, when he had permitted Fascist banners to be borne into the cathedral during the commemoration of Italian victory, in November 1921. The result was a change of tack on the part of both *L'Osservatore Romano* and *La Civiltà Cattolica* in February 1922.[19] Mussolini shamelessly exploited this opportunity. The avowed atheist and anti-clerical, who had written a semi-pornographic novel entitled *The Cardinal's Mistress* in his misspent youth and who had once stated in his newspaper *Il Popolo d'Italia* that the only solution to the Roman Question was 'to invite his Holiness to leave Rome', by 1921 had

[16] Caroleo, *Le banche cattoliche*, pp. 116–17.
[17] Ibid.   [18] Pollard, *The Unknown Pope*, pp. 184–5.
[19] A. C. O'Brien, 'L'Osservatore Romano and Fascism: The Beginning of a New Era', *Church and State* (Spring, 1971).

seen the light and in his maiden speech to Parliament assiduously courted Catholic support.[20] In the November 1922 programme of his government he included the re-introduction of Religious Instruction into primary schools, the restoration of the crucifix to public buildings and increased state payments to parochial clergy. What was not part of the official agenda was the salvation of the Banco di Roma. But in January 1923 a secret meeting took place between Gasparri and Mussolini, the outcome of which was an agreement on Mussolini's part to save the bank, in return for the elimination of the 'Catholic' bankers, Vicentini and Santucci (the latter actually hosted the meeting), and their replacement by Fascist "trusties", Prince Buoncompagni Ludovisi and G. B. Vitali as president and managing director respectively, and the cutting off of the bank's subsidies to the Catholic Partito Popolare and the Catholic press.[21] In fact, the salvage of the bank was bought at a higher price than this, that is the abandonment by the Church of the Partito Popolare, the Catholic trade union organisation Confederazione Italiana del Lavoro, and many of the agrarian co-operatives and credit unions, all of which were demolished by Fascism as it consolidated its totalitarian power in the mid- and late 1920s. On the other hand, other major Catholic banks controlled by clerico-Fascist lay elements close to the Vatican were saved from the effects of Mussolini's monetary policies, his insistence on re-valuing the lira to the unrealistic level of 90 to the pound sterling in the same period.[22] The subsequent support which many Catholic bankers, including Grosoli, Santucci and Buoncompagni Ludovisi, gave to Fascism earned the rebuke of the Christian democratic journalist, Igino Giordani, who described them as 'dei cattolici apostolici (banco) romani'.[23]

Papa Ratti did not like Catholic politicians, especially clerical ones like the leader of the Partito Popolare, Fr. Luigi Sturzo, whose departure into exile in 1924 came as great relief to the pontiff, and he does not seem to have had his predecessor's concern for the welfare of the Catholic economic and social movement either. In 1928 he also forbade bishops and priests to be involved in (Catholic) banking, lest they be held responsible for any bankruptcies and losses to the faithful.[24] Instead, he placed his trust in direct political deals with the dominant secular force of the moment – Fascism – and in an apolitical organisation, Catholic Action, to act as a powerful pressure group inside the Fascist regime. Instead of Catholic co-operativism, the mill manager's son preferred bankers, industrialists and other professional capitalist entrepeneurs.

---

[20] As quoted in Pollard, *The Vatican and Italian Fascism*, p. 22.
[21] Pollard, 'Conservative Catholics and Fascism: The Clerico-Fascists', pp. 38–9.
[22] Ibid., p. 39.   [23] I. Giordani, *La Rivolta Cattolica* (Turin, 1924), p. 72.
[24] Caroleo, *Le banche cattoliche*, p. 120.

Papa Ratti, 'Christian restoration' and a construction spree

Papa Ratti's official motto, as enunciated in his first encyclical *Ubi Arcano dei Consilio* (1922) was 'the Christian restoration of society in a Catholic sense', which signified an intransigent determination to impose a thoroughly Catholic vision of the "common good" upon society.[25] That strategy of re-conquering an Italian society semi-secularised over the preceding seventy-five years or so included both the capillary expansion of the lay Catholic Action association and its ancillary organisations in the youth, labour and women's fields, as a powerful pressure group in Italian civil society, and the promotion of Catholic educational institutions, including the newly established Catholic University of Milan. His plans for Catholic Action extended to all Catholic countries, and his anxiety to provide Rome-educated clerical elites for both Italy and the world-wide Church led to attempts to provide suitable accommodation for the various educational institutions in the Vatican and Rome generally. Consequently, in the latter half of the 1920s, Pius XI embarked upon a massive building programme:

1. 1926 – the restoration of the catacombs of S. Sebastian on the Via Appia Antica.
2. 1926–28 – a building for the School of Christian Archeology.
3. 1926 – a building on the Esquiline Hill for the Institute of Oriental Studies founded by his predecessor.
4. Late 1920s – a new palace in the square facing Santa Maria Maggiore for the Lombard College and the building of the Russicum, the centre of training for priests destined for Russian fields of mission and martyrdom.
5. 1928 – the building of the Pontifical Minor Roman seminary in the Vatican – this was converted in 1929 to become the palace of the governor of the State of the Vatican City.
6. 1928 – the building of the Ethiopian College, also in the Vatican.
7. 1928 – the re-housing of the Jesuit-run Gregorian University in Piazza della Pilotta, and the re-building of the Bohemian College, not to mention the building of a new Propaganda college on the Janiculum for the training of missionary priests.[26]

---

[25] Carlen (ed.), *Papal Encyclicals*, III, pp. 225–39. See also G. Martina, 'L'ecclesiologia prevalente durante il pontificato di Pio XI', in A. Monticone (ed.), *Cattolici e fascisti in Umbria (1922–1945)* (Bologna, 1978), p. 226.

[26] L. Castelli, *'Quel tanto di territorio': ricordi di lavori ed opere eseguiti nel Vaticano durante il Pontificato di Pio XI (1922–1939)* (Rome, 1940), pp. 47–9; and Hachey (ed.), *Anglo-Vatican Relations*, p. 130.

One motive for this very ambitious building programme was undoubtedly a desire to re-assert the visibility of the papal 'presence' in Rome in the face of Fascist, totalitarian influences which, in the late 1920s, led to Mussolini's public works projects to 're-build' the Eternal City, including the demolition of much of the core of medieval Rome in order more fully to expose the antiquities of the Forum and to construct a triumphal road to the Colosseum (later called the Via del Impero) as a parade ground of Fascist triumphs.[27] On the other hand, such construction activities would clearly have exhausted the Vatican's ordinary revenues, that is from its investments and from Peter's Pence, in the latter case, even allowing for the boost which the celebration of 'Holy Year' in 1925 would have given those revenues. According to the British Minister to the Holy See, the Holy Year celebrations, and the attendant Missionary Exhibition and commemoration of the sixteen-hundredth anniversary of the Council of Ephesus, brought one and a quarter million pilgrims to Rome.[28] If Lo Bello is right when he says that the Vatican was virtually down to its last dollar in 1928, then Pius XI was clearly neither an economical nor prudent bourgeois: maybe he simply put his trust in the biblical injunction that 'the Lord will provide'. There is other evidence that the Vatican was facing a serious lack of funding in the mid- to late 1920s, in the form of information from the Commissario del Borgo. In July 1926, in a report on unrest among Vatican employees about their salary levels, the Commissario also explained:

The finances of the Holy See, which suffered a grave blow during the war, as a consequence of which many stocks and bonds, like the Russian ones, have completely lost their value, and others have fallen in value, are in anything but a flourishing condition due to the increase in expenditure which is not matched by a corresponding increase in income. If in fact during the Holy Year the income from the Obolo was significant, a considerable fall has already been noticeable in the first months of this year.[29]

A couple of months later the Commissario reported that Pius XI was anxious that there be a big pilgrimage from the USA 'so that . . . the Vatican can collect from the pilgrims sufficient offerings to re-vitalise the finances of the Holy See which are not flourishing'.[30]

---

[27] On Mussolini's grandiose town planning projects for Rome, see I. Insolera, *Roma moderna* (Turin, 1971).
[28] Hachey (ed.), *Anglo-Vatican Relations*, p. 78.
[29] ACS, MI, DGPS, 1926, b. 113, H 4 Notizie Vaticane, report of 31 July 1926.
[30] Ibid., report of 25 Sept. 1926: Salvemini, *Chiesa e stato*, p. 384, says that in the early to mid-1920s the Vatican had been obliged to borrow from the banks.

The American connection

This increasingly important American dimension of the financing of the Vatican would help to explain Pius XI's ability to finance major building projects in the later 1920s and is confirmed by another source. According to Seldes: 'In 1928, through Cardinal Mundelein, a Vatican loan of 300,000 [approximately 3 million lire] pounds five per cent sinking-fund twenty-year bonds was floated, backed by Church property worth many millions in Chicago.'[31] The story is corroborated by both the *New York Times* and the biographer of Cardinal Mundelein, archbishop of Chicago.[32] Along with Cardinal William O'Connell, archbishop of Boston, and Francis Spellman, later archbishop of New York, Mundelein was one of the most vigorous and dynamic of the American cardinals, and his archdiocese was indeed already very wealthy.[33] Cardinal Spellman is usually regarded as the classic, American 'bricks and mortar' bishop, able to raise large sums from the mass of the faithful and charm even larger ones out of the pocket books of the wealthy, Catholic and non-Catholic alike, for the various diocesan building projects, churches, rectories, schools, seminaries and hospitals, etc.[34] In fact, Mundelein was really the first of these men by twenty years, and the first to create what was in effect a diocesan 'bank', which borrowed in bulk and cheaply from the commercial market and lent out to individual parishes at a slightly higher rate,[35] and so successful was he that at the time when he re-launched a bonds issue, *Time* reported that 'No one in Chicago has better credit than the cardinal.'[36] The bulk of the Chicago loan went to pay for the missionary college of Propaganda Fide.[37]

The Chicago loan also confirms the strengthening of a tendency which had become apparent in the reign of Benedict XV, that the Vatican was becoming increasingly dependent on the largesse of American Catholics. In 1920 the Chicago archdiocese alone sent $100,000 in Peter's Pence to Rome, and averaged $120,000 through the 1920s as a whole.[38] And in 1926, it raised $167,000 for Catholic missions, a figure only exceeded by New York, Boston, Philadelphia and Rochester.[39] A sign of Mundelein's 'muscle' in Rome is provided by the fact that in 1930, over the heads

---

[31] Seldes, *The Vatican*, p. 249.
[32] Seldes provides no documentary evidence for the loan, but confirmation is provided by the *New York Times*, and by Mundelein's biographer, E. R. Kantowicz, in *Corporation Sole: Cardinal Mundelein and Chicago Catholicism* (South Bend, Ind., 1982), p. 47.
[33] Kantowicz, *Corporation Sole*; and *New Catholic Encyclopedia*, III (New York, 1967), p. 562: 'Despite the Depression, Bishop of Chicago bonds remained at par throughout.'
[34] Gannon, *The Cardinal Spellman Story*, p. 252.
[35] Kantowicz, *Corporation Sole*, p. 47.
[36] Ibid., p. 42.   [37] Ibid.   [38] Ibid.   [39] Ibid.

of the Sacred Congregation for Seminaries and Universities, the archbishop of Chicago managed to persuade the Vatican to grant his newly founded diocesan seminary at St Mary of the Lake the status of pontifical university, a status that eluded many much more well-established and prestigious institutions and that the first eucharistic congress to be held in the USA took place in Chicago in 1926.[40] With that event, it might be said that the American church had come of age.

Though there might be disdain and dislike of Americans in Roman ecclesiastical circles,[41] the fact was that US Catholics were paying a lot of the Vatican's bills. Inevitably, this meant a growing American influence in the Vatican. We have further evidence in the annual report for 1923 written by the British Minister to the Holy See. Commenting on the elevation of Archbishops Mundelein of Chicago and Hayes of New York to the cardinalatial purple shortly after Benedict's death, he claimed: 'It was declared in Rome, and probably with some truth, that American gold had something to do with the promotion of the two archbishops.'[42] He went on to explain to his superiors in the Foreign Office that American Catholics contributed as much to Catholic missions as all other countries put together and concluded by saying:

America has deserved well of the Holy See, seeing that she has furnished vast sums for distribution among the poor in Russia and Germany, and especially for the foreign missions. Apart from these special collections, the Catholics of Chicago and New York are by far the largest contributors towards Vatican funds. It is indeed, difficult to see how the present administration could be preserved without their support.[43]

It is therefore impossible not to concur with another of his statements, 'and it is not so much of an exaggeration to say that the United States is now looked up to as if it were the leading Catholic nation'.[44] The increasing strength of the American Catholic Church meant increasing influence at the Vatican. By the middle of the 1930s, the importance of Catholic laymen and their contribution to the financing of both the American Church and the Vatican was demonstrated by the fact that 100 United States citizens were listed in the *Annuario Pontificio* as having papal orders and seven of them held titles of papal nobility.[45] According to another acute observer of the papacy in these years: 'In the latter years of the long reign of Pius XI (1922–1939), however, American Catholicism began to take

[40] Ibid., p. 49.
[41] See for example J. Cooney, *The American Pope* (New York, 1983), p. 52, where he discusses the difficulties encountered by Cardinal O'Connell of Boston and his auxiliary, the then Bishop Francis Spellman when they worked in Rome.
[42] Hachey (ed.), *Anglo-Vatican Relations*, p. 71.
[43] Ibid.   [44] Ibid., p. 70.   [45] Seldes, *The Vatican*, p. 23.

the place in the Vatican councils to which its growing numbers, wealth and prestige entitled it.'[46] The fact that Papa Ratti created two American cardinals (including Mundelein) in one year, 1924, when there had only been three in the whole previous history of the American Church, and the fact that he also changed the rules of the conclave, thus prolonging the interregnum in order to allow the American cardinals more time to reach Rome, was the clearest demonstration of the growing American influence in the Vatican.

Conciliazione

In less than a year from the Chicago loan, Pius XI had no more need of loans because a final agreement with Italy to settle the 'Roman Question' put an end to the Vatican's financial problems.[47] It seems likely that one of his chief motives for seeking the agreement was precisely the state of the Vatican finances; there has even been a suggestion that he was prepared to embark on a spending spree and take out the Chicago loan in anticipation of a generous financial element in the settlement.[48]

The origins of the *Conciliazione* of February 1929 can be traced back to the failed efforts of Pius's predecessor to resolve the dispute with Italy a decade previously. By the end of the First World War, despite conflict over a number of serious issues, relations between the Vatican and Italy had enormously improved, so much so that in the spring of 1919, behind the scenes at the Versailles Peace Conference, the Under-Secretary of State, Msgr Cerretti, engaged in talks for a definitive settlement with Italian Prime Minister Vittorio Emmanule Orlando. The talks resulted in a broad agreement, more or less along the lines achieved in 1929, but the difficult parliamentary situation, and the resistance of the king prevented a successful outcome: nevertheless, talks continued in the early 1920s.[49] Pius XI's opening towards Fascism from the beginning of his reign, and his acquiescence in Mussolini's conquest and consolidation of power between 1922 and 1925, including the abandonment of the Partito Popolare, and the salvage of the Banco di Roma, cleared the way for further progress. Though he rejected a unilateral attempt by Italy to revise its ecclesiastical legislation in the Church's favour, in 1926, he also made it clear that the way was open for bilateral discussions to resolve

[46] John P. McKnight, *The Papacy: A New Appraisal* (London, 1953), p. 315.
[47] Curiously, Teeling in *The Survey of International Affairs* for 1929, p. 158, says that the *Conciliazione* was prompted by Vatican worries about its dependence on US money.
[48] ACS, MI, DGPS, 1929, b. 187, H 4, Notizie Vaticane, report of an article in *The Tribune*, 15 Feb. 1929.
[49] Pollard, *The Unknown Pope*, pp. 19–20.

the 'Roman Question' as a whole.[50] As a result of nearly two and a half years of difficult negotiations, which were suspended on several occasions because of disputes between Mussolini and the pope over Fascist attacks on various branches of the Italian Catholic movement, an agreement was finally reached in the form of the Lateran Pacts signed on 11 February 1929. The Pacts consisted of the Treaty, which set up the independent and neutral State of the Vatican City, the Concordat, which regulated Church–State relations within the Italian peninsula, and the Financial Convention, which liquidated the outstanding financial obligations of the Italian state towards the Holy See by means of a cash payment of 750 million lire and one of 1,000 million lire in Italian government bonds.[51]

The financial settlement was one of the most difficult dimensions of the long-drawn-out negotiations between the autumn of 1926 and February 1929. Only the fate of the Catholic youth organisations, the international legal status of the Vatican – King Victor Emanuel opposed conceding outright sovereignty to the State of the Vatican City – and, in the ratification stage, the complex problems of reconciling canon law and civil law on the question of marriage, caused more difficulties.[52] At the beginning of the negotiations, Pius XI tried to extract a larger sum from the Italian state than that eventually agreed. According to Francesco Pacelli, the brother of Eugenio Pacelli later Pius XII, the Vatican lawyer who did most of the negotiating for the pope, the original request of November 1926 was for 2 milliards of lire, payable in twelve yearly instalments, 1.25 milliard lire in state securities and the rest in cash.[53] He justified this claim on the grounds that the operations of the Vatican had increased enormously since 1870, citing the increase in the number of nunciatures from ten to thirty-four, as an example of this.[54] Mussolini initially agreed to this figure.[55] Then he changed his mind, saying that 2 milliards was excessive and that 1 milliard had to be the limit.[56] At the end of the year, he was declaring that his final offer was 2 milliards to be paid in twenty annual instalments, without interest; he was prepared, however, to accept the pope's suggestion that the Vatican find an American bank which would discount the operation in cash.[57] According to Pacelli, Pius XI did, in fact, make soundings via the apostolic delegate in America, Bonzano, and the result was that Msgr Francis Spellman's friend, the papal marquis Patrick Brady, who had banking interests in Philadelphia and was president of

[50] Pollard, the Vatican and Italian Fascism, pp. 39–41.
[51] For the texts of the treaties, see ibid., Appendix III.
[52] Ibid., pp. 44–6 and 67–852.   [53] Pacelli, Diario della Conciliazione, p. 24.
[54] Ibid.   [55] Ibid., p. 19.   [56] Ibid., p. 26.   [57] Ibid., p. 39.

the Edison Electricity companies of New York and Brooklyn,[58] expressed a readiness to make the necessary arrangements.[59]

The problem for Mussolini was the precarious state of Italian finances in the wake of the re-valuation of the lira; Pacelli reported to the pope that in his conversation with the Duce, the latter 'added that he would have happily agreed to give more, but the grave condition of Italian finances would not permit it'.[60] As Pius XI pointed out, this problem was being carefully concealed in official government communications.[61] The arguments dragged on throughout 1927, and in November of that year the Italian government's financial difficulties had become such that its negotiator, Barone, went so far as to suggest that the 2 milliards of lire be raised by an appeal to the world, rather than paid by Italy: Pacelli warned that such a suggestion would elicit a very dusty answer in the Vatican.[62] Rumours that the Italian state would raise the funds to pay the Vatican its compensation by means of a public loan persisted until just before the announcement of the *Conciliazione*.[63]

At the beginning of 1928, despite his repeated protestations that nothing less than 2 milliards would suffice, the pope had retreated and was considering the alternative of $80 million (roughly equivalent to 1.6 milliard lire) paid over eight years, without interest. By the end of that year, the problem had still not been resolved, and the apostolic delegate in America was instructed by the pope to explore the possibility of an American bank loan to Italy to cover its payment to the Vatican.[64] The size of the financial indemnity remained a major negotiating problem until almost the last moment: on 19 January 1929, with only three weeks to go before the signing of the Lateran Pacts, a compromise was finally reached on the total to be paid.[65] Even then, as late as 11 April 1929, during the course of the process of ratification, the Italian Minister of Justice, Rocco, was obliged to ask that the Vatican forego the immediate payment of the whole of the cash sum as this would have put the Italian government's 1928–9 budget into the red.[66] Pius XI, on the advice of the Italian financial expert Bernardino Nogara, agreed that the payment should be postponed until 1 July rather than on the day of formal ratification, 7 June.[67] It is indicative of the fears on the part of the Italians about the potential for monetary destabilisation which such a large cash transfer might

---

[58] For details of Brady's career, see *Who Was Who in America*, I (Chicago 1943), p. 129.

[59] Pacelli, *Diario della Conciliazione*, pp. 374–6.   [60] Ibid., p. 39.   [61] Ibid.

[62] ACS, Segreteria Particolare del Duce, Carteggio Riservato (SPD, CR), 6/97/R, Questione Romana, SF.8, Carteggio Barone, letter to Pacelli of 17 Apr. 1928; and Pacelli, *Diario della Conciliazione*, p. 39.

[63] ACS, MI, DGPS, 1929, b. 187, H4 Notizie Vaticane, report from Paris of 19 Feb. 1929 and radio interception from the Naue press agency, 12 Feb. 1929.

[64] Pacelli, *Diario della Conciliazione*, p. 103.

[65] Ibid., p. 454.   [66] Ibid., p. 135.   [67] Ibid.

create that, in the end, Bonaldo Stringher, the governor of the Bank of Italy, intervened and persuaded Nogara that the payment should be made in instalments between June 1929 and December 1930.[68] Despite Stringher's efforts, there were falls on the Italian stock exchanges.[69]

Who got the better of the bargain in this deal, and how did Italy find the funds to pay the Vatican? Mussolini argued that the amount paid was much less than the compensation for the payments that the Vatican would have received under the terms of the Law of Guarantees over the fifty-nine-year period since 1870.[70] Francesco Pacelli's calculations of how much that would have been, using the official Italian coefficient to take into account inflation and a six-monthly capitalisation of 5 per cent, reached the figure of nearly 4 milliard lire.[71] What Pacelli did not take into account was the fact that Italian law permits only five years of unpaid instalments to be recovered.[72] And the official calculation of the Corte dei Conti, Italy's equivalent of the Auditor General's Office, was a total of 2.270 billion lire.[73] On the other hand, Mussolini agreed that the Italian state would pay for the public works necessary in order to provide the Vatican with a proper water supply, a railway station and link to the Italian state railways and cover the cost of the expropriation and/or demolition of properties on Vatican territory in the ownership of private individuals; in addition, the tax immunities granted to ecclesiastical bodies under the Law of Guarantees of 1871 were continued by the terms of articles 6, 7 and 16 respectively of the Lateran Treaty.[74] So, in the longer term, whichever figure is taken into account, it can be said that the Vatican did get a good bargain and it is evidence of the pope's concern not to be seen to be extorting too much from an impoverished and struggling Italy that he agreed to insert the following preamble into the Financial Convention:

the Supreme Pontiff, considering on the one hand the enormous damage suffered by the Apostolic See by the loss of St. Peter's Patrimony, consisting of the ancient Pontifical States, and of the possessions of ecclesiastical institutions, and on the other the ever increasing needs of the Church if only in the city of Rome, and at the same time taking into consideration the financial position of the State and the economic conditions of the Italian people, especially after the war, has decided to limit his request for an indemnity to the strictest necessary amount.[75]

---

[68] For an overview of the Italian financial crisis, see G. Toniolo, *L'economia dell'Italia fascista* (Bari, 1980), ch. 2.

[69] ACS, SPD, CR, 6/97/R, Questione Romana, Stringher to Mussolini, 16 May 1929.

[70] *Opera Omnia di Benito Mussolini*, ed. E. D. Susmel (32 vols., Florence, 1952–), XXIV, p. 79.

[71] Pacelli, *Diario della Conciliazione*, p. 422 n. 1.   [72] Seldes, *The Vatican*, p. 392.

[73] ACS, SPD, CR, 6/97/R, Questione Romana, Sott. 5, varia, unsigned memorandum from Corte dei Conti, 6 Feb. 1928.

[74] Pollard, *The Vatican and Italian Fascism*, pp. 201–3.   [75] Ibid., p. 215.

Even if we assume that the 1,000 million lire worth of bonds was really only a paper transaction, there was an agreement with the Vatican about the speed at which it could sell off its bonds, thus protecting Italy from a sudden loss of financial confidence and in any case the real value of the bonds was 83 per cent of the nominal one, the cash payment of 750 million lire was still a lot of money by Italian standards (the exchange rate between the Italian lira and the pound sterling and US dollar in 1929 was 92 and 19 respectively). The 1929–30 Italian state budget was only 20,000 million lire; thus the cash payment alone was equal to 3.7 per cent of that budget.[76] Where did the Italian government get the money from given its acute financial difficulties? That the payment to the Vatican was a heavy burden on Italy's already strained finances is clear from Mussolini's speech to Parliament on the ratification of the Lateran Pacts. As Pallenberg points out, Mussolini went through various rhetorical contortions and juggling of figures in order to minimise the size and consequences of the payment to the Vatican:

This juggling, the almost country-market-vendor skill of Mussolini in first pretending that 2 billion lire were involved, and then reducing it to 1,750 million, then again to 1,550 million, then again converting the reduced figure to 400 million gold lire and finally comparing it to the 200 billion of the public debt, is self-evident, even if naïve.[77]

In his speech, despite his previous anxiety to persuade the Vatican to accept an instalment plan, he claimed that the payment was no problem because the Italian state had a liquid reserve of 2,000 million lire, and he also pointed out that the Italian government bonds given to the Vatican were only really worth 800 million lire.[78] Finally, he explained that the billion lire of state bonds would be borrowed from the Loans and Deposits Fund, 'which has stacks of them anyway', and be given back by buying bonds worth 100 million at face value in the market every year for ten years.[79] All this is indicative of Mussolini's anxiety to reassure the anticlerical critics, both Liberal and Fascist, that the Lateran package was not a sell-out to the Church.[80]

A factor which genuinely offset the financial cost of the *Conciliazione* of 1929 to the Italian state was the fact that a significant part of the money received by the Vatican went back indirectly into the coffers of the Italian state: for example, Cipolla estimated that the building operations in and around Vatican City were employing 3,000 men in 1931.[81]

---

[76] *Opera Omnia*, ed. Susmel, XXIV, p. 80.
[77] Pallenberg, *Vatican Finances*, p. 67.   [78] *Opera Omnia*, ed. Susmel, XXIV, p. 80.
[79] Ibid.   [80] Pollard, *The Vatican and Italian Fascism*, pp. 70–2.
[81] Cipolla, 'Due giorni in Vaticano', *La Stampa*, 16 Nov. 1931.

Seldes suggests a much higher figure, 8,000.[82] It is a fair assumption that most of the building materials were bought in Italy as well. Here was perhaps an unintended application of the principles of 'Keynesianism' before Keynes.

Bernardino Nogara and the Special Administration

1929 marked the advent of one of the most important of all financiers, lay or ecclesiastical, ever to be associated with the modern papacy – Bernardino Nogara. It was in order to invest and administer the indemnity provided by the Financial Convention that the Amministrazione Speciale per la Santa Sede (the Special Administration of the Holy See) was set up by *motu proprio* in June 1929,[83] and that Bernardino Nogara was appointed to head it. Pius XI's decision to create the Special Administration, rather than entrusting the new endowment to existing Vatican agencies like the ABSS or the Commissione per le Opere di Religione, suggests that he did not have full confidence in them. It also fits with his rather authoritarian temperament to have desired that the administration of the new endowment should be directly subject to his oversight.[84] Throughout the 1930s, the Special Administration operated in considerable secrecy and with a very small staff – rarely more than a couple of dozen employees. As far as Nogara is concerned, he was a *uomo di fiducia* ('a trusty') and a Lombard, Milanese one at that. From his election in 1922, Pius XI tended to bring in his own, trusty milanesi to fill many important posts in the Vatican: Msgr Caccia-Dominioni was appointed Maestro di Camera; Count Ratti, Pius XI's brother, was given a leading position in the civil administration; and Giuseppe Colombo and Adelaide Coara were put in charge of various branches of the Italian national Catholic Action organisation.[85] This provincial 'favouritism' was increased in the late 1920s when the firm of Ing. Castelli, another Milanese, got most of the construction contracts in and around the Vatican, a situation continued after 1929.[86] The Milanese architect Momo designed three major Vatican buildings – the Ethiopian College, the Governor's Palace and the Railway Station – and in 1930 another famous Milanese architect Beltrami was commissioned to design the new Vatican picture gallery.

Nogara's appointment also marked a decisive break in the long-standing, traditional links between the Vatican and the Banco di Roma.

---

[82] Seldes, *The Vatican*, 253.   [83] *Annuario Pontificio*, 1948, p. 687.
[84] Pollard, *The Vatican and Italian Fascism*, pp. 23 and 25.
[85] Hachey (ed.), *Anglo-Vatican Relations*, p. 226.
[86] Ibid., where the British Minister to the Holy See complained that Milanese firms had a virtual monopoly in the Vatican.

Illustration 10 Bernardino Nogara

In the first place, investment advice, and more general financial advice, instead of being sought from the managers of that bank, would now be provided 'in house' by Nogara.[87] Secondly, the Italian financial institution with which he was linked, the Banca Commerciale, had long been one of the Roma's main competitors, especially in foreign markets; the Roma's agent in Istanbul, for instance, had complained about Comit's activities in that city where, ironically, Nogara was its chief representative.[88] The Banca Commerciale was a northern, Milan-based operation, with strong Jewish and German links, unlike the Banco di Roma. Announcing Nogara's appointment as head of the Special Administration to the board

---

[87] Ibid., p. 202, where the minister reported that Nogara also advised the ABSS on its investments.
[88] Webster, *Industrial Imperialism in Italy*, p. 158.

of directors of the bank, the managing director Toeplitz proudly informed them that 'our bank will have the honour to consider itself bankers to the Holy See, receiving on deposit considerable funds which will follow the [Vatican's] agreement with the Italian Government'.[89] In fact, things did not quite work out as Toeplitz had so confidently predicted; the bank only ever received a small fraction of the Vatican's funds, the rest being spread by Nogara around a number of other banks both in Italy and abroad (see Chapter 8, p. 170), and perhaps this constituted the biggest change which Nogara brought to the Vatican's finances, the links with foreign, and especially Swiss and French, banks which were actually represented in the composition of the staff of the Special Administration. Nevertheless, the association with the Vatican was undoubtedly a very useful card in the coming years when complete collapse stared the Banca Commerciale in the face.

The career of Nogara was a very interesting and spectacular one. Trained as an engineer at the great Politecnico of Milan, the nursery of so many Italian industrialists and entrepeneurs, Nogara managed mining operations in Britain (hence his excellent English), Bulgaria and the Ottoman Empire. As a result of his contacts there, he was appointed representative of the Italian Banca Commerciale in Istanbul and then Italian representative on the International Committee whose task it was to oversee the Public Debt of the Ottoman Empire, and in 1913 he was one of the Italian delegation who negotiated the Treaty of Ouchy which brought an end to the Italo-Turkish war over Libya. Such was the reputation he had developed for his financial knowledge and skill, especially in the fields of gold and currency operations, that Nogara was appointed to the Italian delegation to the Economic Comittee at the Versailles Peace Conference of 1919, was an Italian representative on the permanent reparations committee thereafter and between 1924 to 1929 managed the industry section of the Inter-Allied Commission to execute the Dawes Plan in Berlin.[90] He was a member of the board of directors and later (1945) a vice-president of the Banca Commerciale Italiana, which was Italy's largest private bank, and a member of the board of Comofin, representing the consortium of controlling share-holders.[91] Nogara's career had brought him into contact and friendship with many of the leading lights in the Italian financial establishment – such as Count Gioacchino Volpi, who

[89] ASBCI, Fondo SOFINDIT, 1926–37, Cart. 417, fasc. 4–6, Santa Sede, batch 5, VCA, 1, 86.29 (p. 38).
[90] There is no biography of Nogara; most of the biographical information used here comes from *L'Italia*, 16 Nov. 1958, and Belardelli, 'Un viaggio di Bernardino Nogara negli Stati Uniti (novembre 1937)', *Storia Contemporanea*, 23 (1992), pp. 321–38.
[91] Lo Bello, *L'oro del Vaticano*, p. 21.

became Mussolini's finance minister in 1926, Alberto Pirelli, head of the Milan-based rubber conglomerate, Bonaldo Stringher, who, as has been seen, was governor of the Bank of Italy, and Carlo Beneduce, the economic 'technocrat' who led the efforts to salvage major Italian industries and banks during the 1930s and thus became the head of the state agency controlling the process, the IRI (Industrial Reconstruction Institute) which would ultimately control a vast swathe of the Italian banking, insurance and manufacturing sectors. He was thus perfectly placed to promote and protect the Vatican's financial interests in Italy. It was the Istanbul connection which first made Nogara known in Vatican circles; in 1914, he bought various bonds on the behalf of Pope Benedict XV.[92] But it was his long-standing relations with the family of Achille Ratti, elected pope in 1922, which led to his involvement in the finances of the Vatican.[93] The fact that he was a devout Catholic and that one of his brothers, Bartolomeo, was superintendent of the Vatican museums, and would thus have known his opposite number in the Library very well, that another was an archbishop, two more were rectors of seminaries in southern Italy, a third was a missionary priest and that his sister was superior of a convent, made Nogara's entry in the world of the Vatican a very easy and natural one.[94] Though subject to more restrictions and surveillance after the death of Pius XI in 1939 and the election of his successor, Nogara remained in charge of the Special Administration until 1954, when he was succeeded by his deputy, Henri De Maillardoz, a director of Credit Suisse, one of the Vatican's leading Swiss bankers. Until his death in 1958, however, he continued to be consulted by the papal administration.

Given the important implications of the Vatican's investment strategy for the financial stability of the Italian state – to have sold large amounts of its holding in Italian government stocks would obviously have precipitated a serious Italian financial crisis – Nogara's appointment was agreed with Mussolini beforehand, as Francesco Pacelli's *Diario della Conciliazione* indicates.[95] It has even been suggested that Nogara was actually involved in the negotiations for the Financial Convention; there is no firm evidence for this, but it is likely that he advised the chief Vatican negotiators, Gasparri and Francesco Pacelli, as well as the pope, on the financial

[92] Webster, *Industrial Imperialism in Italy*, p. 158, says that he had previously been involved in the finances of the Vatican but does not provide further details.

[93] *Annuario Pontificio*, 1955, p. 869. Martina, 'L'ecclesiologia prevalente durante il pontificato di Pio XI', p. 224, claims that Pius re-habilitated Giuseppe Nogara, one of Bernardino's brothers, after he had fallen under a cloud in Pius X's reign, and made him archbishop of Udine.

[94] A. Kersevan and P. Visintin (eds.), *G. Nogara: luci e ombre di arcivescovo, 1928–1945* (Udine, 1997), pp. 10–11.

[95] Pacelli, *Diario della Conciliazione*, p. 141, 14 May 1929.

aspects of the settlement. Nogara was known and acceptable to the Italian head of the government, though there is absolutely no evidence that he was a member of the Fascist Party, or, even less, as Seldes claims, that he was a personal friend of Mussolini.[96]

Nogara kept a 'diary' from 1931 to 1939, and though it does not tell us exactly how the 750 million lire were originally invested (the bulk of the 1,000 million lire remained in government bonds for some time to come), it does provide a broad picture of the investment operations. Nogara appears to have followed a broad strategy of investing in gold, currencies, railway and utility companies, and government securities throughout the world, if only to mitigate the effects on the Vatican's finances of further fluctuations in the value of the Italian lira after those of the mid- to late 1920s, with a particular concentration of investments in sterling securities, and this is confirmed by Seldes.[97] In these operations, Nogara used his strong connections in the markets in Switzerland, France, Britain and the USA, and especially in the last case, the House of Morgan.[98] Despite claims to the contrary, Nogara invested little in Germany.[99] Though he was friendly with Bertha Krupp, he was not keen on the Germans and unimpressed by their financial institutions, probably because his experience in the Dawes Commission left him sceptical about Germany's economic future.[100] Until the diary entries for 1932, there is no evidence of any investment in either industrial shares or property, but it is known from other sources that Nogara made investments in Italian companies in the 1930s (see Chapter 8, pp. 171–7). While the diary does not include the balance sheets of the Special Administration, it does provide a detailed account of Nogara's day-to-day financial activities for the Holy See – the size of the accounts he administered; their diversity; the nature of the

---

[96] Seldes, *The Vatican*, p. 253.

[97] Ibid., p. 252; and Hachey (ed.), *Anglo-Vatican Relations*, p. 204, where the British minister says that, 'the Vatican, in various forms and under various names have [*sic*] large holdings in sterling securities'.

[98] See Chernow, *The House of Morgan*, p. 286, for the full list of banking institutions with which Nogara dealt.

[99] M. Aarons and J. Loftus, *Unholy Trinity* (New York, 1998), pp. 294–5, where they claim, *inter alia*, that 'Following the $26 [*sic*] million cash settlement with Mussolini over the disputed lands in 1929, the Vatican invested nearly all of the proceeds in German industry as well', and 'The Vatican merely proved its heavy financial investment in Germany.' They provide no documentary evidence for either of these claims.

[100] Ambassador Osio, in a conversation with the author in October 1996, said that despite the friendship with the Krupp family, his grandfather was wary of economic involvement in Germany, and that he later disliked the Nazi dictatorship as much as the Soviet one. Chernow, *The House of Morgan*, p. 437, also says: 'It is also likely that Nogara was secretly hostile to the Germans, for neither before nor after the War did he invest Vatican funds in German securities.'

pope's own accounts; papal spending on construction works; and, above all, Nogara's various new investments.

Strictly speaking, the diary is a record of Nogara's audiences with Pope Pius XI; although the Special Administration was nominally answerable to a supervisory board consisting of Secretary of State Gasparri and two other cardinals, in reality Nogara reported directly to the pope: there is not even any mention of the board in the *Annuario Pontificio*. It should be noted that he had an audience with Pius XI on average once every ten days. This tells us just how important he was; of the curial cardinals and other leading officials of the Roman congregations, only the Cardinal Secretary of State, the Under-Secretary of State, the Substitute Secretary of State (*Sostituto*) and the Secretary of the Holy Office saw the pope more frequently than that.[101] In addition, Nogara was given an apartment in the newly built Governor's Palace, a sure sign of his extremely important role in the papal administration and of his high standing in the pope's esteem.[102]

Conclusion

The signing of the Lateran Pacts marked a very important turning point in the history of the modern papacy. At last the vexed 'Roman Question' with Italy had been resolved. The papacy had now been re-clothed with a little territorial sovereignty and the Vatican's diplomats hoped and believed that its new status would preclude the kind of problems and inconveniences which it had faced in the past, and especially during the First World War. The papacy and Italy were reconciled and that country now had the opportunity to take its place as *the* European Catholic power. It was also a diplomatic triumph for Pius XI and Gasparri in a broader sense, giving them more confidence and more prestige internationally, and therefore making it inevitable that more states would seek to establish relations with the Vatican, and that even the new Nazi regime in Germany would seek a sort of 'papal benediction' by means of the *Reichskonkordat* in 1933.

But the impact of the *Conciliazione* on the state of the Vatican's finances was no less dramatic; after sixty years of uncertainty and difficulty, the papacy was now financially secure, it would never be poor again. And the forms which Nogara's investment of the money received from Italy took also marked an important development in the Vatican's financial

---

[101] *Annuario Pontificio*, 1931 and 1932.
[102] According to the *Acta Apostolicae Sedis*, 21 (1929), p. 613, in August 1929 Nogara was made a Commendatore of the papal order of St Gregory the Great.

history. Henceforth it would no longer be tied to the Banco di Roma and its dependencies, and be at the mercy of an amateurish and incestuous clique of Catholic aristocratic financiers. Indeed, it seems more than likely that Pius XI appointed Nogara to head the Special Administration precisely in order to cut those ties. Even more significantly, its investment operations would no longer be restricted to a provincial (Roman) or even Italian economic milieu. From June 1929 onwards, the investments of the Vatican, following the strategy of Benardino Nogara, moved into the financial markets of the world.

7   The Wall Street Crash and Vatican finances in the early 1930s

> The Greatest human calamity since the Flood.
>
> (Pius XI on the Great Depression)

After the *Conciliazione*, Pius XI embarked upon a spending spree. The sudden availability of large amounts of cash following the signing of the Financial Convention made it possible to expand the building programme which he had initiated in the mid-1920s. Assuming an average 5 per cent return on its investments, from 1930 onwards, the Vatican's new-found capital funds would have yielded a maximum annual income of over 87 million lire in addition to the existing revenues, a very considerable sum by the standards of that time, though it is unlikely ever to have reached such a figure given the pope's short-term spending. But very soon, all of Nogara's financial skills were to be called upon to preserve the Vatican's newly found wealth because Pius XI's ambitious building plans, the Holy See's chaotic budgeting and accounting practices and, above all, the effects of the Wall Street Crash, quickly threatened to destroy it.

The creation of the 'Vatican City'

In order to give credibility to that minimum of territorial sovereignty which Pius had sought, the establishment of the Vatican state necessitated the creation of an appropriate infrastructure, as laid down in the Lateran Treaty: a telegraph and post office, a railway station and track (all built by Italy) and other living and working accommodation, etc., not to mention the completion of the walls required to set it apart from the rest of the city of Rome. A whole new north-eastern 'industrial quarter' was created to provide shops, garages, workshops and a small power station.[1] But Pius XI's ambitions stretched further than that. He insisted on converting the building originally constructed as the Roman Minor Seminary on the Vatican Hill into a massive palace for the governor of the new Vatican state, with sumptuously appointed apartments for visiting

[1] Castelli, '*Quel tanto di territorio*', pp. 47–9.

Catholic sovereigns and heads of state, and others for Vatican officials.[2]
He constructed what are now the Mosaic Workshop, the Ethiopian College, law courts and a prison, accommodation for both *L'Osservatore Romano* and the Vatican printing press, and a building for the new Vatican Radio Station. Admittedly, the radio equipment was supplied free by Marconi, and a most up-to-date telephone switchboard was donated by I T & T.[3] Similarly, after the Vatican's abandonment of horse-driven vehicles in 1926 (the first royal household in Europe to do so) following an accident,[4] Italian and American car manufacturers competed to supply the pope, who had a penchant for fast cars, with their vehicles, sometimes free.[5] After literally decades of neglect due to a lack of funds, Pius XI was also obliged to spend enormous amounts of money simply on repairs to buildings in the Vatican and at the papal villa of Castelgandolfo in the Alban Hills outside of Rome.[6] He also lavished new electrical and heating plants on the Vatican Library, of which he had been prefect until 1917, which then had to be reconstructed after the collapse of a wing in 1931;[7] he extended the Vatican museums and built a new picture gallery, designed by the Milanese architect Beltrami. For two or three years, the Vatican and its environs were one enormous building site and in the process small streets of mean houses, like Via Sciaccia, that had previously accommodated the *sanpietrini* and other Vatican employees, were demolished to make way for the new public buildings.[8] With the small houses went the homely, rustic air that had prevailed in the Vatican for decades.[9] The British minister to the Vatican was not impressed by the 'improvements'; he described them as 'disfiguring the previously beautiful gardens of the Vatican'.[10]

Pius XI's vision did not stop at the walls of his new domain: large buildings were erected in the neighbourhood of the Vatican, in a hideous, neoclassical style not dissimilar from the Fascist version but even heavier and more pompous, and adorned by Papa Ratti's coat of arms. Other areas in Rome granted extra-territorial status in the Treaty were also endowed with new buildings, like the enormous Palazzo San Calisto in Trastevere,[11] built to house the burgeoning bureaucracy of several of the Roman

---

[2] Ibid.   [3] Hachey (ed.), *Anglo-Vatican Relations*, p. 195.
[4] ACS, MdI, DGPS, b. 113, 1926, H4, 31 Mar. 1926.
[5] V. Moretti (ed.), *Le Auto dei Papi: settant'anni di automobilismo Vaticano* (Rome, 1981), p. 7.
[6] Castelli, '*Quel tanto di territorio*', pp. 118–19.
[7] Hachey (ed.), *Anglo-Vatican Relations*, p. 219.
[8] Castelli, '*Quel tanto di territorio*', p. 70.
[9] Ibid.   [10] Hachey (ed.), *Anglo-Vatican Relations*, p. 228.
[11] Hebblethwaite, *John XXIII*, p. 355, singles out Palazzo San Calisto for its hideous monumentalism.

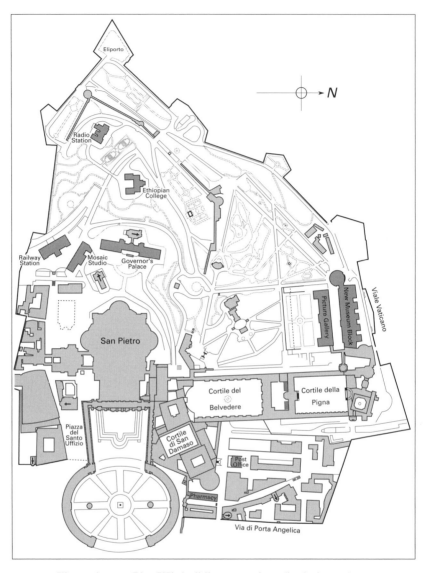

Illustration 11 Pius XI's building operations (in dark tone)

congregations and to accommodate some cardinals, and considerable construction work was carried on at the papal villa of Castelgandolfo, including the new observatory fitted with the latest lenses from Zeiss.[12] The pope also used his new-found wealth to fund the construction of works not strictly connected with the Vatican. In his Consistorial Allocution of June 1930, he spoke of the need to construct houses for the desperately disadvantaged clergy of southern Italy and the islands, and of the pressing need to provide new churches for the expanding suburbs of Rome, including the new Cathedral of Our Lady of the Sea at Ostia; the latter was not unconnected with his growing concern about the spread of Protestant proselytism in the Eternal City.[13] This ambitious programme cost 75 million lire in 1931 alone, not far short of the total increased annual income, and the rhythm of building continued into the following years with even larger budgets.[14]

Pius XI's building plans were indicative of a new phase in the history of the Vatican, a kind of 'imperial papacy', expansionistic, ambitious, even aggressive, after the years of retreat, defensiveness and isolation under Pius IX and his successors. They were a fitting, if belated, physical manifestation of the papal supremacy over the Roman Catholic Church which had been established by the promulgation of the dogma of Infallibility in 1870. They were perhaps also an instinctive response to, and imitation of, the increasing demonstration of Fascist power in the form of massive, monumental public buildings in Rome and the Italian provincial capitals. In this way, Pius XI transformed the Vatican, leaving it looking much as it does today. No longer was it, as Gasparri had once described it, 'merely a palace with a garden on the edge of Rome'.[15] And when the monumental Via della Conciliazione, connecting Piazza San Pietro to the River Tiber, was constructed from the mid-1930s onwards,[16] which, incidentally, involved demolishing much of the medieval Borgo, it then became immediately accessible by a broad, triumphal avenue from the Tiber. The new face of the Vatican, the true face of the modern papacy, was complete.

[12] AFN, Nogara's diary, 7 June 1932.

[13] ACS, PS, b. 453, H4. 30 June 1932; on the Vatican's apprehensions about the Protestant 'peril' in Rome, see Pollard, *The Vatican and Italian Fascism*, pp. 108–11.

[14] AFN, Nogara's diary, entries for 22 Dec. 1931, 25 Feb. 1932, 23 Mar. 1932 and 7 June 1932.

[15] As quoted in Spadolini (ed.), *Il Cardinale Gasparri*, p. 234.

[16] C. Rendina (ed.), *La grande enciclopedia di Roma* (Rome, 2000), p. 327, says that workmen began to demolish the 'spine' of the Borgo to make way for Via della Conciliazione in 1936.

Other problems

Pius XI had other calls upon his purse; he regularly used the funds of the Special Administration to help out diocesan administrations, seminaries and the religious orders, though he was anxious to avoid saddling the Vatican with long-term financial obligations. Thus in 1932, during discussions about the setting up of what was in effect a building society for the religious orders in Italy, he told Nogara to make 'a careful study of the effects of the moral and legal responsibility, which the Holy See would have to assume in relation to third parties even if it limited its involvement to symbolic patronage'.[17] He was later to make even sharper comments about the need to prevent Italian dioceses automatically turning to the Vatican to solve their financial problems.[18] Like his predecessor, he could not escape the moral, and sometimes legal, obligations which tied the Holy See to Catholic credit institutions in Italy. As the general crisis of Catholic banking institutions deepened in the late 1920s, the Vatican was called upon to help out. From the published records of the Banca d'Italia we know that in December 1929 the Vatican offered 50 million lire as a contribution to the capital of the Istituto Centrale di Credito, the organism created by clerico-Fascist bankers to bail out Catholic banks and *casse di risparmio*; the governor of the Bank of Italy made it clear that there was no guarantee that the Vatican would get its money back, but the pope had little choice in the circumstances – it was the only way to ensure the survival of many Catholic banks.[19] It is very likely that the Special Administration was involved in other analogous operations at this time.

According to Seldes and Cipolla, a further cause of spiralling costs was the fact that the permanent staff of the Vatican increased significantly between 1929 and 1931: Cipolla put the final figure at 500.[20] The diary of Msgr Domenico Tardini (later Cardinal Secretary of State to John XXIII), who as *Sostituto* was at the centre of affairs in the Vatican from 1929 onwards, which contains some sharply critical comments on the overall financial management of the Vatican in the early 1930s, also makes this point. Talking of the Lateran Pacts and the State of the Vatican City to which they gave rise, Tardini wondered whether it, 'was really such a good thing to organise this state, so miniscule yet so pretentious, so

---

[17] AFN, Nogara's diary, entries for 6 Mar. 1932 and 20 Apr. 1932.
[18] Ibid., entry for 12 Oct. 1933.
[19] G. Guanno and G. Toniolo (eds.), *La Banca d'Italia e il sistema bancario, 1919–1936* (Bari and Rome, 1993), pp. 582–3; on the broader problems of the crisis of the Catholic banks, see Caroleo, *Le banche cattoliche*, chs. 3 and 4.
[20] Cipolla, 'Due giorni in Vaticano', *La Stampa*, 16 Nov. 1931.

poor, yet so wasteful, so lilliputian yet so saturated with employees and burdened with salaries'.[21]

Another problem, which very clearly emerges from the pages of Nogara's diary and other sources, was that the Vatican had no unified budgeting or accounting system at this time, a fact which gave rise to considerable disquiet among American Catholics who were, after all, the main providers of free-will offerings to the Holy See.[22] Today, thanks to the curial reforms of Paul VI in 1967, the finances of all the various Vatican departments (except, significantly, the Vatican bank) are supervised and co-ordinated by the Prefecture of the Economic Affairs of the Church.[23] But in the 1930s, in a manner typical of an unreformed absolute monarchy, the heads of the various spending departments reported directly to the pope. And though the traditional papal equivalent of the peasant keeping money under the mattress, Leo XIII's famous brass chest, seems to have been abandoned, Tardini's diary makes it clear that the custom of dispensing funds from a box in the drawer of the pope's desk was not entirely discontinued even in Pius XI's reign.[24]

Uginet argues that 'The multiplication of the economic organisms [of the Holy See] does not seem to have been a problem during the reign of Pius XI, who dominated the complex mechanisms of the papal administration with great ability.'[25] Nogara's diary suggests otherwise. Nogara was clearly not happy with the way in which other Vatican departments quickly came to expect subsidies from the funds of the Special Administration, and he frequently lamented the fact that building contractors in the Vatican were massively overspending on estimates, the result, he claimed, of a lack of adequate financial oversight on the part of Vatican officials.[26] For example, whereas in March 1932 the pope had confidently predicted that in the following year the cost of building works would have fallen by three-quarters, from 80 million to 20 million lire, in June 1933 Nogara was forced to explain to the pope that far from falling, the costs

[21] C. F. Casula, *Domenico Tardini (1888–1961) e l'Azione della Santa Sede nella crisi fra le due guerre* (Rome, 1988), p. 294.
[22] Seldes, *The Vatican*, p. 251: 'The absence of public and regular bookkeeping at the Vatican has caused for a long time remarks and occasionally protestations from foreign cardinals, and especially American cardinals. This is explained by the fact that the Catholics of the United States promised, at least morally, to furnish the pope with all the funds that he needed. Clearly, the periods of economic crisis must be excepted because there is no way of doing the impossible.'
[23] G. Cereti, 'The Financial Resources and Activities of the Vatican', *Concilium*, 116–20 (1978), pp. 3–15.
[24] Casula, *Domenico Tardini*, pp. 291–2.
[25] F. C. Uginet, 'Le finanze pontificie', in P. Levillain (ed.), *Dizionario storico del papato* (Milan, 1966), p. 603.
[26] AFN, Nogara's diary, entry for 6 Oct. 1933.

of construction had actually risen by 18 million lire.[27] Tardini implies that this state of affairs was largely the fault of Ing. Castelli, the main building contractor, though this is probably a typical manifestation of Roman resentment against the influx into the Vatican at the beginning of Papa Ratti's pontificate of large numbers of Milanese, of whom Castelli was one.[28] On the other hand, the fact that Castelli's firm had a virtual monopoly of building operations in and around the Vatican must have rather limited the scope for competitive tendering.[29]

Nogara tried very hard to bring some order into the Vatican's finances, as his diary shows. He got himself appointed to the Consulta Tecnica (technical committee) overseeing the construction works and he also tried to establish some proper budgetary procedures; in January 1933, he agreed with the pope that in future every spending department in the Vatican must provide him with an annual budget, calculated according to monthly income and expenditure, and that the Special Administration would make payments to them only on that basis.[30] But it is difficult to judge how successful Nogara was in bringing order into the finances of the Vatican. Ironically, Arnoldo Cipolla described him as 'The Pope's Minister of the Treasury',[31] and the British minister to the Holy See called him 'the State Treasurer' of the Vatican.[32] He was neither of those things. As is evident from the following diagram, Nogara had only very limited control over the Vatican's finances: other than the Special Administration itself, the only bodies on which he exercised some very limited influence were the ABSS, and the Commissione per le Opere di Religione, the Vatican's embryonic bank.[33] But this might explain why the attempt in 1930 on the part of the Anglo-French Banking Corporation, backed by the British Legation, to provide banking facilities, was spurned by the Vatican.[34] Nogara was, presumably, more than content with the arrangements he had established with his banking contacts in Italy, Switzerland, London and New York.

The Wall Street Crash

But the foregoing problems pale into insignificance when compared with the impact of the 'Great Depression'. The biggest problem facing the

---

[27] Ibid., entries for 6 Mar. 1932 and 6 June 1932.
[28] Casula, *Domenico Tardini*, p. 293.   [29] Hachey (ed.), *Anglo-Vatican Relations*, p. 226.
[30] AFN, Nogara's diary, entry for 18 Jan. 1933.
[31] Cipolla, 'Due giorni in Vaticano', *La Stampa*, 16 Nov. 1931.
[32] Hachey (ed.), *Anglo-Vatican Relations*, p. 174; in 1944, Roosevelt's Personal Representative at the Papal Court, Myron Taylor, described Nogara as 'the Vatican's Minister of Finances', in letter to Mattioli, in *Vaticano e Stati Uniti, 1939–1952: dalle carte di Myron C. Taylor*, ed. with an introduction by E. Di Nolfo (Milan, 1978), p. 418.
[33] Hachey (ed.), *Anglo-Vatican Relations*, p. 202.   [34] Ibid.

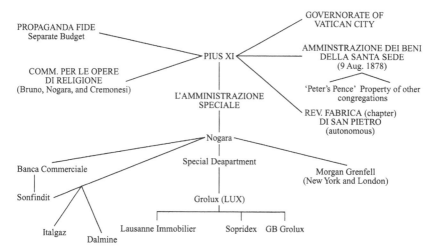

Illustration 12 The structure of the Vatican finances, 1933

Vatican finances in the early 1930s was undoubtedly the longer-term effects of the Wall Street Crash. By the end of 1931, the world economic crisis was beginning to damage seriously the financial structures of the Vatican. In 1931, the British minister to the Vatican reported that the change of administration and the general election in Britain 'were followed with interest, the fluctuations in sterling with apprehension' in the Vatican, but that 'So far as is known, they did not betray any signs of panic.'[35] A year later the minister reported that the depreciation of the pound had caused further anxiety, as had the fact that 'subscriptions [*sic*] are no longer flowing in on the old scale'.[36] The fall in 'subscriptions', i.e. Peter's Pence, was inevitable given the gravity of the unemployment problem in Germany and America, both of which had long been major contributors to the Vatican's coffers, and the extraordinary Holy Year of 1933–4 did little to ameliorate the situation. In the autumn of 1932 there was anxiety in the Vatican about the 'Hunger Marches' in Britain and the fall in the value of the pound, whether out of concern for British social and political stability or for the financial consequences for the Holy See it is difficult to say.[37] The worries about the financial situation in the Vatican reached such a point in 1933 that a general reduction in wages was decreed for all Vatican employees, 10 per cent for those receiving under 2,000 lire per annum and 15 per cent for those receiving in excess of that figure.[38] And by the end of 1934, the pope had voiced his financial worries both to the British ambassador and to Msgr Tardini; the latter

[35] Ibid., p. 204.   [36] Ibid., p. 228.   [37] Ibid., p. 229.   [38] Ibid., p. 259.

wrote of an audience with the pope, 'He talked for the umpteenth time about his lack of money.'[39] In 1932, Pius wrote to Cardinal Mundelein, requesting him to help the Vatican out by sending an advance on the Chicago diocese's usual offering of Peter's Pence.[40] In a further letter to Cardinal Mundelein of 12 December of that year, he thanked him for the 'conspicuous sum' sent by way of Peter's Pence.[41]

Nogara's diary makes it possible to follow in detail the impact of the Great Depression upon his investment strategy. In February 1931, he was forced to explain the large losses suffered by the Special Administration due to the fall in the value of the pound sterling in that financial year, and Pius XI acknowledged that they were not the result of bad management on Nogara's part.[42] On 23 March 1932, he warned the pope that they needed to start re-building abundant reserves because it was extremely probable that countries like Brazil, Chile, Peru, Hungary, Bulgaria, Greece and Austria would default on their payment of loan interest and that the big international firm, Kreuger and Toll, would also be unable to pay its creditors: this was serious because by now the Holy See derived a significant proportion of its annual income from these investments.[43] Nogara was quickly proved correct on all counts. On 20 April he had to inform the pope that Kreuger and Toll had indeed gone bankrupt, as a result, 'of losses in all markets'.[44] In fact, the collapse of this company was only partially the result of the worsening economic situation. As the *Financial Times* explained, Nogara and other investors were the victims of a massive international fraud, one of the biggest in the twentieth century.[45] Kreuger, 'the Swedish Match King', committed suicide. The failure of the Missouri-Pacific Railroad Company, in which the Vatican had invested 100,000 dollars, and the falls in the value of the dollar itself, in April and September 1933 respectively, inflicted further damage on Nogara's investment strategy.[46]

By the summer of 1933, Nogara estimated the Vatican's losses as follows: the devaluation of sterling in 1931 had cost the Special Administration 60 million lire, and a further 30 million in 1932; losses from the

---

[39] As quoted in Casula, *Domenico Tardini*, p. 293.
[40] AAC, Pius XI to Cardinal Mundelein, 28 May 1932.
[41] Ibid., Pius XI to Mundelein, 12 Dec. 1932.
[42] AFN, Nogara's diary, entry for 25 Feb. 1931.   [43] Ibid., entry for 23 Mar. 1932.
[44] Ibid., entry for 20 Apr. 1931; according to C. P. Kindleberger, *The World in Depression* (London, 1978), p. 179 n. 29, 'Kreuger organised Kreuger and Toll, a match conglomerate, which lent money to governments on favourable terms in exchange for the grant of match monopolies. When tight credit made it difficult for Kreuger and Toll to borrow money to re-lend, Kreuger forged collateral.'
[45] *Financial Times*, 18 Apr. 1932, 'Ivar Kreuger and the European Problem'.
[46] AFN, Nogara's diary, entry for 6 Apr. 1933.

depreciation of the dollar in the same year cost 60 million lire, with a permanent loss of revenue of 7 million lire annually.[47] He predicted that the situation would worsen in 1934, obliging the Special Administration to use up reserves of another 26 million lire.[48] The pope was so alarmed by the rise in losses that he actually suggested seeking a loan of 2 million dollars in the USA through the good offices of the influential Msgr Francis Spellman, at that time auxiliary bishop of Boston and later cardinal archbishop of New York.[49]

Nogara's new investment strategy

Nogara's ultimate response to this very serious situation was to elaborate a new investment strategy. First of all, he advised cuts in the pope's building programme, for which Pius XI volunteered a halt to the construction of clergy houses.[50] Secondly, he proposed to transfer funds into gold, a policy which according to the diary, began in earnest in September 1933, by which time the Vatican already had a gold reserve worth 100 million lire.[51] The third element in his new strategy was to diversify into property. Following the maxim 'safe as houses', Nogara decided to seek more security for at least some of the Vatican's money in bricks and mortar, a natural reaction in a time of economic recession. While the nature of the business into which he entered was not unusual, the *way* in which he entered into it was. Hitherto, in harmony with Antonelli's fundamental guidelines for Vatican financial ventures (see Chapter 2, p. 52), Nogara had never entered *directly* into business on behalf of the Vatican. He had always bought shares, a large or even controlling share-holding in an *established* company, and this was, as far as is known, what he was to do in the future; but in regard to his property ventures, Nogara actually set up companies directly controlled by the Amminstrazione Speciale. It is indicative of the unprecedented nature of Nogara's activities in 1932–3 that even the pope demurred.[52] By April 1932, Nogara was already studying plans to go into the property business in Britain, France and Switzerland.[53] Eventually, in Paris, he purchased shares in the Société Hôtel D'Albe, and bought the whole share-holding of the Union Foncier de Paris, both property companies.[54] He went further by setting up a completely new company Société Privée d'Exploration Immobilière (SOPRIDEX), which acquired a range of properties, mainly housing for both middle-class and working-class tenants, and in the summer of 1932 he even contemplated buying

---

[47] Ibid., entries for 19 Aug. 1932 and 30 July 1933.
[48] Ibid.   [49] Ibid.   [50] Ibid.   [51] Ibid., entry for 21 Sept. 1933.
[52] Ibid., entry for 20 Apr. 1932.   [53] Ibid.   [54] Ibid., entry for 27 June 1932.

both the offices of the Wagons Lit company and those of the French National Tourist Office.[55] In Britain, he established British Grolux Ltd.[56] British Grolux is the only one of these foreign property companies whose history has been possible to investigate in any detail. Using the records of Companies House in the City of London, its history can be plotted down to the present day. The entries in Nogara's diary for 27 May and 27 June 1933 tell us that he tried to buy the massive London headquarters of Thomas Cook, the major British travel agent (just as he also tried to buy the Wagon Lits offices in Paris), but decided that it was overpriced.[57] He eventually settled for residential property in London and Coventry, which the company still owns.[58] In Switzerland, he bought out several existing property companies in the city of Lausanne, most notably Société Immobilière de la Promenade, of which Nogara himself became chairman and which had an initial capital of 390,000 Swiss francs,[59] the Société Florimont and the Société Immobilière sur Collanges, based in a village on Lake Geneva near the eponymous city.[60] All three companies continue to operate.[61] In one buying spree alone, Nogara purchased 640,000 Swiss francs worth of property for these companies.[62]

In the establishment and operation of these foreign property companies, he relied on his specialist expertise, knowledge and contacts, which were considerable, given his international activities; as his diary shows, Nogara was always travelling.[63] All the initial foreign property ventures were in places – Paris, Lausanne and London – on Nogara's normal circuit of foreign visits – the Reparations Committee in Lausanne and London and the Ottoman Bank in Paris – and were well known to him. On the board of the company created to run the property portfolio in Paris he placed Messieurs Lefèvre and Erpinier, the latter an official of the Banca Francese e Italiana with which the Vatican had dealings, and which was used for banking purposes; on that of the Swiss companies he appointed himself and two colleagues, Messieurs Duriaux and Dennicel de Monte, and for British Grolux Ltd he chose two members of a long-established northern English Catholic family, the Radcliffes.[64] Indeed, the list of people appointed to the board of the last-named company over

---

55 Ibid., entry for 5 Aug. 1932.   56 Ibid., 2 Dec. 1932.
57 Ibid., 27 May and 27 June 1933.   58 Ibid.   59 Ibid.
60 RdeCVV, dossier 1446, Profima, memorandum of 10 Oct. 1932.
61 Ibid., memorandum of 13 Feb. 1998.
62 AFN, Nogara's diary, entry for 24 July 1933.
63 In a conversation with the author in October 1996, Ambassador Osio said that he remembered that 'Grandfather was always travelling.'
64 AFN, Nogara's diary, entry for 18 Jan. 1933.

the years reads like a roll-call of the English Catholic aristocracy and gentry.[65]

He then chose to establish a holding company, into which the profits of the property companies would be channelled, and which would act on behalf of the Special Administration. In August 1931 Nogara and Maillardoz acquired an 'off the shelf' company, Serilux, in the Grand Duchy of Luxembourg.[66] The choice of Luxembourg was, at first sight, a surprising one. There is no evidence that Nogara had any particular links with the Grand Duchy, which in the 1930s was still a bit of an economic and financial backwater, whereas his links with Lausanne were well established – in 1913 Nogara had been involved in the negotiation of the Treaty of Ouchy (on Lausanne's lake shore) to bring to an end the Italo-Turkish War over Libya (see Chapter 6, p. 145). On the other hand, with his encyclopaedic knowledge of financial markets and the social and political milieu of various Western European countries, Nogara knew that Luxembourg had a favourable financial climate deriving from its social and political stability and that the Grand Duchy had been pursuing a policy of attracting capital for investment in its holding companies.[67] Indeed, in 1929 the Luxembourg Chamber of Deputies had passed legislation on holding companies domiciled in the Grand Duchy which was every bit as up-to-date as those in Liechtenstein and Switzerland; foreign-owned holding companies were allowed considerable fiscal advantages, on condition that they did not engage in industrial activity or have offices open to the public.[68] These terms were ideal for the operations which Nogara wished to pursue through his company. Nevertheless, it is still perhaps surprising that he did not choose somewhere in Switzerland as the location of his holding company, since he already had many financial contacts and operations there, but this perhaps can be explained by the fact that two of the property companies he eventually founded were in London and Paris, both of which were closer to Luxembourg. Only the third was in Switzerland itself. He may even quite simply not have wished to put too many eggs in one basket. Two and a half weeks after its acquisition, Serilux had changed its name to Groupement Financier Luxembourgeois (Grolux), S. A. Holding.[69] By 1934/5, Grolux and its subsidiary companies, like other similar companies, were experiencing fluctuating fortunes (see Table 5).

---

[65] Companies House, London, file 270820, British Grolux Ltd, Annual Returns, 1932, 1933, 1936 and 1945.
[66] *Mémorial du Grand Duché de Luxembourg, Recueil Spécial*, 1931, pp. 1037–44.
[67] See E. Muhlen, *Monnaie et circuits financiers au Grand Duché de Luxembourg* (Luxembourg, 1968), p. 105.
[68] Ibid.   [69] *Mémorial*, 1931, pp. 1177–8.

Table 5 *Grolux: operations from 1932 to 1935*

Year	Turnover	Value of portfolio	Profit
1932	$16,505,821	$15,414,000	$118,600
1933	FL22,934,752	FL17,816,77	FL474,131
1934	FL16,924,334	FL12,277,778	FL159,504
1935	FL17,793,394	FL13,024,476	FL109,210

Source: Mémorial, 1932, p. 1050, 1933, pp. 1707–8, 1934,
Annexe, p. 1146, and 1935, Annexe, p. 55.

Nogara's investment policies and Catholic social doctrine

In his diary, Nogara frequently records the fact that Pius XI showed a great interest in the Italian and international economic situation. Thus, on his return from trips to financial conferences and meetings Nogara was asked by the pope to brief him on their outcome, and also on the general development of the Italian and world economic situation. For example, at the end of October 1931 he asked Nogara what economic effects he anticipated would ensue from Mussolini's speech in Naples earlier that month,[70] and in June 1933, in response to the pope's questions about the Conference on Economic and Monetary Matters that was taking place in London at that time, Nogara replied that he very much doubted that it would have positive results, and he was proved right.[71] As well as the information which he received on a regular basis from Nogara, Pius XI received first-hand accounts from other quarters. But the letter to Cardinal Mundelein of 12 December 1932 reveals that he had hitherto not grasped the seriousness of the economic crisis in America. In the same letter in which Pius XI thanked the cardinal for the 'conspicuous sum' sent by way of Peter's Pence, he went on to say that 'I must say that I would not have made that request [for an advance on Peter's Pence] if I had known before what I learnt in recent weeks about the terrible dimensions of the impact of the world crisis in the United States.'[72] Eighteen months later, he wrote to Mundelein congratulating him on the 'slow and partial improvement in the economic situation of the United States of America'.[73]

How did these 'lessons in applied economics', so to speak, at the hands of Nogara, not to mention the enormous losses which the Vatican

[70] AFN, Nogara's diary, entry for 31 Oct. 1931.
[71] Ibid., entry for 23 June and 6 July 1933.
[72] AAC, Mundelein papers, 1872–1939, 3/36, Pius to Mundelein, 12 Dec. 1932.
[73] Ibid., 3/73, Pius to Mundelein, 28 May 1934.

suffered, influence Pius XI's public pronouncements on economic and social matters?

In the period between May 1931 and May 1932, Pius XI issued three encylicals on such matters:

1. *Quadragesimo Anno* of May 1931
2. *Nova Impendet* of October 1931
3. *Caritate Christi Compulsit* of May 1932

Quadragesimo Anno is not the best document to use in this investigation because, as its title suggests, it was issued on the fortieth anniversary of Leo XIII's great social encyclical, *Rerum Novarum*, and was, as a result, long in preparation, and largely the work of hands other than the pope's – the Jesuit father, Nell-Brunning.[74] Nevertheless, it contains a very strong condemnation of what can only be described as anonymous, monopoly capitalism: 'In the first place, it is obvious that not only is wealth concentrated in our times but an immense and despotic dictatorship is consolidated in the hands of a few, who are often not owners but only the trustees and managing directors of invested funds which they administer according to their arbitrary will and pleasure.'[75] And the encyclical goes on to stigmatise: 'A no less deadly and accursed internationalism of finance or international imperialism whose country is where profit is.'[76] Where Pius XI thought that the Vatican fitted into this picture is not clear but Gollin claims that Nogara only agreed to become head of the Special Administration on two conditions:

1. That he not be restricted by religious or doctrinal considerations in his investment-making.
2. That he be free to invest funds anywhere in the world.[77]

'Religious and doctrinal considerations' would surely cover the Church's *social* doctrine, so Nogara was presumably exempt from its dictates. On the other hand, there was not much in the way of social doctrine that covered investment matters. As Miller, an expert on Catholic social doctrine, argues:

The words 'bank' and 'banking' are almost nonexistent in the documents of modern Catholic social teaching. Perhaps because the medieval teaching was never formally retracted that money was unproductive and therefore money lending at interest was therefore immoral, yet the church itself became an active investor

---

74 P. J. Chimielewski, SJ, 'Nell-Brunning, Oswald Von', in Dwyer (ed.), *New Dictionary of Catholic Social Thought*, pp. 676–8.

75 As quoted in Carlen (ed.), *Papal Encyclicals*, III, p. 431.

76 Ibid., p. 432.   77 Gollin, *Worldly Goods*, p. 440.

(Maritain) . . . Or perhaps it was because the church was deeply involved in financial matters at the highest levels that it was in no position to criticise.[78]

Nova Impendet, which was written specifically to address the growing problem of unemployment, contains no clear references to the evils of the capitalist system. *Caritate Christi Compulsit*, issued five months later, is, like *Nova Impendet*, also concerned about the dangerous social and political consequences of mass unemployment, and bears the clear imprint of Papa Ratti's style. It also harps on the theme of monopoly capitalism:

> those few men, very few indeed, who since they are endowed with immense riches, seemed to control the government of the world, those very few, moreover, who being addicted to excessive gain, were and are in great part the cause of such evils; these very men – we say – are often with little honour, the first to be ruined, grasping the goods and fortunes of the very many unto their own destruction . . . 'The desire for money is the root of all evil.'[79]

What was he thinking of as he wrote these words, perhaps of the Kreuger and Toll disaster, and his other massive losses which Tardini says he frequently lamented in his interviews with him?[80] He presumably did not see *himself*, or Nogara, as one of those 'very few men'. In this encyclical, he finally *seems* to have learnt something from his (vicarious) experience of the markets. Talking of remedies to the economic crisis he declared, 'What is needed is the restoration of the divine and human moral law . . . this is the soundest rate of exchange.'[81]

All in all, this seems to indicate a curious blindness on Pius XI's part to the nature of the financial activities in which Nogara was engaged on the Vatican's behalf. For a mill manager's son from Lombardy, there appears to have been a complete lack of understanding of the possibly intimate connection between those activities and the economic fate of nations and individuals.

Nogara's investment policies and canon law

Tardini was very critical of the management of the Vatican finances in the early 1930s, though, curiously, he attributes all the decision-making to Pius XI; he does not once mention Nogara. The entry in Tardini's diary for 30 November 1933, is typical of his criticisms:

[78] A. Miller, 'Banks and Banking', in Dwyer (ed.), *New Dictionary of Catholic Social Thought*, pp. 676–8.
[79] Carlen (ed), *Papal Encyclicals*, III, p. 475.   [80] Casula, *Domenico Tardini*, p. 292.
[81] Carlen (ed.), *Papal Encyclicals*, III, p. 481.

Was it really prudent to invest the money of the Holy See in certain bonds, foreign currencies etc.? And is it prudent now to buy real estate in various countries? Has there not been just too much speculation? Were there not other areas of investment, more stable and less risky . . . If there have been mistakes, the Holy See will have to suffer the consequences for a long time to come.[82]

Tardini's reference to speculation is very significant; it was not simply a question of the wisdom or otherwise of Nogara's investments but its morality, and perhaps most important of all, its *legality*, whether that is, it was in conformity with Catholic canon law. In 1917, Benedict XV had promulgated the Code of Canon Law for the Western Church, a Code which had been drawn up by Cardinal Pietro Gasparri, assisted by Eugenio Pacelli (later Pius XII) since 1907 and which provided rules and regulations for all aspects of the Church's life, including the administration of its property.[83] A number of writers have questioned whether Nogara's operations were indeed licit by the terms of canon law, in particular, Gollin argues: 'Under both civil and canon law, the Ordinary of a see is required to act as the trustee of the property he nominally owns. He is forbidden to engage in financial speculation and is accountable to his superiors, and very often to the civil courts as well, for the financial transactions he conducts or authorises.'[84] Gollin's view is borne out by several leading canonists. The Rev. Harry Byrne, who wrote a doctoral thesis entitled, 'The Investment of Church Funds', for the Catholic University of America in 1951, is very clear on the matter of speculation, claiming that: 'The Holy See has indicated that speculation is a form of business activity prohibited in clerical and religious affairs . . . Further, speculation is illicit in ecclesiastical administration for another reason, viz., the excessive degree of risk generally present.' And he goes on to cite decrees of the Sacred Congregation of the Clergy.[85] In the case of Nogara's activities, it is clear that he engaged in one of the riskiest forms of financial speculation – arbitrage. On 16 February 1932, for example, Nogara explained to the pope:

We have sold $220,000 worth of North American bonds: meanwhile we have bought $240,000 worth of first class bonds at a price of $188,000 . . . Another arbitrage operation is in progress to sell £100,000 of Australian loan stock in order to buy $300,000 of Australian stock. The purpose of this operation is to profit from the greater depression of the New York market in comparison with the London one.[86]

---

[82] As quoted in Casula, *Domenico Tardini*, p. 292.
[83] Pollard, *The Unknown Pope*, pp. 194–5.　　[84] Gollin, *Worldly Goods*, p. 131.
[85] As quoted in ibid.　　[86] AFN, Nogara's diary, entry for 15 Feb. 1932.

While another canonist, Woywood, does not actually say that speculation is illicit, he does claim that ecclesiastical trustees must, 'observe the rules of both Canon and civil law . . . invest the surplus revenue of a church . . . to the benefit of the church'.[87] And a third, Ayhrinac, says that trustees have 'To invest for the benefit of the Church . . . the surplus revenues or disposable funds that admit of safe and profitable investment.'[88] But, while all affirm that these rules of canon law were applicable to dioceses, parishes and other ecclesiastical jurisdictions, they do not say whether they were also applicable to the Holy See. As far as Gollin's point about civil law is concerned, the Holy See was obviously not answerable to any civil courts after 1929, but even though canon law was primarily intended for the parochial and diocesan levels of the ecclesiastical hierarchy, the Holy See, and therefore the Roman curia and even its financial agencies – like the Special Administration – was presumably also bound by canon law. So if Gollin is right when he says that Nogara only agreed to his appointment on condition that he would not be restricted by religious or doctrinal considerations, then it would appear that Pius XI had given the Vatican's financier complete exemption from both the dictates of Catholic social teaching and the explicit law of the Church. And, of course, it was much easier to do that with a *layman*, outside of the circle of curial officials and papal courtiers involved hitherto in Vatican financial administration, and in a separate administration solely responsible to the pope.

The aftermath of the Wall Street Crash

Tardini was very genuinely concerned about the long-term consequences of Nogara's investment strategy, doubting the wisdom of the essential elements of that strategy, as others have since. There had indeed been speculation, massive speculation. Given the extraordinary circumstances and terms of his appointment, it was Nogara's job to speculate, to employ the Vatican's capital in the most profitable way in the financial markets. Some of that capital would have been invested in the short period between the receipt of the funds from Italy in June 1929 and the Wall Street Crash at the end of October, in a mixed portfolio of government stocks and bonds, gold and currencies. This was almost certainly done at least in part on the advice of Morgan Grenfell and Co. in London and New York. It was, therefore, a very sound, sensible and prudent strategy by the standards of the day, and the Wall Street Crash of October 1929

---

[87] Woywood, *A Practical Commentary on the Code of Canon Law* (2nd edn, New York, 1926), pp. 180–1.
[88] A. D. Ayhrinac, *Legislation in the New Code of Canon Law* (New York, 1930), p. 431.

itself would undoubtedly have appeared to re-inforce the wisdom of the strategy in the short term. Could anyone, even Nogara, have foreseen the Crash, and could they have anticipated its catastrophic long-term effects on financial markets, manufacturing industry and governments? It is interesting in this regard to note that Nogara never criticises other economic players, except governments, for whose immorality in refusing to honour debt repayments and interest he has some very sharp words indeed.[89] It is also clear that Nogara had not mismanaged the Vatican's finances, the precious nest-egg of the Special Administration. On the contrary, when the crisis hit, Nogara used his knowledge, expertise and contacts to embark on a policy of diversification which was to have long-term success. Other authors, however, have criticised even the policy of diversification, arguing that had he invested all of the money paid by Italy in 1929 on the New York Stock Exchange, the Vatican's investments would have been worth far more than they actually were in 1988.[90] Apart from the fact that it is not known exactly how much they were worth in 1988, hence we cannot make a useful comparison, it seems unlikely that he could have invested all of those monies on Wall Street between June and October 1929; there simply was not enough time. That he did not might also suggest that he suspected that all was not well with the markets there. In any case, in the short term, the results of the Crash would have had far more serious consequences for the Vatican's financial position than those it actually experienced between 1930 and 1934. Finally, it is, of course, easy to say with the benefit of hindsight that by keeping his nerve and leaving the funds in New York, Nogara would have won out in the end. It would have required nerves of steel in this period.

By the end of 1934, the worst was over for the finances of the Vatican, and by 1937, as Belardelli has demonstrated, Nogara was ready to lay the foundations for a policy of blue chip investment in the USA which was eventually to provide one of the biggest pillars for the Vatican's Second World War and post-war financial strength.[91]

---

[89] Casula, *Domenico Tardini*, p. 292.
[90] A. Jones, 'Sixty years of inept management, bad investments lead to Vatican deficit', *Republic*, 11 Mar. 1988, pp. 1 and 23; see also Rees, *Inside the Vatican*, p. 219.
[91] AFN, Nogara's diary, entry for 22 May 1933.

8   Vatican finances in an age of global consolidation (1933–1939)

As far as the development of the finances of the Vatican was concerned, the period of the mid- to late 1930s was characterised by two divergent trends. On the one hand, the globalisation of Nogara's investment activities continued, and indeed towards the end of the decade actually intensified. On the other hand, the Vatican's penetration of the Italian economy, in particular of the financial and manufacturing sectors, gathered pace. The balance between the two trends was, almost always throughout the decade, determined by the international situation.

The Vatican's world-wide financial network

By the middle of the 1930s, the Vatican, thanks to Nogara and his links with the Banca Commerciale, was placed at the centre of a world-wide network of banking, and other financial institutions. The post-Second World War Italian politician, Ugo la Malfa, who worked for the bank in the 1930s, once described the Commerciale as a school of economic education, a window on the world, particularly the Anglo-Saxon world.[1] Given its German, Jewish origins, the Commerciale was the only Italian bank with strong international connections; indeed, it was the hub of a network of banks stretching across both Europe and Latin America, and to a lesser extent North America, the Middle East and North Africa, as can be seen from Illustration 13.

The two strongest sections of the Commerciale network were the string of banks in the Balkans, and those in Latin America. The former were evidence of long-standing Italian attempts at economic penetration of countries there, and those in Latin America were based on the lucrative exploitation of the financial needs of the large communities of Italian immigrants which had been established in several Latin American countries in the decades leading up to the First World War, most especially that of sending remittances back to their families at home.

[1] From ASBCI, Collana Inventari, Serie 7, vol. 2, p. LXVI.

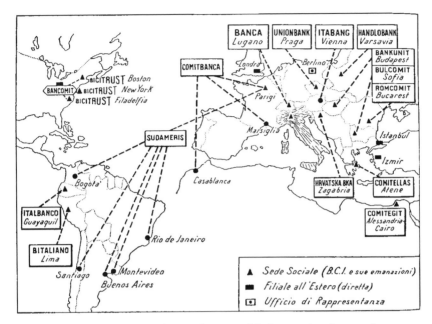

Illustration 13 The Banca Commerciale international network

As a member of the management board of the Banca Commerciale, Nogara would have had some knowledge of all of them, but the two institutions with which he had the closest links were the Banca della Svizzera Italiana, based in Lugano, Switzerland, and Sudameris which, as Illustration 13 shows, had branches in several South American countries, especially in Brazil. Nogara was a director of the Swiss bank, which carried out various banking operations for the Special Administration, and the Vatican had a small share-holding in the bank from the beginning of the 1930s.[2] Sudameris, or to give it its full name, Banque Française et Italienne per l'Amérique du Sud, was actually a joint operation of the Banca Commerciale and Paris-based Banque de Paris et des Pays Bas (Paribas).[3] Though he never actually visited Sudameris, Nogara knew its managing directors, Cavin and Malagodi, and through its Swiss holding company, Profima, the Vatican had a share-holding package in the bank.[4] Nogara became closely involved in its management from 1942 onwards

---

[2] ASBCI, Fondo AD2, Cart. 15, fasc. 40–50, Nogara, letter of Nogara to managing director of the bank, 16 Aug. 1938. See also NARA, JAGO, RG 153, Library, entry 135, L60, 'Italy: Money and Banking', p. 65.

[3] See ASBCI, Collana Inventari, Servizio Estero e Rete Estera, p. 61.

[4] NARA, OSS, box 168, XL 1257, report from Berne of 7 July 1945.

(see Chapter 9, pp. 191–2). The Vatican's financial involvement in South America also stretched to Peru, where Nogara acquired for it a substantial stake in the Banco De Credito De Peru.[5]

The Banca Commerciale itself acted as an international banker for Nogara and the Special Administration from 1929 onwards, and in 1935 kept accounts for the Vatican in Hungarian pengos, Reichsmarks, French and Belgian francs, as well as Austrian Schillings.[6] Remittances from the Vatican property companies in Britain, France and Switzerland were also lodged in lira accounts at the Commerciale.[7] But Nogara did not depend solely upon this bank to conduct his foreign financial transactions; by the mid-1930s, apart from the Banca d'Italia, House of Morgan branches in New York, London (where it kept part of its gold reserve and several hundred thousand pounds worth of securities) and Paris, he was keeping accounts in G. Mees & Co., Holland, the Union Bank of Switzerland, Credit Suisse (where it held another stock of gold) in Geneva and Wallenberg's Enskilda Banken in Sweden.[8]

Due to lack of published accounts, it is difficult to know how the individual property companies in Britain and France were doing in the late 1930s, but the accounts of the Grolux holding company in Luxembourg suggest that they did not do at all well in 1934;[9] in 1935 they briefly recovered, but in 1936 and 1937 they registered significant losses.[10] In the case of the French company, the reasons were fairly obvious; whereas in 1932 France, of all the Western economies, appeared to have strongly resisted the effects of the Great Crash, by mid-1937 economic conditions had deteriorated and political instability persisted, which probably explains why Nogara eventually decided to reduce his involvement in the Paris property market. In Lausanne, on the other hand, economic conditions actually appear to have improved, which would explain why he transformed Profima from being purely a property company into a holding company able to participate in 'all forms of commercial, industrial, property and financial enterprises, in Switzerland and abroad', and increased its capital from 390,000 to 500,00 Swiss francs in September 1938.[11] The Swiss Bank Secrecy Act of 1934, which made it unnecessary to publish

---

[5] NARA, JAGO, RG 1533, Library, entry 135, L60, 'Italy: Money and Banking', p. 65.
[6] ASBCI, Fondo SOFINDIT, Cart. 417, fasc. 5, memo of 23 Nov. 1935, 'Al Dott. Majnoni. Le cifre di questi elenchi arrotondate [sic]', p. 2.
[7] Ibid.   [8] Chernow, *The House of Morgan*, p. 96.
[9] *Memorial*, 1935, Annexe, p. 55, indicates a profit of 160, 000 Luxembourg francs.
[10] Ibid., 1937, Annexe, p. 320, indicates a profit of 5.74m Luxembourg francs; 1938, Annexe, p. 793, indicates a profit of of only 1.55m Luxembourg francs for 1937; 1939, Annexe, p. 802, indicates a loss of 377,000 francs for 1938, and 1940, Annexe, p. 667, registered a loss of 517,133 francs.
[11] RdeCCV, dossier on Profima, Procès-Verbal of 20 Sept. 1938.

annual accounts, the growth of Lausanne as a centre of banking and insurance, as well as the portents of war in Europe, made the concentration of commercial activities in the western Swiss city a very sensible step to take.[12]

The Vatican and the Italian economy

Though Vatican financial activities had an increasingly global dimension to them under Nogara's management, the Italian peninsula also remained a major target of Nogara's financial initiatives in the early to mid-1930s. Grilli has argued that the Lateran Pacts of 1929 allowed 'Vatican financial groups to officially take part in the management of the Italian economy'.[13] This may be an exaggeration, but there certainly is clear evidence that the Vatican, under Nogara's direction, began to buy share-holdings in various major Italian companies from 1929 onwards. By the middle of the decade, he had acquired substantial share-holdings on behalf of the Vatican in an increasing number of Italian financial institutions, manufacturing and utility companies and had become a member of their boards of directors, including the Istituto di Credito Fondiario (bank), Assicurazioni Generali (Italy's major insurance company), the Società Italiana per le Strade Ferrate Meridionali, otherwise known as Bastogi (since the nationalisation of all Italian railways in 1907, essentially a holding and finance company for electrical and electronic industries), the Istituto Romano per i Beni Stabili (property company), the Società Electrica ed Electrochimica della Caffaro (electricity and chemicals), the Società per l'Industria Petrolifera (petrochemicals), the Società Mineraria e Metallurgica di Pertusola (mining), the Società Adriatica di Electricità (electricity supply), and Cartiere Burgo (paper manufacture).[14] In addition, Nogara acquired the controlling interest in the Rome-based Società Generale Immobiliare (property and building, with later diversification) for the Vatican and became its president.[15] Eventually, the Immobiliare became Italy's largest property and construction company, and one of the largest in the world when it extended its operations to North and South America after the war.[16] When the fact that all this was in addition to established Vatican holdings in the appropriately named Banco di Spirito Santo, the Banco di

---

[12] *Regards sur la ville: Lausanne, 1900–1939*, Catalogue of an exhibition at the city historical museum (Lausanne, 2001), section on 'Commerce', reveals that in the period 1900 to 1939 banks in Lausanne increased from twelve to twenty-two, and that in the latter year there were ten insurance companies in the city and no less than fifty-eight property companies.

[13] Grilli, *La finanza vaticana*, p. 61.

[14] ASBCI, ScdA, 'CV di Bernardino Nogara', 14 Nov. 1958.   [15] Ibid.

[16] Pallenberg, *Inside the Vatican*, p. 96.

Roma and the Cassa di Risparmio di Roma, not to mention the Società Molini e Panifici Pantanella and the Società Romana del Gaz is taken into account, it is clear that the Vatican had consolidated its hold over the economy of the Italian capital city.

To take advantage of the especially favourable circumstances for company development in Milan, Italy's commercial capital and the seat of its main stock exchange, in 1935 Nogara set up another holding company, the Società di Partecipazioni Finanziarie Industriali e Commerciali (PARFINCO), with a capital of 5m lire, placing his son-in-law on the board. Over the years, PARFINCO made substantial and increasing profits and by 1939 they were equivalent to nearly 10 per cent of the original investment.[17]

The crisis of the major Italian banks – the Banca Commerciale, Banco di Roma and Credito Italiano – which was provoked by the longer-term effects of the Great Depression, was also very skilfully used by Nogara to the Vatican's financial advantage. Between 1931 and 1933, these banks were faced by a situation in which their major creditors, manufacturing and other companies in which the banks were themselves also the main share-holders, were bleeding them dry of funds due to the collapse of markets and consequent cash-flow problems. The various efforts on the part of the banks themselves between 1931 and 1933 to off-load their liabilities were not successful. Nogara was himself initially to have directed the Banca Commerciale's operation to liberate the bank of its loss-making shares in companies through the establishment of the Società Finanziara Industriale (SOFINDIT),[18] but Guido Jung, later Mussolini's minister of finance from 1932 to 1935, was appointed the head of that organisation instead. Similar organisations were set up for the Banco di Roma and the Credito Italiano. Eventually only a national, government-sponsored plan could resolve the problems of these loss-making companies and save the banks from collapse. In 1933, the Industrial Reconstruction Institute (IRI) was founded to take over the share-holdings of the three banks and by the Bank Act of 1936 Italian banks were forbidden from accumulating major company share-holdings again.[19]

As a vice-president of the Banca Commerciale and a member of the board of management of COMOFIN, the holding company into which many of the bank's industrial shares were placed, Nogara was obviously thoroughly au fait with the massive and delicate operation being carried

---

[17] AFN, Nogara's diary, entry for 4 Nov. 1931.
[18] For an account of these operations, see Zamagni, *The Economic History of Italy*, pp. 300–3; and Toniolo, *L'economia dell'Italia fascista*, pp. 312–19.
[19] Ibid.

out between 1931 and 1933 to save the Italian banking system from collapse. He consequently sought to benefit the Vatican from this situation in
two ways. First, he knew that the IRI had managed to revitalise several ailing companies by a capital injection, thus guaranteeing their future health
as re-privatised companies. In June 1933 Nogara negotiated the purchase
of a majority share-holding in one such company, the Dalmine iron and
steel complex, and a large packet of shares in another, the Società Italiana
del Gaz, a utility company with an effective monopoly in Turin, Florence
and Leghorn.[20] As a result of his work for the Banca Commerciale,
Nogara knew that the Italgaz had recently been put back on its feet, after
a series of difficulties, by Senator Frassati; indeed, Nogara had taken part
in the operation as a representative of the bank, a major share-holder. To
protect his investment, Nogara then chose four of the board of directors,
including two well-known Catholic laymen, the Counts Di Rovasenda
and Pace, and his own son-in-law Umberto Osio, a lawyer.[21] He carried
out a similar operation in relation to the privatisation of Bastogi, and, as
a result, the Vatican's Special Administration was listed alongside such
Italian blue-chip companies as FIAT, Pirelli, Assicurazioni Generali and
Monte dei Paschi di Siena among the chief share-holders of Bastogi.[22]
Nogara sat on the board along with the cream of the Italian economic
establishment: Toeplitz and Conti of the Banca Commerciale; Frigessi
and Mopurgo who were the dominant force in Italian insurance; Pirelli of
the rubber giant; Volpi di Misurata who was Mussolini's finance minister
between 1926 and 1929; and Giovanni Agnelli of FIAT.

The IRI was not so successful with the bulk of the ailing companies
whose share-holdings it took over from the three major banks; it was,
therefore, not possible to re-privatise them and most of them stayed
within the state sector for a long time to come with the result that by
the end of the 1930s Italy had the largest state sector outside of the Soviet
Union: the state holding company owned 10.3 billion lire or 21.5 per
cent of the nominal capital of all Italian firms.[23] The same was true for
the banks themselves. The problems of the Banca Commerciale, Credito
Italiano and the chronically ailing Banco di Roma could not be solved by
the banks' own efforts, even after they had been relieved of their share-
holding liabilities and so they were also taken over by the IRI. At the end

---

[20] AFN, Nogara's diary, entry for 3 June 1933.   [21] Ibid., entry for 21 Sept. 1933.
[22] ACS, IRI, Cart. 17, Cda, 2 July, 1935. Acccording to the ASBCI, Cart. 82, Sindacato
azioni SFM, fasc. 45, 3 Jan. 1949, in that year the Special Administration's share-holding
amounted to 5.68 per cent, one of the largest. Cited in G.-D. Piluso, 'Un centauro metà
pubblico e metà privato. La Bastogi da Alberto Beneduce a Mediobanca (1926–1969),
Annali della Fondazione Luigi Einaudi, 26 (1992), p. 377.
[23] Toniolo, L'economia dell'Italia fascista, pp. 248–9.

of the Fascist period in 1943, the state, through the IRI and other para-statal bodies, controlled 80 per cent of Italian banking operations. This secured the safety of the Vatican's deposits in the Banco di Roma (it is extremely unlikely that Cremonesi would have sat on the board of directors of this bank unless the Vatican had had a share-holding in it), and also another bank in which the Vatican had a major stake, the Banco di Santo Spirito, and a number of authors have argued that Nogara even succeeded in negotiating with Mussolini a swap on very favourable terms of the Vatican's shares in the bank for the new IRI bonds which were used to raise capital for the companies and which yielded interest at 5 or 6 per cent.[24] The essence of the Italian Fascist form of 'nationalisation' was majority state share-holding (through the IRI) not compulsory acquisition of assets, lock, stock and barrel, as in the case of the nationalisation policy pursued by the British Labour government of 1945–51. This meant that there continued to be a role (albeit minor) for private capital, either in the form of IRI bond issues, which could in any case be converted to shares, or in shares themselves. Nogara almost certainly acquired a significant portfolio of IRI bonds for the Vatican, a useful form of diversification from the massive holding in government stock which Pius XI had had to accept in 1929 as part of the Financial Convention. It was also one that would have been acceptable to the Italian government.

According to Grilli, the Vatican's penetration of the Italian economy continued through the mid- and late 1930s.[25] By analysing the changing composition of the boards of directors of a number of companies during the course of the decade, he identified those in which the Vatican established a significant share-holding, and consequently Nogara's strategy for protecting Vatican investments in them:

From this point onwards (1929) there begin to appear on the boards of directors of numerous Italian companies the names of eminent lay persons closely linked to the Vatican. It is significant that Nogara's name very rarely appears among them. From this we may deduce that Nogara sought to place his own men at a decision-making level in all of the companies in which he invested Vatican capital.[26]

Remarkably energetic and industrious though he was,[27] Nogara was quite simply not physically capable of sitting on the boards of all the companies

---

[24] Ibid., p. 135.   [25] Grilli, *La finanza vaticana*, p. 71.   [26] Ibid.
[27] In 1931, on top of all of his other very demanding tasks, Nogara undertook to save the troubled Sardinian mining company, Montevecchio, from collapse. Through no fault of his own, he failed. See P. Fadda, 'Il banchiere del Papa al capezzale del Montevecchio', *Argenteria*, new series, 1 (1992), p. 110.

in which the Vatican had an interest. Instead, he appears to have 'planted' more than half a dozen key 'uomini di fiducia' on the boards of those companies: Count Paolo Blumensthil, Filipo Cremonesi, the Marquis Giuseppe Della Chiesa (nephew of Benedict XV), Count Franco Ratti (Pius XI's nephew), Ing. Giuseppe Gualdi, Francesco Mario Odasso and Giovanni Rosmini.[28] All were tied into the Vatican in some way or another, and eventually obtained papal titles, decorations or honorary positions in return for their services. When Eugenio Pacelli was elected pope in 1939 they were joined by others such as his particular protégé, Count Enrico Galeazzi, and by his nephews, the brothers Marcantonio, Carlo and Giulio Pacelli.[29] What then becomes obvious is that the Vatican spread a very wide net of share-holding across the Italian economy. For example, Cremonesi and Rosmini sat on the board of the Banca Nazionale dell'Agricoltura, along with Ratti and another major Catholic figure, Prince Boncompagni Ludovisi.[30] Della Chiesa was president of the Cassa di Risparmio di Roma and other savings banks in the region around Rome; he was to play an even bigger role in undertakings with a Vatican interest after the end of the Second World War.[31] Gualdi was president of the Società Generale Costruzioni di Roma (building), the Società Cemento Armato di Roma (re-inforced concrete) and the Società Costruzione ed Esercizio Ferrovie di Palermo (railway construction and operation).[32] In addition, he and the Marchese Francesco Pacelli, the Vatican negotiator of the Lateran Pacts, sat on the boards of the Società Elettro-Ferroviara, Roma-Ostia (electric railways).[33] In 1939, Odasso became managing director of SNIA-Viscosa, which was the result of the merger of a number of major Italian textile manufacturing companies.[34] Franco Ratti sat on the boards of the Banco Ambrosiano, the major Catholic bank in Milan, of the Dalmine (see above, Chapter 7, p. 173), the Officine Meccaniche Reggiane, a munitions company, the Compagnia Nazionale Aeronautica (aircraft production) and the Società Agricola Lombarda (food processing).[35] By the end of the 1930s, there was hardly a sector of the Italian economy in which the Vatican did not have a share-holding of some sort or another, except farming, and it is indicative of this extraordinary success on the part of Vatican/Catholic finance under Fascism that in 1936 Count Blumensthil was actually appointed to the Board of Governors of the Banca d'Italia.[36]

[28] Grilli, *La finanza vaticana*, pp. 66–7.   [29] Pallenberg, *Inside the Vatican*, pp. 106–7.
[30] Grilli, *La finanza vaticana*, p. 67.   [31] Pallenberg, *Inside the Vatican*, pp. 125–6.
[32] Grilli, *La finanza vaticana*, p. 66.   [33] Ibid., p. 67.   [34] Ibid., p. 72.
[35] Ibid., p. 71.   [36] Ibid., p. 66.

Table 6 *Some of the major Italian companies with a Vatican share-holding in 1934*

Company name	Vatican director	Capital
Banca Commerciale	Nogara	Lit. 700m
Banca di Roma	Cremonesi	Lit.?
COMOFIN	Nogara	650m
Istituto di Credito Fondiario	Cremonesi	60m
Assicurazioni Generali	Cremonesi	60m
Ass. Forlanini	Cremonesi	60m
PRAEVIDENTIA	Ratti	7.5m
Elettro. Ferr. Italiane	F. Pacelli	18m
Soc. Romana Tramways & Bus	Pacelli	8.4m
Soc. Molini & Pasticceria Pantan	Cremonesi	15m
Soc. Romana del Gaz	Pacelli	85m
Soc. Italiana del Gaz	Di Rovasenda; Osio; Ratti	288.5m
Soc. Immob. Generale	Cremonesi; Nogara	72m
Dalmine	Ratti	75m
Ferro E Metalli	Ratti	8m
Acqua Pia Marcia (water in Rome)	Blumensthil	100m
Caffaro		21m
Bastogi	Ratti	219m

Source: Notiziarie Statistiche, 1934 (the presence of Nogara on the boards of the Banca Commerciale and COMOFIN may not necessarily mean that the Vatican had a share-holding: he had already been a director before 1929).

Grilli makes the further point that, a number of Fascist *gerarchi* having managed with as much success as Catholics to penetrate large parts of Italian business, by the end of the decade it was frequently the case that representatives of the Vatican and the regime sat alongside each other on boards of directors, citing the membership of Ratti and of Emilio De Bono (a leading Fascist boss) on the board of the Istituto Italiano di Previdenza (insurance) as a case in point.[37] This Catholic–Fascist *condominium* over the Italian economy mirrored the 'marriage of convenience' which endured between the Church and Fascism for most of the 1930s, despite the crises of 1931 and 1938 in their relations and Mussolini's growing relationship with Hitler (which largely provoked the 1938 crisis). Convergence on such important issues as 'public morality', the subordinate role of women, the outlawing of contraception and abortion, 'ruralisation' (privileging of rural, agrarian over urban, industrial society) and the struggle against Communism made it possible for Church and State

[37] Ibid., p. 73.

to work together reasonably harmoniously in Fascist Italy and made it possible for the Church to develop the various specialist associations of Catholic Action, the only non-Fascist organisation to enjoy any autonomy under the regime.[38] Until 1943, and the emergence of an Armed Resistance against the Germans which was dominated by the parties of the Left, Italy was therefore under a kind of joint Catholic–Fascist hegemony in all spheres, political, social, cultural and economic.

Certainly, by 1935, the Vatican was more closely tied to the Italian state and economy, and heavily dependent upon Italy's political stability, and consequently its financial and economic health, than ever before. The Vatican therefore had more than simply a political/religious stake in the survival of the Fascist regime; its financial prospects were also involved. Thus, in 1931, as the first serious effects of the Great Depression, unemployment and resulting social unrest began to be felt in Italy, according to Giorgio De Vecchi di Val Cismon, Mussolini's ambassador at the Vatican, the Cardinal Secretary of State, Eugenio Pacelli, 'has asked me several times whether the government felt itself to be strong',[39] and in a letter from the pope to the ambassador Pius XI declared that 'Fascism has already lost a lot of ground and it loses more everyday. Listen carefully to this advice which is given in a friendly spirit.'[40] While De Vecchi gives no indication of the nature of the advice, it undoubtedly *was* given in a friendly spirit; though there was a serious dispute between the Vatican and the regime over Catholic youth and labour organisations in 1931, the pope for his part did not desire the downfall of the regime. The Vatican had too much to lose, in all sorts of ways, from the collapse of Fascism and the ensuing turmoil, which, it was generally believed, would inevitably result in the triumph of Communism.

The Italo-Ethiopian War

The closeness of the tie-up between Vatican finances and the Italian economy in the early 1930s lends credence to the claims that the Vatican was aligned with Italian foreign policy in this period.[41] It would help to explain Pius XI's anxiety over the outbreak of the Ethiopian War in October 1935, and his policy of benevolence towards Italy. That policy was strongly criticised in Britain and France, and led to accusations that Italian companies part-owned by the Vatican helped provide Mussolini with munitions for

---

[38] Pollard, *The Vatican and Italian Fascism*, pp. 187–9.
[39] As quoted in ibid., p. 154.   [40] Ibid.
[41] P. Kent, *The Pope and the Duce: The International Impact of the Lateran Pacts* (London and Basingstoke, 1981), pp. 173–81.

the war.[42] That was almost certainly true given the extent of the Vatican's stake in the Italian manufacturing economy. It could hardly have been otherwise, because of the fact that a number of companies in which the Vatican had invested – Reggiane, Compagnia Nazionale Aeronautica and Breda, for example – produced munitions for the government. It has even been alleged that the pope helped directly to finance the Italian invasion through a substantial loan.[43] Murphy comments: 'Ironically, Mussolini had been forced to come to the papacy for significant financing for his war with Ethiopia. Even though Christ was the Prince of Peace, the Vatican, seeing war as a profitable business, had seized the opportunity and made huge loans to the Fascist government.'[44] This is highly unlikely, but it could be argued that the Vatican was *indirectly* propping up the war effort through its massive holding of Italian government stock and IRI bonds, thus justifying the concerns of many people in the Vatican. Pius was clearly concerned that Italy would be defeated, and feared the consequent collapse of the regime with all the dangerous possibilities outlined above. During the course of the Italo-Ethiopian crisis, Nogara was himself involved in various peace moves, as his diary testifies.[45] As a result of his frequent trips abroad, he was able to keep the pope informed about the attitude of his high-level contacts in Britain and France towards the impending crisis in July 1931.[46] He urged both the pope and Guariglia, the head of the 'Special Office for the Ethiopian Question' in the Italian Foreign Ministry, on a number of occasions to seek mediation through President Roosevelt, assisted by the pope's good offices, something which Pius tried without success.[47] In all of these efforts, he showed himself to be a loyal, patriotic Italian who was outraged by what he regarded as the obstinate, intransigent egoism of British policy towards Italy. But he was also very concerned about the effects of the cost of the war, and League of Nations sanctions on the Italian economy and state finances. In the end, he feared that an Italian defeat in Ethiopia, or a peace imposed by the League 'would be disastrous for Italy and for the European balance of power'.[48] He was equally afraid that even a long-drawn-out war would result in economic chaos and the arrival in power of 'The extremist party which would take Italy [along the path] of State collectivism.'[49]

---

[42] Murphy, *La Popessa*, p. 138.   [43] Ibid, p. 139.   [44] Ibid., p. 140.
[45] For a full account of his peace-making efforts, see R. De Felice, 'La Santa Sede e il conflitto Italo-Etiopico nel diario di Bernardino Nogara', *Storia Contemporanea*, 8 (1977), pp. 823–34.
[46] AFN, Nogara's diary, entry for 20 and 27 July 1935.
[47] Ibid., letter to Guariglia 14 Oct. 1935.
[48] Ibid., Nogara's diary, entry of 23 Nov. 1935.   [49] Ibid., nota of 8 Jan. 1936.

And that, of course, would have had catastrophic consequences for the Vatican.

Prelude to war

Nogara's concerns for the international effects of the Ethiopian War were effectively proved justified when it became clear that one of the major consequences of that conflict was the emergence of a closer relationship between Fascist Italy and Nazi Germany, the so-called Rome–Berlin Axis, which the pope so deplored.[50] The British and French policy of imposing League of Nations sanctions on Italy for her aggression against Ethiopia threw Mussolini into the arms of Hitler, a development that was consolidated by the outbreak of the Spanish Civil War in 1936, in which both Fascist dictators intervened on the Nationalist side. Given Pius XI's mounting apprehension about the nature of the new National Socialist dictatorship in Germany, which had begun to violate the terms of the *Reichskonkordat* almost as soon as it was signed in 1933, this was not a reassuring development. From 1936, Vatican diplomacy began to draw closer to Britain and France, and eventually the USA. The Cardinal Secretary of State, Eugenio Pacelli, had already visited France for the Lourdes celebrations in the pope's stead (Pius XI was unwell) and the Vatican continued to seek closer ties with France, as a way of opposing Hitler, despite the advent of a Popular Front government in 1936.[51] It pursued a similar policy towards Britain, to which it sent an apostolic delegate, a papal representative without diplomatic status but nevertheless with a covert diplomatic role, for the first time in November 1938.[52]

The most significant diplomatic move on the Vatican's part in the midto late 1930s was undoubtedly Pacelli's visit to America in October 1936.[53] The visit was officially supposed to be a purely 'private' one under the wing of Msgr Francis Spellman, Pacelli's friend and now auxiliary bishop of Boston. But Pacelli's whistle-stop tour of the major cities of the United States which, as the British minister to the Vatican pointed out,[54] included

---

[50] Ibid., 'the problem of Austria is developing in a way which is favourable to German National Socialism, but will prove damaging for Italy in the future'.
[51] Kent, *The Pope and the Duce*, p. 179.
[52] Moloney, *Westminster, Whitehall and the Vatican*, p. 93.
[53] For an account of the visit, see Gannon, *The Cardinal Spellman Story*, ch. 8; and Fogarty, *The Vatican and the American Hierarchy*, pp. 246–51. According to Gannon, *The Cardinal Spellman Story*, p. 110, Enrico Galeazzi (a friend of both Pacelli and Spellman) accompanied the cardinal to America. It is likely that Nogara used him to visit J. P. Morgan in New York and get a sense of the situation in the markets there.
[54] Hachey (ed.), *Anglo-Vatican Relations*, p. 363.

twelve out of the sixteen Roman Catholic ecclesiastical provinces in America, was in the first place meant to be a sign of recognition by the Vatican of the demographic and financial importance of the American Church. It was also clearly intended as a way showing off Papa Ratti's designated successor to the American Church and people, and it provided an opportunity for Pacelli to meet Roosevelt, just re-elected to a second term. In this way, the visit laid the foundations for what eventually became a close relationship between Washington and the Vatican.[55]

A year later, Nogara followed Pacelli to the United States.[56] Though he had long maintained close relationships with J. P. Morgan of New York, and other American financial institutions, he had never visited the country himself; now he was accompanied by J. P. Morgan's representative in Rome, Giovanni Fummi.[57] As the links between Hitler and Mussolini tightened, following the latter's visit to Berlin in September 1937, and the international situation in the Old Continent darkened, it is clear that Nogara went to America 'on a voyage of economic and financial study',[58] as he put it, seeking investment opportunities there in order to diversify away from Italy and Europe, for he knew that by late 1937 the economic giant was already showing signs of recovery from the slump, thanks in part to Roosevelt's policies. His visit was not as extensive as Pacelli's, but included major financial/industrial centres like New York, Chicago, Cleveland, Philadelphia and also Washington. In New York he had lengthy consultations with his advisers at the House of Morgan and with Cardinal Hayes and the financial advisers of the archdiocese and in Chicago with Cardinal Mundelein and his financial advisers.[59] The advice that he received from them on the effects of government policy and future economic prospects in America was mixed but gloomy which left him feeling perplexed. Nevertheless, despite his natural caution, he worked out plans for new investments in manufacturing shares and treasury bonds totalling three and a half million dollars, to be made within a period of three to six months from his visit.[60] The bulk of the eventual investments were in electricity supply companies, and by 1942 the

---

[55] Fogarty, *The Vatican and the American Hierarchy*, pp. 251–1.

[56] For an account of the visit, and the text of the journal which Nogara wrote during the course of it, see Belardelli, 'Un viaggio di Bernardino Nogara'. The original of the journal is to be found in the AFN.

[57] The visit was very carefully prepared in advance by the Vatican Secretariat of State. See, for example, AAC, Mundelein, 4/50 Pizzardo to Cardinal Mundelein, 29 Oct. 1937, in which the Vatican Under-Secretary of State gave his recommendation of Nogara: 'He enjoys the entire confidence of the Holy Father who has entrusted to him the most delicate financial affairs . . . please assist him in every way that is in your power.'

[58] Belardelli, 'Un viaggio di Bernardino Nogara', p. 327.

[59] Ibid., journal entries for the 12, 13, 15 and 20 Nov. 1937.

[60] Ibid., journal entry for 20 Nov. 1937.

Special Administration, via J. P. Morgan and the apostolic delegate in Washington, was receiving annual dividends worth over $56,000.[61]

The death of Pius XI

In February 1939 Pius XI died. His death, and the election of Cardinal Pacelli as his successor, had very swift repercussions for the Vatican's investment manager. Pius XII was a Roman and the other Romans in the Vatican quickly took the opportunity to settle scores with their Milanese rivals.[62] One wonders what part Msgr Tardini, himself a Roman, and the very powerful number two in the Secretariat of State took in these events. The cry went up, 'Fuori i milanesi dal Vaticano!' (The Milanese out of the Vatican!).[63] In the ensuing 'purge', Nogara and his Special Administration were subject to an investigation by a commission of cardinals. In the event he escaped with his reputation and position intact, for the claims of incompetence made against him were unproved.[64] But in the longer term, his influence in the Vatican began to go into decline. He did not have that cosy relationship with the new pope that he had had with his Milanese predecessor. In fact, Nogara's diary ceased after the death of Pius XI, presumably because Pius XII saw no value in maintaining such close and frequent contact. The Special Administration came under a commission of cardinals, whose leading light, Cardinal Nicola

---

[61] NARA, FBI, J. E. Hoover to Adolf Berle, Assistant Secretary of State, 22 May 1942:

As of possible interest to you, information has been received from a reliable and confidential source to the effect that J. P. Morgan and Company, Inc. NY City, sent to the apostolic delegate at Washington, coupons for the following bonds

Bonds	Number	Date of expiry	Interest
Adriatic El. Co. SF 7%	3,000	Jan. 4. 1952	$315
Meridionale Co. 7%	89,000	Jan. 2 1952	$9,345
Terni Indust. Co. 61/2%	338,000	2.1.1952	$$32,955
United El. Co. 7% 'A'	117,000	12.1.1956	$12,285
Int. Power securities Corp. 61/2% 'C'	14,000	15.1.1955	$910
Ibid 7% 'F'	3,000	15.1.1955	$210
Total		$56,335	

[62] Falconi, *The Popes in the Twentieth Century*, p. 241.
[63] Author's interview with Nogara's grandson, Bernardino Osio, Oct. 1996.
[64] Ibid. See also Lo Bello, *The Vatican Empire*, p. 25. Murphy, *La Popessa*, p. 76, ascribes the investigation to Mother Pasqualina; she 'had heard whispers of what she considered the loose handling of the $91 million the Church had received from the Lateran Treaty. She had learned of a so-called "man of mystery", an Italian banker by the name of Bernardino Nogara, had been granted sole control by the papacy over the entire fortune.'

Canali (another Roman), became a very powerful figure in the Vatican during the war.[65] Moreover, Pius XII brought members of his family into Vatican service, his nephews the Princes Pacelli, who also became powerful forces inside the various financial agencies of the Vatican. Nogara's dominant influence over the finances of the Vatican was beginning to come to an end.

[65] Pallenberg, *Inside the Vatican*, p. 78.

9 Vatican finances in the reign of Pius XII: the Second World War and the early Cold War (1939–1950)

Introduction

Papa Pacelli is usually seen as the dominating figure of the twentieth-century papacy, before the election of his successor, John XXIII, that is.[1] He is chiefly, and especially today at the height of the 'Hitler's Pope' controversy, remembered for his alleged silence over the Holocaust.[2] He was also the pope of the Cold War, protesting against the persecution of the 'Church of Silence' in those eastern and central European countries like Czechoslovakia, Hungary, Poland and Yugoslavia after their liberation by the Red Army in 1945 and leading the anti-Communist crusade against the threat of the Left in Italy itself.[3] In addition, he made major doctrinal pronouncements, the most important of them being his declaration in 1950 of the dogma of the bodily Assumption of the Blessed Virgin Mary into Heaven, and took important initiatives in the fields of liturgy and biblical studies. But, like Benedict XV, his first great trial came during war, the second total war to engulf the world in the twentieth century.

The position of the Vatican at the outbreak of war in 1939

The situation in which the Vatican found itself at the beginning of the Second World War was different in several important respects from that which it faced at the outbreak of the First World War.[4] Pius XII was in a much stronger diplomatic position in 1939 than Benedict XV had been in 1914. Whereas Benedict's predecessor, Pius X, and his Secretary of State,

---

[1] There is no good biography of Pius XII: probably the best biographical sketch in English is to be found in Falconi, *The Popes in the Twentieth Century*, pp. 234–304.
[2] Cornwell, *Hitler's Pope*.
[3] P. Hebblethwaite, 'Pius XII: Chaplain of the Atlantic Alliance?', in C. Duggan and C. Wagstaffe (eds.), *Italy in the Cold War: Politics, Culture and Society, 1948–1958* (Oxford, 1995).
[4] For a comparison of the wartime roles of the two popes, see J. F. Pollard, 'The Papacy in Two World Wars: Benedict XV and Pius XII Compared', in R. Mallett and G. Sorenson (eds.), *International Fascism, 1919–1945* (London, 2002).

Illustration 14 Pope Pius XII

Cardinal Merry Del Val, had left the Holy See in relative isolation – in diplomatic relations with fourteen, mostly minor, states – Pius XII inherited from his predecessor, Pius XI, a very healthy and extensive network of diplomatic relationships, which he as Secretary of State had helped to nurture. The Holy See had relations with the all the major powers except the Soviet Union, the United States and Japan; in the last case, matters were rectified in 1942 when relations were established at the request of the Empire of the Rising Sun. The Vatican's diplomatic leverage was further re-inforced by the international reputation which Pacelli had established for himself between 1930 and 1939, and by his extensive foreign travels in the later 1930s, the first embarked upon by any Vatican Secretary of State. In particular, as has been seen (Chapter 8, pp. 180–1), he visited America in 1936, met Roosevelt and maintained relations with him not only through the official Vatican envoy, Apostolic Delegate Cicognani, but also privately through Msgr Francis Spellman, whom Pius named as archbishop of New York in 1939. Eventually, in the winter of 1939/40, Spellman was able to engineer the establishment of diplomatic relations of a sort with the USA when Roosevelt appointed Myron Taylor as his 'personal representative' at the Papal Court.[5] This close relationship with the 'great neutral' was a far cry indeed from Benedict XV's very troubled and unsatisfactory relationship with Woodrow Wilson during the First World War and as we shall see, relations with the United States were to be of crucial importance to the financial operations of the Vatican during the war.

As far as its relationship with Italy was concerned, the Vatican's experience of the 'phoney war', from September 1939 to May 1940, was to be virtually a re-run of its experience between August 1914 and May 1915. Pius XII, however, was more active in seeking to persuade Italy to remain neutral before the outbreak of the Second World War than Pius X had been before the outbreak of the First.[6] As in 1914, so in 1939 Italy declared its neutrality, or rather 'non-belligerence', neutrality being anathema to an old interventionist like Benito Mussolini. He found even non-belligerence extremely galling, and after Hitler's blitzkrieg on Denmark, Norway, the Benelux countries and France in the spring of 1940, he could not wait to join in before the spoils of war were divided up without him. So Italy's declaration of war on France, Belgium, Britain, the Netherlands and Poland on 10 June threatened to renew all the problems

[5] Gannon, *The Cardinal Spellman Story*, ch. 11; and Fogarty, *The Vatican and the American Hierarchy*, pp. 248–57 and 258–66.

[6] O. Chadwick, *Britain and the Vatican during the Second World War* (Cambridge, 1986), pp. 57–8.

which the Vatican had faced after Italy's intervention against Austria-Hungary in May 1915. Would the Lateran Pacts of 1929 prove more effective in preserving the Holy See's neutrality and independence than the Law of Guarantees had done during the First World War? The Pacts did at least ensure that the ambassadors of Italy's four new enemies would be able to retreat into the independent and neutral State of the Vatican City,[7] rather than have to withdraw to Switzerland for the duration of the hostilities, as the Austro-Hungarian, Bavarian and Prussian envoys had been obliged to do in 1915. The Vatican was also subject to Italian surveillance and espionage, and virtually all of its codes were cracked, as in the First World War.[8] The Secretariat of State seems to have learnt surprisingly little from the First World War experience and, in particular, it failed to invest in more sophisticated codes, radio transmitters for its nuncios and other representatives abroad and its own courier service.

In one sense, the Vatican's situation was worse in the Second World War. The Fascist regime, and particularly some of its more extreme elements, like Roberto Farinacci, the *ras* (Fascist boss) of the city and province of Cremona in the Lombard plain, were very suspicious of the Vatican's proclaimed neutrality,[9] and Mussolini himself was less favourable towards the Church in the late 1930s than he had been earlier in the life of the regime; in his diary, Ciano, Mussolini's son-in-law and foreign minister, repeatedly refers to the Duce's outburst against the papacy.[10] Mussolini claimed to have plans to 'settle accounts' with both the monarchy and the papacy after the end of a victorious war.[11] There was consequently strong pressure from the Fascist regime for the Vatican to accommodate its policies to those of Italy, and L'Osservatore Romano was subject to censorship, and was frequently burnt on the streets by enraged groups of Fascists because of its frank reporting of the war.[12]

Nazi Germany was no friendlier to the Vatican either,[13] and one particular reason later in the war was its suspicion that the Vatican was pro-American because it believed that the Vatican's main financial support was American Catholics, and even United States government funds.[14]

---

7   Ibid., chs. 6, 7 and 8.
8   Alvarez, 'Vatican Communications Security, 1914–1918'; and Alvarez and Graham, *Nothing Sacred*, ch. 5.
9   Chadwick, *Britain and the Vatican*, p. 156.
10 *Ciano's Diary, 1937–8*, ed. with an introduction by M. Muggeridge (London, 1952), pp. 179 and 204.
11 *Ciano's Diary, 1939–45*, ed. with an introduction by M. Muggeridge (London and Toronto, 1947) entry for 2 Jan. 1939.
12 Chadwick, *Britain and the Vatican*, pp. 104–14.
13 Alvarez and Graham, *Nothing Sacred*, pp. 48–9.
14 A. Rhodes, *The Vatican in the Age of the Dictators, 1922–1945* (London, 1973), p. 264.

This became problematical when the Germans occupied Italy in September 1943 and the Vatican City was surrounded by their troops.

The financial consequences of the war for the Vatican

The Achilles heel of the Vatican was that it remained dependent on Italy for its material survival. Surrounded by Italian territory, it was at the mercy of the Italian government as far as food, water and energy supplies were concerned, and also in regard to communications with the rest of the world by telegraph and telephone; even Vatican radio was to be effectively censored by Fascist Italy.[15] Owen Chadwick has gone so far as to say that 'The Italian Government could switch off its [the Vatican's] electric light, or its water supply or even its food. It could refuse it banking facilities and bankrupt the Pope's government.'[16] In the light of what was known at the time of his book's publication in 1986 about the Vatican's financial operations during the Second World War, the assertions about its financial vulnerability were a reasonable conclusion to draw; the information that is now available suggests that the Vatican was in fact rather less financially dependent on Italian goodwill than this quotation suggests. As Chadwick himself points out, in May 1940 Nogara negotiated the transfer of a substantial part of the Vatican's gold reserve, valued at $7,665,000, from Morgan Grenfell's office in London to the United States Federal Reserve administration.[17] At the same time, along with Giovanni Fummi, Morgan's representative in Rome, he supervised the 'repatriation' to the Vatican of hundreds of pounds' worth of securities.[18] Other sources suggest that the Vatican went further than that, but there is no corroborating information. Msgr Vagnozzi of the apostolic delegation in Washington, writing to the US Treasury in May 1942, declared:

At the very outset of the present war, the Holy See transferred all its foreign assets into American dollars. In this step it was motivated by implicit confidence in the security of the American dollar, as well as by the clear-sightedness and spirit of cooperation of the Government of the United States regarding the use of the said funds in countries whose assets had been frozen, or in countries which had been invaded by the enemy.[19]

Whatever the precise scale of these transactions, they effectively made the Holy See independent of Italy in financial terms, even though the Vatican

---

[15] Chadwick, *Britain and the Vatican*, pp. 141–9.
[16] Ibid., p. 132.   [17] Ibid., p. 117.
[18] PRO, FO, 371/2519, Removal of Gold from Morgan Grenfell to the USA, Kingsley Wood [Chancellor of the Exchequer] to Halifax [Foreign Secretary], 20 May 1940.
[19] NARA, RG 131 (Dept of Justice, Foreign Funds and Control Records), box 487, letter from Vagnozzi, 21 Sept. 1943.

State's currency was tied to the Italian lira and thus affected by the infla-
tionary spiral that beset it during the war. According to Vagnozzi, 'the
special currency proper to the Vatican City is, practically speaking, at the
present time devoid of value on the international exchange'.[20] Despite
some misgivings, the Federal Reserve effectively became the Vatican's
major international banker for the duration of the war, on the grounds that
the possible economic disadvantages to the Allied cause were trivial and
were outweighed by the other important policy considerations, an indication of the special place which the Holy See occupied in Roosevelt's diplomacy.[21] Via the apostolic delegation in Washington, Nogara used the gold
deposited in the Federal Reserve, plus other assets, to buy Swiss francs,
Portugese escudos and Spanish pesetas to cover expenses incurred in Italy
for the provisioning of Vatican City and its extra-territorial dependencies, for its international postal, telegraph and other services, for funding the operations of the 'Vatican Bank' (see below, pp. 197–200), for
the expenditure of nunciatures on mainland Europe (and presumably in
Latin American after a number of countries there declared war on Italy
in late 1942) and for relief operations in various occupied countries.[22] In
1943 these costs came to a total of $1,300,000 and since the Italian and
Swiss governments would only accept gold-backed currency, a substantial
part of this, $576,000, was in Swiss francs.[23]

The Vatican's externally based gold reserve was all the more essential
to its financial operations because, as a result of the outbreak and spread
of hostilities, the flow of Peter's Pence to Rome must have been seriously
disrupted. We have no actual figures to illustrate this situation but the
defeat and occupation of countries such as Czechoslovakia, Poland,
France, Belgium, the Netherlands and Luxembourg by Nazi Germany
and the temporary occupation of Lithuania and parts of Poland by the
Soviet Union must have diminished the ability of the local churches both
to make collections from the faithful and transmit them to Rome. Italy's
declaration of war on the USA in December 1941 also disrupted communication with that great provider of financial sustenance for the Holy See.
In these circumstances, the only substantial and reliable sources of Peter's
Pence during the course of the war were probably the Latin American
states, and relations with even some of these countries must have been
affected by their declaration of war on the Axis in 1942. And of course, a

[20] Ibid. Zamagni, *The Economic History of Italy*, p. 255, provides a table showing that between
the outbreak of the war and the end of 1943, prices in Italy had risen by 80 per cent.
Inflation over the next two years' of Allied occupation was to be even more spectacular.
[21] NARA, RG 131 (Dept of Justice, Foreign Funds and Control Records), box 487, letter
of J. W. Pehle to Morgenthau, 21 Apr. 1942.
[22] Ibid., letter of Vagnozzi, 21 Sept. 1943.   [23] Ibid.

major channel for the transmission of the financial support of the faithful, *ad limina* visits by bishops, was as badly affected by the Second World War as they had been in the First.

The effect of the war on Vatican investments outside Italy

If the United States Federal Reserve helped finance some Vatican needs, it could not resolve all the difficulties which Nogara faced in his management of the Vatican finances in a time of war; a serious problem was posed by the German invasion and occupation of France and Luxembourg, and by Italy's declaration of war on Britain. There is some evidence of how he sought to salvage Vatican assets in Luxembourg and Great Britain. In the case of Luxembourg, it is clear that he was already beginning to wind down operations there early in 1939. At an extraordinary general meeting of Grolux in March of that year, which was attended by De Maillardoz, various amendments were made to the statutes of the company, most notably the giving of discretion to the president to call meetings of the board of directors outside of the Grand Duchy 'in case extraordinary events compromise the management and activity of the company inside the Grand Duchy'.[24] Clearly, even at this early stage, Nogara thought that war was inevitable and that, as in 1914, Luxembourg would be one of the first victims of German aggression. In October 1939, the capital of Grolux was reduced from 36 million Luxembourg francs to 10 million.[25] What happened to the company and its assets thereafter is not known. Given the fact that the Vatican had some prior warning of the imminent attack, there is a strong possibility that Nogara liquidated it before the Germans invaded the Grand Duchy in the spring of 1940. Alternatively, he may have done so at the end of the war. Certainly, there is no further trace of the company in the Luxembourg records after the annual meeting in March 1940. In the case of British Grolux, communication with the Vatican was carried on via the apostolic delegation in London. When the Trading with the Enemy Branch of the Foreign Office became concerned about the connections with Italy, ownership of the Vatican share-holding in the company was transferred to Morgan's Bank.[26] As has been seen, the Paris-based property company, SOPRIDEX, was reduced in importance

[24] *Memorial*, 1939, pp. 634–5.   [25] Ibid., p. 2285.
[26] PRO, FCO, 371/30197, letter of P. W. Dixon to F. W. W. Combe, Trading with the Enemy Branch, 27 Aug. 1941, in which he says that the Hon. H. E. Fitzalan Howard had asked whether the accounts of a real estate company owned by the Vatican in this country could be sent to the Vatican. Usually they had been sent to Nogara via the Apostolic Delegate in London. There would be no mention of war damage in the accounts which might 'give away information which might be of value to the enemy in the sense of indicating the value of real estate in this country under wartime conditions'.

and brought under the control of its Swiss sister in Lausanne, and after the German occupation of France and Luxembourg, Switzerland became the centre of financial operations for the Vatican in Europe. A Foreign Office memorandum of 19 January 1942 says that British Grolux was owned by a 'Swiss parent company', presumably Profima, demonstrating that Grolux in Luxembourg no longer figured in this relationship.[27]

Apart from Profima, and its links with Sudameris, Nogara had strong ties with Credit Suisse, in which he had strategically built up a considerable gold account.[28] But the British Ministry of Economic Warfare was not happy with Profima's arrangements for dealing with the affairs of companies in the German-occupied zone of France, in particular the remaining Paris property companies; in a correspondence of 1941–2, they complained about Profima's activities and alleged that it had breached their regulations about trading with the enemy by not declaring the property company assets.[29] Nogara was accused of 'shady activities', and being 'up to some dirty work' to evade Allied controls by the British Ministry of Economic Warfare over the Paris companies.[30] The fact that Profima answered to an Italian, Nogara, based in the Vatican, surrounded by Italian territory, and therefore to the average American or British bureaucratic mind, effectively Italian, did not help.[31] After the war, the Allies continued to treat Profima with great suspicion, believing, apparently without justification, that it had been heavily involved in commercial deals with the Axis powers.[32]

Profima got into even worse trouble when it became involved in the affairs of the South American branches of Sudameris. By 1939, the banking subsidiary held deposits of $10 million for its customers in Argentina, Chile, Colombia and Uruguay, and thanks to a pre-war agreement, control had been devolved to a Frenchman, Cavin, and an Italian, Malagodi, who was an official of the Banca Commerciale, in the event that France and Italy went to war.[33] The problem for Profima arose in late 1942 when the US government put increasing pressure on friendly governments in South America to break off relations with the Axis powers, Italy and

---

[27] Bank of England Archive, EC4/370, memo of 19 Jan. 1942, gives details of the Vatican's investments in the United Kingdom, including the property owned by British Grolux, estimated at £500,000. Another memo, of 12 Jan. of the same year, noted that in Britain the Vatican banked with Morgan Grenfell and Barclays.
[28] Gollin, *Worldly Goods*, p. 458.   [29] NARA, RG 226 (OSS), box 168, XL12579.
[30] PRO, FO, 37150078, Financial Activities of the Vatican, Crump, Ministry of Economic Warfare, to Hebblethwaite at Foreign Office, 29 Mar. 1945.
[31] Ibid.
[32] There is a theory that Vatican-owned financial institutions had been used for the purchase of wolfram, from which came tungsten, which was so vital to the Nazi war effort.
[33] ASBCI, Fondo CM Bernardino Nogara, memo attached to letter of Mattioli to Nogara.

Germany. Clearly, Sudameris would be at risk of confiscation since it was in part owned by a private banking institution of one of the Axis powers. In fact, it was put on the black ('statutory') list by the British in October 1940 because its French parent, Paribas was judged to be a 'willing collaborator with the German occupation authorities'.[34] Moreover, it was also claimed by other sources that 'It [Sudameris] has certainly worked for the enemy . . . perhaps more than any other bank in South America.'[35] According to Cavin and Malagodi, the real reason was that 'someone in Uruguay told the Americans that the bank had bought quartz and diamonds on behalf of the Germans'.[36]

The Allied pressure mounted and Sudameris was actually closed down in Brazil in 1943 and its branches and assets confiscated.[37] In these circumstances, in order to save the remaining branches, Nogara was persuaded by the Banca Commerciale to take over the subsidiary on behalf of Profima. Whereas in November 1942, Profima owned only 30 per cent of the share-holding (in part on behalf of Paribas), Banca Commerciale 30 per cent, Paribas 20 per cent and minor share-holders 20 per cent,[38] it acquired more shares, raising its holding to 42 per cent, effectively a controlling stake.[39] In order to prevent further confiscations, Mattioli, the managing director of the Banca Commerciale, notified Giovanni Malagodi, the chief official in South America, that Vatican control, through Profima, with Nogara as managing director, would effectively render Sudameris 'neutral'.[40] In this telegram, Mattioli more or less confirmed the distribution of shares between Profima and other holders indicated by the Office of Special Services (OSS), but says that Profima now owned 47 per cent of the shares.[41]

This worked in most of the countries concerned, and most especially in Argentina, which, incidentally, never did declare war on Italy and Germany, but not in Brazil where the government insisted on confiscating the assets of Sudameris branches, despite an attempt on Malagodi's part to play the 'Vatican card' by claiming that Sudameris was effectively the property of the Holy See.[42] Both the British and the American

---

[34] NARA, RG 153 (Judge Advocate General's Office), entry 135, L60 'International Banking Connections', Aug. 1943.

[35] NARA, RG 226, Research and Analysis Branch, entry 19, box 90, file XL6425, letter from R. G. Fenton in London, 14 Feb. 1945.

[36] ASBCI, Fondo CM Bernardino Nogara, Malagodi and Cavin to Nogara, 22 Mar. 1944.

[37] Ibid., AD2 (Segreteria degli Amministratori Facconi & Mattioli), cart. 210, fasc. 1, pezzo n.1, allegato, 'Sudameris; rapport sur l'exercise 1945'.

[38] NARA, RG 226, box 168, file 12579, report from Berne of 7 July 1945.

[39] Ibid.   [40] AFN, telegram of 15 Feb. 1942.   [41] Ibid.

[42] ASBCI, Fondo AD2 (Nogara), cart. 15, fasc. 40–5, telegram of Malagodi and Cavin to Nogara, 15 May 1943.

representatives at the Vatican protested about Nogara's activities, claiming that he had acted without the knowledge of his superiors.[43] Osborne, the British minister at the Vatican, challenged Cardinal Maglione, Secretary of State, on the issue in 1943, and reported to the Foreign Office that 'The Cardinal informs me that on enquiry he learns that this is correct. He adds that, had he known of the proposed transaction, he would have forbidden it.'[44] It would appear that Nogara could not disentangle his responsibility to a neutral Vatican from his loyalty to his native country or, as a company man, to the Banca Commerciale. In doing so, he also brought renewed suspicion to fall on Profima in Allied circles. It is significant that throughout the whole episode, Vatican diplomacy was actively used on behalf of Sudameris, thus in 1944, Msgr Lavame, the nuncio in Montevideo, telegrammed the Secretary of State to say that his efforts to via the United States ambassador on behalf of the bank had failed.[45]

Nogara then had to work hard himself to have Sudameris taken off the British and American lists. As early as November 1942 he considered sending Maillardoz to Washington to plead with the American authorities on behalf of the threatened branches in Brazil and to explore the possibility of a North American company buying out the subsidiary.[46] He then tried through Tom Lamont of Morgan and Co., as a *quid pro quo* for his protection of Fummi, the company's Rome agent from the Italian Fascist police. But even that powerful New York banking house was unable to sway the American government.[47] Nogara then turned to Myron Taylor directly, and in late 1942, he made an offer to sell half of Profima's share-holding in return for the removal of Sudameris from the black-lists.[48] Finally, in August 1945, under pressure from the Swiss authorities, he transferred 30,000 Profima shares in Sudameris into the hands of Morgan,[49] but it was not until November 1945 that he was finally able to write to the *chargé d'affaires* of the President's representative at the Vatican, Harold Tittman, to thank him for achieving the de-listing of Sudameris.[50]

43 Ambassador Osio also suggested that his grandfather did not keep Vatican officials entirely informed of his activities; conversation with the author, Oct. 1996.
44 PRO, Ministry of Economic Warfare, letter to Berne Embassy, 10 Apr. 1945.
45 ASBCI, Fondo CM Bernardino Nogara, letter of Lavame to Maglione, 1 Apr. 1944.
46 ASMAE, ApSS (Ambasciata presso la Santa Sede), pacco 71, memoranda to the minister, 4 and 24 Nov. 1942.
47 NARA, RG 84 (Dept of State and Foreign Relations), PRPtPXII (Personal Representative of the President to Pius XII), box 11, 851.6 Vatican Bank, banking black-list, Tom Lamont to Myron Taylor, 12 Aug. 1944.
48 Ibid., RG 226, box 168, XL12579.
49 ASBCI, Fondo CM Bernardino Nogara, Nogara to Mattioli, 28 Aug. 1945.
50 *Vaticano e Stati Uniti*, ed. Di Nolfo, pp. 418, 548, 560, 561 and 592–5, contain documents tracing the development of negotiations over Sudameris.

As a postscript to this saga, it is interesting to note that another bank with which the Vatican had connections (Nogara was one of its directors), the Banca della Svizzera Italiana, was also put on the British 'statutory' list during the war.[51] The justification was that the bank had allegedly done business in Bulgaria and Romania, both allies of the Axis powers.[52] This bank was only finally deleted from the 'statutory list' on 7 November 1945.[53] Fundamentally, of course, the problem was that both Sudameris and the Banca della Svizzera Italiana had close connections with the Banca Commerciale, an Italian, and therefore enemy, bank; as long as this was the case, and Nogara remained a director of that bank, the Allied authorities were bound to be suspicious about Nogara's financial activities on behalf of the Vatican outside of Italy.

The Vatican and Italy, 1942–3

By mid-1942, the diplomatic balance of power between the Vatican and the Italian government had changed, and the latter became very obliging in meeting the financial requests of the Vatican because, despite Mussolini's instinctive anti-clerical belligerence, he realised that at that stage in the war, with the Italian forces encountering defeat on nearly every front, in the interests of national unity and the war effort, it paid to keep on good terms with the pope. He had probably also calculated that the war against the Allies was lost and he saw the possibility of negotiating a peace treaty with them through the good offices of Pius XII.[54] Not least in that calculation would have been his awareness of the possible usefulness of Nogara in peace feelers to the enemy, given his network of influential connections in the Allied countries, as demonstrated by his role during the Italo-Ethiopian War (see Chapter 8, pp. 178–9).

In 1942 the Italian Ministry of Finance, presumably at Mussolini's prompting, resolved a taxation matter to Nogara's satisfaction. In February of that year, a bill had been published which would have imposed a new 10 per cent tax on government stock interest, a 20 per cent tax on dividends, plus a new charge of 10 per cent on current accounts, in order better to finance the war effort.[55] Nogara set to work to win exemption for the Holy See from paying the new taxes, including not only the congregations and offices of the Roman curia, but also the ABSS, the

---

[51] NARA, RG 84, Safehaven Files, entry 323, box 6, Banca della Svizzera Italiana, memo from managing director to the US consul-general in Berne, 30 Mar. 1943, protesting about the listing.
[52] Ibid., letter of HM consul-general in Zurich, 28 Mar. 1946.
[53] Ibid.   [54] Pallenberg, *Vatican Finances*, p. 132.
[55] Ibid., where he also says that an attempt had been made to introduce this in 1935/6.

Special Administration and the Istituto per le Opere di Religione.[56] As correspondence passed between Nogara's office and the Italian Embassy to the Holy See, Nogara argued that Britain, Canada and the USA had all exempted the Vatican from the operation of their tax impositions in these regards, the embassy arguing in reply that the article of the Concordat which Nogara cited in support of his claims, no. 29, could not give the Holy See more favourable treatment than the state itself.[57] In all of this, Nogara seems to have been in somewhat of a hurry. One reason for his impatience may have been the fact that some over-zealous official in the Ministry of Finance had forced the Vatican-owned Milanese company, PARFINCO, to pay the tax on shares which the Vatican owned in the company.[58] But he had more serious motives; he was undoubtedly afraid of the possible negative consequences of the likely collapse of Fascism. Fear of the serious danger of the collapse of the regime prompted tough resistance towards Italy on tax exemptions, probably because there was apprehension in the Vatican regarding the composition of a post-Fascist government which might be more skewed to the Left and therefore less inclined to be accommodating to the Vatican. In any case, clause 29 was clear, the Holy See and all of its immediately dependent organisa-tions were exempt from *all* taxes. Eventually Nogara got his way and by means of a government decree of 31 December 1943 the exemptions were granted.[59] In retrospect, Nogara's victory may not have been such a big deal after all; McGregor Knox in his book on Italy's military perform-ance in the Second World War argues that the Fascist Italy had a very lax wartime tax regime by comparison with other belligerents: 'Overall tax yield, despite a series of wartime increases and surcharges, decreased by 20% between 1939/40 and 1942/3.'[60] And he confirms the view that this was due to Mussolini's desperate desire to preserve political consensus in Italy.[61]

Whatever the significance of the tax concessions, it is clear that at this late stage in the war, Nogara and the Vatican were treated with kid gloves by the Italians; in 1942 he was given permanent use of his own sleeping car on his travels around Italy on Vatican business, an extraordinary conces-sion in wartime.[62] Another example of Italy's willingness to accommodate the needs of the Vatican in the later period of its war can be found in an

---

[56] ASMAE, ApSS, pacco 160.1.3, Special Administration, letter from Nogara to Guariglia of 6 Nov. 1942 and letter from Guariglia to Nogara of 11 May 1943.

[57] Ibid., letter from Guariglia.   [58] Ibid., pro-memoria to Attolico, 29 Apr. 1942.

[59] Pallenberg, *Vatican Finances*, p. 132.

[60] M. Knox, *Hitler's Italian Allies: Royal Armed Forces, Fascist Regime and the War of 1940–1943* (Cambridge, 2000), p. 39.

[61] Ibid.   [62] ASMAE, ApSS, pacco 160.1.3, Embassy memo of 10 June 1942.

episode which again emerges from the records of the Embassy to the Holy See. In November 1942, the Embassy asked the Foreign Ministry to consider a request it had received from Nogara, asking to be allowed to visit the USA because 'he had for some time now been deprived of economic and financial information about North America, which he required in order to carry out his functions (as manager of the Special Administration)'.[63] As his side of the bargain, Nogara promised to try to sort out the troubled affairs of Sudameris which were now adversely affecting one of the parent companies, the Banca Commerciale, by trying to find a North American company to buy the Vatican share-holding.[64] In the event, Nogara decided not to go to the USA, and sent his deputy Maillardoz instead. At least he was Swiss and therefore the citizen of a neutral country. It is unthinkable that the Americans would have allowed a native Italian, albeit with a Vatican passport, i.e. Nogara, to visit their country and, in particular, inform himself about various aspects of the economic and financial situation there! On the other hand, it is just possible that his mission was meant to be a cover for peace feelers to the US, and Nogara's grandson remains convinced that some attempt was made in that direction.[65]

Vatican humanitarian aid and the liberation of Italy, 1943–5

Like Benedict XV during the First World War, Pius XII assumed responsibility for programmes of humanitarian relief to civilian and military victims of the Second World War, and as the war dragged on, the Vatican's relief programmes for civilians, refugees and deportees, including Jews, and prisoners of war expanded enormously.[66] After the Italian peninsula became a theatre of war following the Allied invasion in the summer of 1943 the Vatican increasingly focussed its relief efforts on Italy. After the German take-over of the city of Rome in September 1943, the Jews, anti-Fascist activists and others who took refuge in the Vatican, in its extra-territorial dependencies and in other religious institutions all had to be fed. By March 1944, the Vatican was running forty convoys of lorries carrying flour from Tuscany to re-victual the capital; by May, it was thirty convoys per week, and some of them were bombed by Allied planes

---

[63] Ibid., 'pro-memoria per l'Eccellenza il Ministro', 4 Nov. 1942.
[64] Ibid., letter of Nogara to D'Ajeta, Capo Gabinetto del Ministro, 24 Nov. 1942.
[65] Conversation of the author with Ambassador Osio, Oct. 1996.
[66] See the *Actes et documents du Saint-Siège relatifs à la Seconde Guerre Mondiale* (12 vols., Vatican, 1968–74), vols. VI, VIII, IX and X.

by mistake.[67] As Vatican relief activity expanded, Nogara and the Special Administration sought to buy ex-Italian air-force planes and in September 1944, the Vatican asked permission from the Allied military government to send ships for the repatriation of refugees and the procurement of more foodstuffs for Rome.[68] By March 1945, Vatican agencies were providing 2.75 million meals from their soup kitchens every month.[69] In addition, Nogara exploited the Vatican's ownership of the Società Immobiliare Generale to transport food and other necessities to starving populations outside of the city.[70] The Vatican's own resources were, inevitably, heavily augmented by the offerings of American Catholics, which on more than one occasion, including before the collapse of the Fascist regime, were actually brought to Rome by no less a person than Archbishop Spellman of New York.[71]

Nogara's own position during the months of German occupation must have been a difficult and dangerous one because he was a member of the resistance movement in Rome, effectively the Vatican's 'representative' on the city's Committee of National Liberation.[72] And he and his wife narrowly escaped death when bombs fell outside their apartment in the Governor's Palace, during what turned out to be a German raid on the Vatican City.[73] While his daughter and son-in-law were taking a perilously active part in the Resistance in the north, Nogara was also doing his bit in Rome.[74] During the German occupation of the Eternal City, from September 1943 to June 1944, Nogara, 'Who had contacts and information which few other people could boast',[75] sought to save those at risk, like his colleagues Frigessi and Volpi, from falling into the hands of the Gestapo,[76] all this under the guise of being responsible for the Vatican's humanitarian relief operations in Rome.

In the wake of the collapse of Fascism in July 1943, and the subsequent flight of the Royal Government from Rome in September, the Holy See resumed a role in Italian affairs, and especially those of the city of Rome, which it had not held for nearly a century. Indeed, Chabod has compared that role to the one which the popes inherited on the fall of the Western

---

[67] NARA, RG 84, entry 2789, Records of the Political Adviser to Supreme Allied Commander Mediterranean, General Records, box 47, 1944/5: Myron Taylor to Office, 31 Mar. 1945.
[68] Ibid.
[69] Ibid., letters of 26 June and 17 July 1944.   [70] Gollin, *Worldly Goods*, pp. 462–3.
[71] Ibid.   [72] *Il Corriere della Sera*, 16 Nov. 1958, 'Morte di Bernardino Nogara'.
[73] B. Osio (ed.), *Antonietta Osio Nogara, 1904–1987: diari e lettere sparse* (privately published, 1989), pp. 103–7.
[74] Ibid., pp. 99–146.
[75] S. Romano, *Giuseppe Volpi: industria e finanza tra Giolitti e Mussolini* (Milan, 1979), p. 235.
[76] Ibid., pp. 235–6.

Roman Empire at the beginning of the fifth century.[77] The origins of that role can be traced back to Pius XII's diplomatic efforts to prevent the bombing of Rome by Allied aircraft,[78] and when those efforts failed, by his dramatic visit to the first area of the city to be bombed, the Borgo San Lorenzo near the marshalling yards in July 1943. While Mussolini was away negotiating with Hitler, it fell to Pius XII to visit the ruins and the dead, bringing moral and material aid to the injured, bereaved and homeless.[79] In this way, the pope effectively eclipsed the twenty-one-year 'cult of the Duce' even before Mussolini was voted out by the Fascist Grand Council and Fascism was overthrown. Henceforth, Pius XII would have no rivals in the development of his own cult, which reached its culmination in the film *Pastor Angelicus*.[80] The Roman pope thus became the absolutely dominant personality in the Eternal City, as *Defensor Urbis* and *Salvator Civitatis*, in the immediate post-war years. This was due in no small part to the way in which the Vatican, thanks to Nogara's efforts, had been able to finance its massive relief activities.

Ustasha gold and the Vatican Bank, 1945–6

Against the background of the renewed controversy over the wartime role of Pius XII – 'Hitler's Pope', as one of the authors in this debate has dubbed him – an aspect of the financial operations of the Vatican during and after the Second World War has become a major historiographical and legal issue.[81] In September 1999, a law suit was initiated in the US District Court, Northern District, California, by lawyer Jonathan Levy on behalf of Emil Alperin et al., including Ukrainians, Serbians, anti-Fascist Croatians, Jews and Roma, against the 'Vatican Bank' (Istituto per le Opere di Religione), the Franciscan Order and the Ustasha Organisation. The bank and co-defendants were accused of a

common scheme and course of conduct:
(1) to profit from, both directly and indirectly, the inhumane and genocidal system instituted by the Nazi and Ustasha ideology;
(2) to obtain, accept, conceal and profit from assets looted by the Ustasha Regime and deposited in, or liquidated through, the IOR, Defendant Banks, and Franciscan organisation during the ascendancy of the Ustasha regime and

---

[77] F. Chabod, *L'Italia contemporanea, 1918–1948* (Turin, 1961).
[78] *Vaticano e Stati Uniti*, ed. Di Nolfo, pp. 254–64.
[79] Logan, 'Pius XII: Romanità, Prophesy and Charisma'.   [80] Ibid., p. 238.
[81] The publication of Cornwell, *Hitler's Pope*, re-ignited the historiographical debate around the alleged silence of Pius XII in face of the Holocaust. Since the book was published, nearly another ten works on the subject have appeared, including R. R. Rychlak, *Hitler, the War and the Pope* (Huntington, Ind., 2000), which is a robust reply to Cornwell's main theses.

following the demise of the regime at the behest of former Nazi and Ustasha leaders through the offices of the Franciscan Order; and

(3) to retain and convert assets deposited in their institutions by the Ustasha and Franciscan Order.

Upon the demise of the Ustasha government in 1945, assets valued at between 50 and 180 millions of dollars were transferred from the capital Zagreb. The majority of these funds, estimated at more than 80 million dollars were transferred to Vatican City with the assistance of Roman Catholic clergy and in particular members of the Franciscan Order part of or sympathetic to the Ustasha.

Moreover, 'Many officials of the Ustasha government including the war criminals like Pavelic, were secretly housed by the Franciscan Order in the Vatican or Rome. The Ustasha treasury with the assistance of the IOR and Franciscans was used to resettle the Ustasha fugitives in Spain, Argentina, the United States and other sympathetic countries.'[82]

The basis of the suit is the claim that the Ustasha had stolen gold, currencies and other valuables from the victims of their atrocities – Ukrainians, anti-Fascist Croatians, Serbs, Jews and gypsies.[83] These claims are based on documentary evidence found in both the US National Archives and the British Public Records Office, from US and British secret service agents to the effect that before the collapse of the 'Independent Croatian State', the Ustasha leadership had smuggled gold and other valuables out of their capital, Zagreb. Some had been taken to Switzerland where it was deposited in banks, and the rest, it was alleged, had been taken directly to the Vatican. In October 1946, Emerson Bigelow, an OSS officer, wrote to an official of the US Treasury in these terms:

The following has been received from a reliable source in Italy. It is sent to you in the belief that it may be of interest. The Ustasha organisation [a Croatian fascist organisation, headed by Ante Pavelic] removed funds from Yugoslavia estimated to total 350 million Swiss francs. The funds were largely in the form of gold. Of the funds brought from the former Independent Croat State where Jews and Serbs were plundered to support the Ustasha organisation in exile an estimated 150 million Swiss Francs were impounded by the British authorities at the Austro-Swiss frontier; the balance of approximately 200 million Swiss Francs was originally held in the Vatican for safe-keeping. According to rumour, a considerable portion of this latter amount has been sent to Spain and Argentina through the Vatican's 'pipeline', but it is quite possible that this is merely a smokescreen to cover the fact that the treasure remains in its original repository.[84]

---

[82] From a copy of the indictment sent to the author via email by Mr Jonathan Levy, co-attorney in the suit, 3 Oct. 2000.
[83] Ibid.   [84] NARA, RG 226, entry 183, box 29, report from Bigelow of Oct. 1946.

There were other, rather more vague, claims in 1945 that the Vatican might be 'aiding and abetting Fascists to transfer their funds elsewhere' and the British Foreign Office warned that 'Moscow telegrams . . . make a number of allegations against the Vatican' in this respect.[85] But it is equally true that at the same the British Ministry of Economic Warfare argued that 'We have no evidence that the Vatican has played a role in transferring Fascist wealth from Europe.'[86] Since the end of the war, these claims have been aired again, most notably in 1991 by Aarons and Loftus in their book, *Ratlines*,[87] but there are a number of problems with the story. The first relates to the quantity and quality of the evidence offered in support, and amounts of gold and currencies alleged to have been transferred to Swiss banks/the Vatican Bank. 150 million dollars – or even 80 million – was an awful lot of money by the standards of the time; at present-day prices it would be worth the equivalent of 20 billion dollars. It is inconceivable that the Ustasha could have amassed such a treasury. Croatia, even the 'Greater Croatia' including largely Serb-inhabited Slavonia and Bosnia-Herzegovina, created by the Ustasha regime, was a fairly medium-sized, rural agrarian country. The Ukraine was less so, but the activities of the Croats, though they were there for only a few months as part of the 'crusade' against Bolshevism during Russia's war with the Soviet Union, seem unlikely to have harvested such amounts of assets. Only if the Ustasha had managed to loot the Yugoslav National Bank in Belgrade, and we have no evidence that they did so, would it have been possible to arrive at such a figure. This does not mean, of course, that smaller sums were not transferred to Swiss banks/the Vatican Bank.

Another problem is the fact that both Aarons and Loftus and the lawyers in the California court case speak of the 'Vatican Bank', i.e. the IOR, as if it possessed the funds and international contacts, and operated as a merchant as well as a clearing bank, which it does today, as has been revealed by the literature on the Calvi/Banco Ambrosiano and Sindona scandals.[88] The IOR, which had been founded by a chirograph of Pius XII of 27 June 1942 'to provide for the custody and administration of capital destined for religious works' in a difficult time of total war,[89] was essentially a re-organisation of the former Amministrazione

[85] PRO, FO, 371/50078, Financial Activities of the Vatican, Crump, Ministry of Economic Warfare to Hebblethwaite, 10 Apr. 1945.

[86] Ibid.

[87] M. Aarons and J. Loftus, *Ratlines: How the Vatican's Nazi Networks Betrayed Western Intelligence to the Soviets* (London, 1991), ch. 5.

[88] See, for example, Raw, *The Moneychangers*, especially ch. 15.

[89] *Acta Apostolicae Sedis*, 8 (1942), Chirographus, p. 1.

per le Opere di Religione referred to earlier (see pp. 65–7). According to the chirograph, which conferred on the IOR the status of a legal entity, the purpose of the re-organisation was to give it 'a set of regulations more befitting to the needs of the time and to make the responsibilities of the aforementioned administration appear even more separate and distinct from those of the Holy See'.[90] This, and the fact that same chirograph downgraded the body administering the IOR from a cardinalatial to a prelatial one, suggests that the ultimate purpose was to give the IOR as much independence in financial dealings as possible, while at the same time protecting the Holy See from any unpleasant publicity that might be generated by such transactions, especially in the delicate and difficult wartime conditions. But the IOR was still largely underdeveloped during and immediately after the Second World War, and it was the other Vatican financial agencies like the ABSS and, more importantly, the Special Administration under the management of Nogara, which possessed the funds and international contacts (see above Chapters 6 and 7). The ABSS was recognised after the Second World War by the International Monetary Fund as a central bank, not the IOR.[91] As late as May 1960, Benny Lai, one of the most reliable journalistic observers of Vatican affairs, wrote: 'No, the IOR is not a bank, even though all, or nearly all, banking transactions are carried out there. It is a financial institution.'[92] So it seems unlikely that the IOR, the 'Vatican Bank', was really involved in the Ustasha gold transactions. But whichever Vatican agency might have been involved in these putative transactions, it has to be said that the further allegation that the Vatican used the gold from the Ustasha to finance the 'ratlines', that is the escape route for Ustasha leaders, including Ante Pavelic, and other war criminals, to South America, is, however, perfectly plausible.[93] The Vatican's obsession with the threat of Communism in Italy, and its fears for the consequences for the Church in those eastern and central European countries liberated and occupied by the Red Army at the end of the Second World War, guaranteed on which side it would end up at the beginning of the Cold War. Though Pius XII may not have been exactly the 'chaplain of NATO', as some described him,[94] the Vatican's behaviour in 1948, when Italy seemed to face a real threat of an electoral victory of the Marxist Left, demonstrates the lengths which it was prepared to go to fight Communism: we know, for example, that at that time Pius XII received money from Ireland and other countries to

---

[90] Ibid., p. 2.
[91] M. Walsh, *Vatican City State* (Oxford, 1983), p. xxxii where he says: 'APSA is the Vatican's central bank as far as international financial institutions are concerned.'
[92] Lai, *Vaticano aperto*, p. 176.   [93] Aarons and Loftus, *Ratlines*, pp. 56–7.
[94] Hebblethwaite, 'Pope Pius XII: Chaplain of the Atlantic Alliance?', p. 75.

give to the Christian Democrats' fighting fund, and that Msgr Montini, Under-Secretary of State in the Vatican, established a 'slush fund' account in the IOR using the receipts from the sales of US Army surplus.[95] The victory of Tito and the Communist partisans in Yugoslavia was a terrible blow to the Vatican. Apart from bringing the iron curtain to the eastern borders of Italy, it meant the destruction of the Croatian Independent State. Pius XII's attitude to that state had been ambivalent to say the least. Though he refused to recognise it officially, and his representative in Zagreb, Fr. Marcone, did not even have the status of an apostolic delegate, there can be no doubt that the Vatican shared the hopes of the Catholic clergy in Croatia, led by Archbishop Stepinac of Zagreb, that Pavelic's Ustasha regime marked a new era of Catholic freedom from Serbian, Orthodox control from Belgrade.[96] As the bestiality of Ustasha treatment of Serbs, gypsies and Jews became apparent – even the German Nazis were horrified by the barbarism of the Ustasha who included Franciscan priests in their number – there was silence from the Vatican; indeed, this silence on the part of Pius XII is even less explicable than his alleged silence over the Holocaust, because Stepinac *did* protest at some atrocities.[97] Inevitably, the new Communist authorities in Croatia – Tito was himself Croatian – were determined to put Stepinac and other clergy on trial – some of the worst collaborationist clergy like Bishop Rosman of Lubliana escaped to Austria.[98] We know that US and British Intelligence made use not only of Ustasha but also Nazi war criminals as the Cold War intensified,[99] and there is evidence that Pavelic's concealment in the Illyrian College in Rome was known to the Allied authorities but that they did nothing. According to the Slaney Report: 'Pavelic hid in Rome in various locations from 1946 until his flight to Argentina in November 1948 without any decisive action by the US or British authorities to apprehend him or to make him available for a war crimes trial.'[100] Though the Slaney Report further claims that 'There is no evidence in US archives that the Vatican leadership knew or gave any support to the Ustasha activities outside its walls, but given the location

---

[95] D. Keogh, 'Ireland, the Vatican and the Cold War: The Case of Italy', *Historical Journal*, 34 (1991), pp. 931–52.

[96] S. Alexander, *Church and State in Yugoslavia since 1945* (Cambridge, 1979), p. 19.

[97] Falconi, *The Popes in the Twentieth Century*, p. 260.

[98] Alexander, *Church and State in Yugoslavia*, ch. 3; for an account of Vatican diplomacy towards Tito's post-war Yugoslav regime, see C. Gallagher, 'The United States and the Vatican in Yugoslavia, 1945–1950', in D. Kirby (ed.), *Religion and the Cold War* (London, 2003), pp. 118–45.

[99] S. E. Eizenstat and W. Z. Slany, *Supplement to Preliminary Study on US and Allied Efforts to Recover and Restore Gold and Other Assets Stolen or Hidden during World War II* (Washington, DC, 1998), p. 9.

[100] Ibid., p. 10.

of the College [Croatian] troubling questions remain',[101] the affair was almost certainly known about inside the Vatican, and it may be that the Secretariat of State calculated that Pavelic and his cronies might come in handy one day in helping to overthrow the Tito regime. So the Vatican had the motive for giving financial and other material help to those passing down the 'ratline'. It also had the means to do so: it would have been perfectly possible to channel funds to escaped war criminals in South America from the Vatican's Swiss bank accounts, or indeed any other bank accounts in Switzerland in which the Ustasha had deposited money, through the branches of Sudameris. Again all this would have been possible without the involvement of the 'Vatican Bank' as such. But we shall not know the truth until, as the State Department report into the fate of Holocaust assets states, the Vatican opens up its archives for the post-war period, which is highly unlikely in the foreseeable future.

Vatican finances in the early Cold War period

The financial activities of the Vatican became a matter of great significance for Italian politics in this period, playing an important role in the propaganda battles between the two sides of the Cold War divide. As the Cold War intensified from early 1947 onwards, Italy found herself on the 'front line' in two senses. On the one hand, the southern end of Churchill's 'iron curtain', Trieste, was on Italy's re-drawn frontier with Yugoslavia. It was still in Italian hands, but only just, and it continued to be disputed with Tito's new Communist regime until 1954. Even more significantly, it could be said that the 'front line' in the Cold War actually passed through Italy itself and that the war was 'fought' on Italian territory because Italy possessed the second largest Communist Party in the West. Allied in a Popular Front with the still strongly Marxian Italian Socialist Party, it presented a formidable challenge in the crucial 1948 general elections. Pope Pius XII and the Italian Church hierarchy viewed this situation in apocalyptic terms, especially in 1948. The Catholic Action Movement, with its massive presence in most areas of Italian civil society, was summoned to battle. A huge propaganda effort was launched in 1948 and, in the longer term, popular devotions and the papal cult of the personality were employed against the 'enemy', along with the unleashing by the Holy Office in 1949 of the Church's ultimate weapon – excommunication of all those involved in any way with the Left.[102]

---

[101] Ibid.
[102] For accounts of the impact of the Cold War on Italy, see J. F. Pollard, 'The Vatican, Italy and the Cold War', in D. Kirby (ed.), *Religion and the Cold War* (London, 2003), pp. 103–18.

As well as the threat of Communism, at the end of the Second World War, Italy, in common with other European countries, faced serious economic and social problems indeed, the problem of economic reconstruction itself. But the most pressing and immediate problem in 1945 was relieving the human misery caused by destitution and hunger. Put in social historians' terms this meant that 'the years from 1945 and 1946 were the hardest . . . two years of hunger . . . as seen not only from the alarming drop in average calorie intake . . . but also in the fall in the consumption of individual products'.[103] In response, the charitable activities of the Vatican had grown enormously by the war's end. After the liberation of Rome in June 1944 there was an expansion and intensification of a variety of charitable/relief activities on the part of the Vatican. According to the British minister to the Holy See, D'Arcy Osborne, 'As Bishop of Rome, His Holiness was constantly preoccupied with the food situation of the city.'[104] By the end of the year, foodstuffs and medicines were being sent by the Vatican to France, Belgium and Greece, as well as Italy.[105] Much of the money for this relief work came from America, and often directly from Catholic sources there – 5 million dollars in 1944 alone – and the British minister to the Holy See wondered whether it might not have had something to do with Roosevelt's anxiety to win Catholic/Italian immigrant votes for his re-election campaign.[106] But the rest of the money came from the Vatican's own funds and according to the minister, 'The wide variety of expenditure on charitable objectives was a severe strain on papal resources, already greatly reduced by the war and by the difficulties of communication.'[107] These were sorts of financial problems that had confronted Benedict XV at the end of the First World War, though probably on a much larger scale. A further problem was the depreciation of the lira; in July 1945, the Vatican complained that inflation, and the large amounts of Italian lire it was consequently forced to hold, was hampering its welfare and religious activities.[108]

The Pontifical Relief Organisation – Pontificia Opera d'Assistenza – was founded in 1944, and now played the major role in distributing papal charity.[109] By 1945, throughout Italy it was providing help to 90,000 refugees and displaced persons; it distributed two and a half meals a

[103] Zamagni, *The Economic History of Italy*, p. 323.
[104] PRO, FO, 371/50084, Annual Report of the Minister to the Holy See, 1944, p. 12.
[105] Ibid., p. 15.   [106] Ibid., p. 14.   [107] Ibid.
[108] Ibid., 371/50078, Financial Activities of the Vatican, letter to Osborne from AFHQ, 18 July 1945.
[109] For an assessment of the role of the POA, see A. Giovagnoli, 'La Pontifica Commissione d'Assistenza e gli aiuti americani (1945–1948)', *Storia Contemporanea*, 9 (1978), pp. 1081–111.

month and clothing to a value of quarter of a million pounds.[110] In addition, in the city of Rome, it was providing meals for thousands of factory and office workers, as well as waifs and strays, and providing relief and assistance to soldiers and sailors returning to Italy and to the inmates of prisons, many of them Fascist 'political prisoners'.[111] In 1948, the activities of the Pontificia Opera d'Assistenza (POA) became even more extensive; for example, the Vatican was sending 1 million children to the seaside every summer and assisting another 100,000 persons in other ways, and the British minister made the point that 'The political effects of this charitable activity are not likely to be negligible.'[112]

While the very obvious and widespread charitable activities of the Vatican were indeed a powerful electoral card in the hands of the Church-sponsored Christian Democratic Party and its allies in the 1948 elections, they were not enough. Vatican money was also needed by the opponents of the Italian Left for directly political purposes. As the electoral campaign hotted up in early 1948 the Christian Democrats (DC) sought funding from any source and received it, in particular from the USA and Ireland (see above, p. 196). The Vatican was especially well organised on this occasion because it believed it was facing a titanic, cosmic struggle between life and death, Christ and Anti-Christ for the soul of Italy.[113] It mobilised the vast panoply of Catholic institutions distributed through 24,000 parishes in the Italian peninsula. Catholic Action was the key to this effort. With over two and a half million members in mid-1943 organised into youth, adult, male, female, student, graduate groups, and groups for very profession and occupation, plus sporting, cinematic and other leisure groups, it was a formidable national organisation, and its most potent outreach arm was the Civic Committees who directly organised the clarion call to Italian Catholics to vote.[114] But all this required financing. The Vatican provided much from its own financial resources, and topped this up with the income both from abroad and from appeals to the great and good in Italian society.[115] On the eve of the 1948 elections, Virgilio Scatolini, a Vatican observer who had already earned a lot of money during the war by supplying the American OSS with false information called 'Vessel', about the Vatican's diplomatic relations with a number of states, produced another forgery, *Documenti della Diplomazia Vaticana*, which claimed that by February 1948, the Jesuit Order had already collected

[110] PRO, FO, 371/60803, Annual Report of the Legation to the Holy See, 1945, p. 8.
[111] Ibid., p. 9.
[112] Ibid., 371/79874, Annual Report of the Legation to the Holy See 1948, p. 10.
[113] Pollard, 'The Vatican, Italy and the Cold War', pp. 108–9.
[114] P. Scoppola, *La proposta politica di De Gasperi* (Bologna, 1977), p. 46.
[115] S. Magister, *La politica vaticana e l'Italia, 1943–1978* (Rome, 1979), p. 105.

1 million dollars, mainly from America, to fund the Catholic Electoral Commission, a body specifically set up by the Vatican to support the DC electoral campaign.[116] He also claimed that the Vatican had managed to raise a large amount of cash by then, 853 million lire, from 'big Catholic industrialists, friends of Catholics', with a final target of 1 milliard lire.[117] While these claims are almost certainly false, there can be no doubt that Nogara, and all the other leading Vatican financial figures, would have played their part in the fundraising for the Catholic party in 1948.

But if the Vatican's own innate financial strength, combined with its ability to fundraise among its friends and allies, was a major advantage in the battle with the Communist enemy in 1948, its financial activities could also be a potential liability in the political propaganda war at that time. Both the Soviet press and the Italian Communist Party newspaper *L'Unità* seized on the Vatican's wealth, the fact that it was both a large share-holder in capitalist enterprises and large owner of landed property to argue that it was so enmeshed in the net of capitalism that it 'could not take a line independent of the capitalist powers'.[118] In the course of its campaign to establish a clear identity for the Vatican as 'the organ of the militant imperialist reaction', the Soviet publication *The Literary Gazette* displayed an accurate knowledge of the sources of the Vatican's income claiming that it controlled thirty joint stock companies in Italy worth a total of 300 billion lire.[119] Whether, as it also claimed, the Vatican had big interests in 'Brazilian rubber, Bolivian tin, American ores, French textiles, the Swiss electrical industry and gaming houses in Biarritz and Vichy' and a share-holding in Sinclair Oil is less certain, but by no means unlikely; that it was 'one of the greatest financial trusts in the world' was absolutely true by 1948, thanks to Nogara.[120]

This kind of propaganda was easy to rebut, but two further lines of financial smear-campaigning were potentially more damaging. In 1948, the Soviet press re-hashed claims that the Vatican had been instrumental in transferring Fascist property out of Italy to Latin America.[121] The point of reference was, of course, Sudameris, and all this fitted together nicely with claims about the Vatican's financial holdings in Latin America to

---

[116] Anon, *Documenti della Diplomazia Vaticana: il Vaticano e la democrazia italiana* (Lugano, 1948), pp. 536–8; a report for the Czech Press Agency, to be found in ACMFA, TO-9: 94383, of 24 Apr. 1948, shows that the *Documenti* was a forgery.

[117] Ibid., p. 548.

[118] PRO, FO, 371/73420, Chancery of the British Legation to the Holy See to Bevin, 29 Jan. 1948.

[119] Ibid., British Embassy in Moscow to Western Department, 25 Mar. 1948.

[120] Ibid.

[121] Ibid., 371/50060, Pravda Articles, Osborne to FO, 5 Feb. 1945, and 371/ 50073 Vatican and the Crimea Conference, Osborne to the FO, 14 Feb. 1945.

support the Soviet argument that the Vatican was in close cahoots with 'Fascist' regimes both in that continent and the Iberian peninsula.[122] An even more potentially dangerous propaganda coup lay at hand for the Communists in 1948, the Cippico affair. In November 1947, for the first time since the robbery in the *buco nero* of 1900, the Vatican was faced by a real financial scandal. Msgr Cippico, an official of the ABSS, was found to have defrauded the same highly placed Italian friends on whose behalf he had arranged illicit currency dealings through the Vatican Bank in order to get around Italian restrictions. Naturally, *L'Unità* and *L'Avanti!*, the fellow-travelling daily of the Italian Socialist Party, had a field day about this, and sought to make more embarrassing propaganda out of the story against the Vatican and the DC on the eve of the crucial April elections; only the threat of reviving the scandal surrounding the so-called 'Tesoro di Dongo', valuables allegedly looted by the Communists from Mussolini's possession after they had executed him in the village of that name in April 1945, succeeded in averting this danger.[123]

Vatican finances in the age of Catholic 'triumphalism'

The Christian Democrats and their allies won the 1948 general elections, and a new era of Catholic power, even 'omnipotence', was inaugurated in Italy. Against this background, two new key figures had emerged who came increasingly to dominate the finances of the Vatican for the rest of the reign of Pius XII: the first was the layman Massimo Spada and the second was Cardinal Nicola Canali.[124] Spada began his career with the Vatican in the early 1930s as an assistant in the ABSS.[125] His rise was slow but steady and after 1945 he worked as 'Administrative Secretary' in the IOR, a rather modest title for what was in fact the leading lay position in the Vatican bank,[126] and his name appeared on the boards of several Italian companies, a sure sign of his importance there as a representative of Vatican finance. Among those companies where the Banco di Roma, Italcimenti of Bergamo, Italy's largest cement-maker, Assicurazioni Generali and three companies which operated within the orbit of the IRI, the state holding company – Mediobanca, the powerful Italian merchant bank,

---

[122] Ibid., 371/73420, Chancery of British Legation to the Holy See to Bevin, 29 Jan. 1948.
[123] Ibid.
[124] Another important ecclesiastical figure in post-war Vatican finances was Msgr Alberto di Jorio. He was secretary of the cardinalatial commission of the IOR and secretary of the conclave of 1958, at the end of which he was created cardinal by the newly elected pope John XXIII. By 1961, even before the death of Canali, he had become a powerful force in the Special Administration as well as the IOR: see Lai, *Vaticano aperto*, p. 244.
[125] See *Annuario Pontificio*, 1935, p. 756.   [126] Ibid., 1948, p. 921.

Finelettrica and Finmeccanica.[127] It was Spada who master-minded the passage of the majority share-holding of the Banca Cattolica to the IOR: bishops of the Veneto had feared that it might otherwise pass into non-Catholic hands.[128]

It was also under the direction of Spada, assisted by Nogara, that the march of Vatican finance into the Italian banking world continued. Grilli has identified about seventy-nine Italian banks in the period down to the 1960s in which there were varying degrees of Catholic share-holding: eight, including, naturally enough, the Banco di Spirito Santo, the Banco Ambrosiano of Milan and the Banca Cattolica del Veneta, were under total Catholic control.[129] Three were under partial control, including Mediobanca – the rest of the share-holding of this institution was largely held by the IRI.[130] A further twelve had some Catholic presence on their boards of directors, including the Banca Nazionale dell'Agricultura, which, as its name suggests, had a particular interest in agricultural investments.[131] Finally, another sixty-two banks possessed some connections with Catholic/Vatican finance, including the Banca d'America e d'Italia,[132] which, it has been recently alleged, is partly owned by a share-holding of the Jesuit Order.[133] All in all, by 1950, Vatican finance controlled a very substantial slice of the private banking sector in Italy, as well as being co-share-holders in a number of major banks ultimately controlled by the IRI.

Another significant characteristic of the activities of Vatican finance in the post-war period was the move, spearheaded by Spada and Nogara into the agricultural/food processing sectors of the Italian economy. Nogara became chairman of the Società Industriale Casalese with large estates at Casale Cremasco in Lombardy, and possessed share-holdings in another four major companies in the agricultural sector.[134] All this would make sense in the context of the importance which the Christian Democratic Party gave to its rural/agrarian constituency and its close relationship with Catholic peasant-farming associations and the incestuous relationship between both and the semi-official agricultural co-operative, Federconsorzi.[135]

---

[127] Grilli, *La finanza vaticana*, p. 91.

[128] G. De Rosa, *Una banca cattolica fra cooperazione e capitalismo: La Banca Cattolica del Veneto* (Bari and Rome, 1991), p. 222. Ironically, in 1971, Archbishop Paul Marcinkus, by then president of the IOR, secretly sold the bank to Roberto Calvi of the Ambrosiano over the heads of the Veneto bishops: see Raw, *The Moneychangers*, p. 70.

[129] Grilli, *La finanza vaticana*, p. 102.   [130] Ibid.   [131] Ibid.   [132] Ibid.

[133] Same source as n. 82.   [134] Grilli, *La finanza vaticana*, p. 132.

[135] M. Manuzi, 'Politics and the Italian State Industrial Sector, 1933–1980 – With Two Case Studies' (PhD thesis, Anglia Polytechnic University, 1999), pp. 34–5.

The second major new figure in the Vatican financial world, Canali, whose ascent to power had been interrupted in 1914 by the election of Benedict XV, who had been hostile to Canali's patron, Cardinal Merry Del Val, began to recover lost ground after Benedict's death and the election of Pius XI. Despite his patron's own death in 1930, he prospered in the new pontificate, becoming Penitenziere Maggiore in 1935 and a cardinal. The death of Pius XI and the election of his successor brought even greater power and influence. It is likely that he was one of the cardinals who investigated Nogara's stewardship in 1939. Whatever the truth of the matter, the new reign saw him enter the direction of both the ABSS and the IOR, and thanks to the death of the Secretary of State, Cardinal Maglione, who was not replaced: 'in 1944 he was put in charge of the financial aspects of the Church's administration which had been handled by the Secretary of State himself, and thus [he was] virtually the Vatican's Minister of Finances'.[136] By 1952, he had got his hands on the Special Administration itself. Like his predecessor, Mocenni, he had also become the boss of the Vatican City at Maglione's death. Given the fact that this was now a state, with its own not inconsiderable sources of revenue it was a powerful position and according to Lai, he ruled the State of the Vatican City with an iron fist.[137] So, in the later years of Pius XII's reign, along with Count Enrico Galeazzi, Prince Carlo Pacelli and cardinals Micara, Pizzardo and Ottaviani, Canali become the ruling force in the Vatican. His power base was consolidated by the fact that he also had close connections with Cardinal Spellman, the American intimate of Pius XII, with whom he allied in his ultimately unsuccessful effort to bring the Sovereign Military Order of the Knights of St John of Jerusalem, Rhodes and Malta under his control.[138]

It was therefore fitting that in 1948, Bernardino Nogara, together with Cardinal Canali, laid the foundation stones of the two new palaces (I Propilei) to be built in Piazza Pius XII, an extension of St Peter's Square, immediately opposite the Basilica, which, standing on either side of the triumphal Via della Conciliazione, meant the completion of the project of rebuilding the Borgo and opening up the Vatican to the Tiber. By now, much of the Borgo had been 'reclaimed' by the Vatican, that is the latter had purchased large tracts of property and redevelopment sites on which it built offices for more Roman congregations and other agencies, and for the headquarters of Azione Cattolica Italiana (the Italian Catholic Action organisation). General Cadorna's occupation of the Leonine City in September 1870 had thus been effectively reversed. By supplying the

[136] H. J. A. Sire, *The Knights of Malta* (New Haven, Conn., 1994), pp. 258–9.
[137] Lai, *Vaticano aperto*, p. 284.   [138] Sire, *The Knights of Malta*, p. 260.

means to finance these projects, Nogara contributed to the process of providing the necessary location for those carefully choreographed displays of papal supremacy which characterised the post-war years of the reign of Pius XII and outdid the 'oceanic' gatherings produced by Mussolini during the Fascist era. The ultimate example of this, the high point of Catholic 'triumphalism', took place in Holy Year, 1950, when Pius XII promulgated the dogma of the Assumption of the Blessed Virgin Mary into Heaven. According to Hebblethwaite: 'The Church in 1950 had a papal spectacular, the first in the era of the mass media . . . It dramatised the unity of the Church after the last and most terrible "European civil war" . . . it was a marvellous display of the Church triumphant.'[139] It also marked the apogee of the modern papacy; the advent of John XXIII to the papal throne in 1958 and the Second Council of the Vatican, 1962–5, would change at least much of the appearance of the papacy, if not ultimately its centralised control over the world-wide Church.

[139] P. Hebblethwaite, *Paul VI: The First Modern Pope* (New York, 1993), pp. 228–9.

10 Conclusion: money and the rise of the modern papacy

Coming to terms with capitalism

Much of the history of the development of the financial institutions of the Vatican in this period is the story of the papacy coming to terms with capitalism, and as is evident in Chapters 2, 3 and 4 it was quite slow to do so. It was not simply that the increasing success of Peter's Pence collections seemed to make a sophisticated investment policy unnecessary in the early period, the astute realisation of the advantages of relying upon the boundless generosity of the faithful, who, the more than the pope was attacked and reviled, the more he took up a strong stand against his enemies, the more they were willing to give, rather than on the uncertainties of markets. There were also some fundamental theological/ideological reasons why the papacy was slow to accept the benefits of joining in capitalist speculation in financial markets. The theological hang-over from the Middle Ages, the biblical prohibition against 'usury', lending money at interest, was one obvious problem. As has been seen in Chapter 2, it was not until the 1830s that various Roman congregations relaxed this prohibition, already a dead letter in most Protestant countries, and some Catholic ones too, and announced that those who engaged in it should not, in the typically periphrastic style of the Roman curia, 'be unduly vexed' because of their actions, a strange way, admittedly, of signalling a new course in banking ethics.[1] Lending money to governments, by investment in loan stock, which began almost immediately after the fall of Rome in 1870, probably seemed more morally acceptable inasmuch as, by contributing to the financing of the activities of the state, it was helping to promote the 'common good'. It also seemed safer to the Vatican's financial managers, and in the long term, the practice contributed to a further loosening up of attitudes towards money-lending at interest. The experience which gradually developed in Leo XIII's reign of lending to the impoverished sections of the Roman aristocracy, and then to

---

[1] *New Catholic Encyclopedia*, XIV, pp. 345–4.

those who were themselves engaged in speculation, i.e. the Rome building boom, also assisted this process of cultural change. The American Church's experience of financial management, in which income from landed property was almost wholly absent, the collections of the faithful were the source of the overwhelming majority of revenues and investment of surpluses in the financial markets was an established and widespread practice, may also have had some influence on Roman practices. Eventually all these experiences bore fruit in the inclusion of a canon in the text of the Code of Canon Law which emerged from the codification process in 1917, permitting those ecclesiastics responsible for the Church's financial affairs at a parochial and diocesan level to invest its wealth in interest-bearing activities, albeit at modest rates:

When a fungible is given to another in such wise that it becomes his and is later to be returned only *in kind*, no profit may be derived by reason of the contract itself; but in such a loan it is not *per se* unlawful to make an agreement for the legal rate of interest (unless it is evident that the legal rate is exorbitant), or even for a higher rate, provided that there be a just and proportionate reason.[2]

Another more important factor in inhibiting the Vatican from embracing capitalism was its association with the Jews, Protestants and Liberals. The first was an important consideration in the nineteenth and early twentieth centuries, when the Jesuit journal *La Civiltà Cattolica* was forever denouncing the wickedness of the Jews, and their tendency to exploit good Christians economically through their allegedly monopolistic control of finance capital:

It is the giant octopus [Jewry] that with its oversized tentacles envelopes everything. It has its stomach in the banks . . . and its suction cups everywhere: in contracts and monopolies . . . in postal services and telegraph companies, in shipping, and in the railroads, in town treasuries and state finance. It represents the kingdom of capital . . . the aristocracy of gold . . . It reigns unopposed.[3]

This perception of the economic role of the Jews was almost certainly common-place in the Roman curia; the statement was probably not entirely unaffected by a certain envy of the Rothschilds who, as we have seen, helped keep the listing, leaking bark of St Peter afloat for decades, and there is even the possibility that the suspicion that finance capitalism was ultimately run by the Jews persisted down to the pontificate of Pius XI and may have been the unseen motive for the coruscating criticisms of it in *Caritate Christi Compulsit* and *Non Impendet*.

[2] T. L. Bouscaren and A. C. Ellis, *Canon Law: A Text and Commentary* (Milwaukee, 1957), p. 825.
[3] As quoted in Kertzer, *The Popes against the Jews*, p. 145.

Roman ecclesiastical anti-Protestantism was as virulent as anti-Judaism and thus may have been a serious factor in the Vatican's early refusal to accept the possibilities of capitalist economics, despite the appeals of Langrand-Dumonceau and other Catholic financiers that it was possible to construct a Catholic alternative (see Chapter 2, pp. 37–8). But the most important ideological factor was the rejection of the liberal capitalist bourgeoisie and all their works. They had effectively destroyed the privileged, entrenched role of the Church in the Ancien Regime after 1789 so many European countries (and Latin American ones as well) and especially in Italy. They had carried through a process of the separation of Church and State and the secularisation of society in those same countries. They had almost entirely confiscated the landed property of the Church and, finally, they had destroyed the temporal power of the popes by absorbing the Papal States into the new Italian Kingdom between 1859 and 1870. It was, therefore, in these circumstances unrealistic to expect the papacy to compromise its principles and position by adapting the economic strategies of the accursed bourgeoisie. Mazzonis has argued that Pius IX and Antonelli fully grasped the seriousness of the threat posed by the rise of the capitalist bourgeoisie but decided to meet the challenge by a slow adaptation to circumstances, including acceptance of the loss of their feudal economic and social base, rather than by a full frontal encounter because the Church was too weak to insert itself into the structures of bourgeois capitalism at this point in its history.[4] Leaving aside the rather heavy dose of Marxist economic determinism in his theories, there is probably more than a shred of truth in this explanation.

An even more compelling explanation of the papacy's slowness to accept capitalism is circumstantial, quite simply the fact of the geographical location of the papacy in Italy, in other words in the economically peripheral zone of southern, Mediterranean Europe. Had the papacy been based in north-western Europe – in Belgium, the first Continental country to industrialise or in northern France, Alsace-Lorraine or the Lille-Roubaix basin, or in the Rhineland, Silesia or Saar areas – then its leaders would have been surrounded by a vital, vibrant Catholic bourgeoisie engaged not only in capitalistic financial and commercial activities, but in manufacturing as well. Contrary to the Weber thesis in *The Protestant Ethic and the Spirit of Capitalism*, these groups were emphatically *not* inhibited by the alleged 'cultural backwardness' of Catholicism.[5] So had the papacy been located in any of these places, it would have more quickly

---

[4] Mazzonis, 'Pio IX, il tramonto del potere temporale', pp. 284–5.
[5] M. Weber, *The Protestant Ethic and the Spirit of Capitalism* (2nd edn, London, 1976).

and more easily taken up the habits of capitalist financing. But it was not.

Even worse, the papacy was not even based in that part of Italy, the north-west, which contained the points of the 'industrial triangle', the cities of Milan, Turin and Genoa, around which large-scale Italian industrialisation would eventually develop in the 1880s and 1890s, and which were already centres of commercial and other capitalist activities at Unification. Judging by the unwillingness of Pius X to invest in capitalist business, especially manufacturing, the small town, rural/agrarian milieu of north-eastern Italy – the Veneto – from whence he came, would not have been a propitious environment for the development of a capitalist 'sense' on the part of Vatican financial managers. But the papacy was, of course, based in Rome, the central/southern part of the Italian peninsula, where it was almost as remote as it could possibly be – unless it had been located in Calabria or Sicily – from the invigorating atmosphere of business and manufacture. There, in Rome, it learnt its 'business' skills from a still partly landed aristocracy with an antiquated and half-developed capitalist sense which largely explains the Vatican's long, painful relationship with the Banco di Roma.

The history of that relationship not only exemplifies the backwardness of the economic and cultural milieu in which Vatican finance was operated, it also, on the other hand, demonstrates the remarkable change which nevertheless took place in broader terms in its financial structures and practices in this period. The relationship is undoubtedly one of the most extraordinary features of Vatican finances in the period 1880 to 1933, given the reliance on and vulnerability to the fortunes of the Banco di Roma. It does seem truly amazing that a state of affairs in which the Vatican faced, and indeed on more than one occasion, actually suffered, massive capital losses should have been allowed to continue for so long: over fifty years. Many factors would help to explain this reality.

In the first place, the Banco di Roma was born into and operated inside a peculiarly aristocratic, Catholic and Roman milieu within which a succession of popes felt comfortable and secure. The founders, and many of their successors in the management of the bank over the years, were lay members of the Papal Court – like the Princes Bandinini Giustiniani and Buoncompagni Ludovisi, and Counts Santucci and Soderini and the Marquis Theodoli – and all were good Catholics, good papal courtiers and men of trust. Even Ernesto Pacelli, who was not really a member of the black aristocracy, but who at least came from a family with a long history of service to the papacy, was a discreet, useful and faithful servant of the popes. Another factor was undoubtedly the lack of financial knowledge of the clerics responsible for the Vatican's finances in those times. On the whole, the early popes – Pius IX through to Benedict XV – were old-fashioned, cautious and often uninformed in their attitudes to financial affairs. Pius IX does not seem to have shown very much interest in these matters, leaving them entirely to Antonelli, who was himself very cautious and careful in his administration of the Vatican's finances. Leo XIII was avaricious, old-fashioned, naïve and very trusting of Pacelli, whereas Folchi was sensible and prudent, though he occasionally moved out of the usual Roman *giro d'affari*. Mocenni and Marzolini were certainly not better than Folchi, possibly in some ways worse. Benedict, though not very interventionist, seems to have been a little more canny than his predecessors about the political implications of certain financial operations, e.g. the SER affair (see Chapter 5, pp. 119–21).

The backward state of the Roman and Italian economies was another crucial determining factor in the survival of the Vatican–Banco di Roma link until the early 1900s. This situation allowed little scope for financial innovation and speculation. It therefore seemed safer to stick to a known, trusted and friendly banking institution, even if that friendly institution suffered a series of serious cash-flow crises throughout the life of the relationship. And whenever a crisis arose, there was so much at stake for the Vatican, not only its share-holding but also its cash deposits with the bank. In these circumstances it seemed safer not to pull the plug on the Roma, but to suffer a short-term cash loss in return for the hope of future security. Only Benedict was prepared to break this cycle, and then only in a rather half-hearted, almost accidental, way. And, of course, there was the fear of a loss of prestige on the part of the pope, other Catholic financial institutions and the Church in Italy generally. There was also, undoubtedly, a fear of accusations of betrayal on the part of Catholics who suffered, not to mention the gleeful diatribes of anti-clerical critics.

The election of Pius XI was to be the turning point not only in the Vatican's relationship with the Banco di Roma, but in broader terms the history of the papacy's financial institutions. Coming from a Lombard business/manufacturing family – as well as his father being a mill manager, his brother and nephews were also businessmen – and having lived in and been archbishop of Milan, Italy's greatest commercial centre, Papa Ratti was much better informed on business matters than any of his predecessors. He clearly understood something about financial markets, and his major financial decision, to appoint Nogara, was very sound, not to say, brilliant, for it was Nogara who finally rescued the Vatican from the clutches of the Banco di Roma and its hangers-on. The rather narrow and conservative culture of the Roman curia had encouraged a situation in which ecclesiastical managers relied upon laymen to invest on their behalf. It was their business, after all, was it not? Certainly, both Pacelli and Nogara would have seen through Calvi and Sindona, whereas Archbishop Marcinkus and Papa Montini did not. But compared with Pacelli, Nogara had a much wider and greater array of experience and expertise-experience in mining and manufacturing companies, in Turkey, in international markets and dealings, in property, gold and shares, and through the Banca Commerciale, a very much wider, world-wide stage on which to operate. In part that was simply because he was a *northern* Italian. Another fundamental difference between them was that Pacelli was a bank president who advised the pope on financial matters and thus benefited his bank in the process, whereas Nogara was a completely independent, in-house financial manager. He does not seem to have put much Vatican business the way of the bank with which he had the closest links, the Banca Commerciale, and he worked hard to keep a balanced portfolio of investments for the Vatican. Nogara was obviously not as politically powerful as Pacelli, but clearly had access to much information and some influence in Rome during the Second World War. We have no evidence of Pius XII's involvement in the financial management of the Vatican, other than the thoroughly unreliable story in *La Popessa* (see Chapter 8, p. 181). It seems likely, however, that once Nogara was cleared of incompetence in 1939, Pius left financial matters to him, and to others like Galeazzi, the Pacelli nephews and later Cardinal Canali and Massimo Spada. But whatever his new colleagues achieved, it has to be said, was merely building on Nogara's successes. The 'wind from the North', as Italians describe influences from Milan and the other commercial centres, had brought about a permanent change in Vatican financial culture and practice that would survive even Nogara's death in 1958. Nogara had finally inserted the Church into the structures of international capitalism.

The perils and pitfalls of Vatican financial strategy

On the whole, the financial strategies adopted by the Vatican between 1870 and 1950 were very successful, certainly as measured in terms of providing the popes with the necessary means to sustain them in the policies which they adopted in their governance of the universal Church in this period and in particular to expand their missionary and propaganda activities. Throughout the period, however, the Vatican faced serious perils and pitfalls whatever financial strategy it adopted. As the dust jacket illustration, taken from the German magazine, *Beiblatt des Semplicissimus*, demonstrates, even the spontaneous giving of the faithful could be presented in an unfavourable light. If the Vatican did not invest money it was accused of a modern form of *manomorta*, of wasting opportunities, of leaving capital idle, and if it did invest it was accused of capitalist speculation, as Cardinal Mocenni ruefully complained.[6] So when it did seek to make its money work, it was accused of being an exploitative, capitalist organisation, as for example during the mid-1890s, when the Socialist newspaper *Avanti!* alleged that the capital's bread scarcity was the result of the Vatican's milling 'monopoly' in Rome.[7] Thirty years later, Benedict XV was pilloried in an *Avanti!* cartoon as someone wholly in cahoots with Italian capitalism.

The Vatican's financial strategies at any given time were also potential hazards for its diplomatic stance of neutrality and impartiality in its dealings with states, especially in time of war. Two examples will suffice to illustrate the dangers which this presented. The first relates to the role of the Banco di Roma before and during the Italo-Libyan War of 1911–12 (Chapter 4, p. 105), and the second to Nogara's investments in Italian munition companies and the claims then made about Vatican partiality during the Abyssinian War (Chapter 8, pp. 177–8). In 1963, in Act 2 of his play *The Representative*, which was one of the first major works to accuse Pius XII of not doing enough during the Holocaust, Hochhuth claimed that 'Pius has business interests that preclude any condemnation of Germany.'[8] We now know that this was not even remotely true. But in the present climate of scepticism about Pius XII's policies during the Second World War, this, and claims that commercial institutions wholly or partially owned by the Vatican traded in tungsten and wolfram (see Chapter 9, p. 192), and maybe other key commodities to the Third Reich, would be a very useful stick with which to beat the Catholic Church. In more recent times, Richard Bosworth has claimed not only that the Roman Catholic Church has been thoroughly 'Americanised' in the post-war period, but that because of its financial structures it is essentially little more than a multinational.[9]

Vatican finances and the Church's social teaching

But probably the most serious danger which the modern papacy ran, and still runs, in the management of its finances is that of pursuing

---

[6] Lai, *Finanze e finanzieri vaticani*, p. 171.   [7] Ibid., p. 149.

[8] R. Hochhuth, *The Representative*, translated with a preface by Robert D. MacDonald (London, 1963), p. 88, where Riccardo, the 'dissident' priest also says 'Nowhere is it ordained . . . that the successors of St Peter should present themselves at the Last Judgement as the largest shareholding company in the world.'

[9] R. Bosworth, *Italy and the Wider World, 1860–1960* (London, 1996), p. 159.

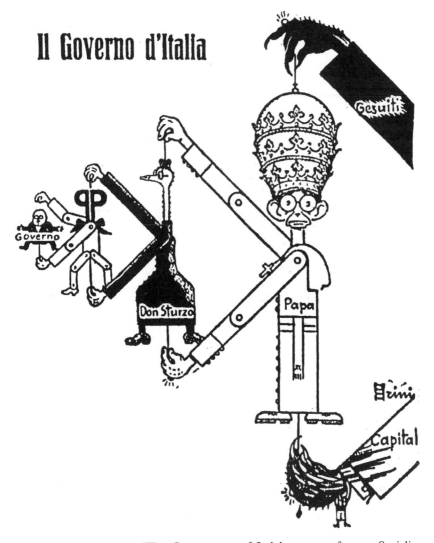

Illustration 15 'The Government of Italy', cartoon from a Socialist newspaper of 1919

strategies which are, or are perceived to be, in conflict with its own teaching. There really seems to have been little attempt on the part of the popes in the period covered to relate the policies pursued by Vatican financial agencies to the concerns they themselves expressed in public statements about the ethics of economic and social matters. Arguably,

this was almost inevitable given the lack of notions of an ethical investment policy before the 1970s. This explains Nogara's lack of concern
about the investment of Vatican capital in munitions industries and the
apparent lack of concern on his part, or indeed that of Pius XI, to enquire
about wages and working conditions in Italian companies in which they
invested. Presumably they were reassured by the Fascist regime's introduction of the Charter of Labour of 1927, which on paper at least guaranteed fair wages and safe working conditions for Italian workers, but was
in reality based on the ruthless suppression of free, i.e. non-state, non-
Fascist, trade unionism, something which even Pius XI had condemned
in *Quadragesimo Anno*.[10] Interestingly, in the United States of America,
Catholic bishops at this time were strongly supporting workers' rights,
trade unions and the New Deal.[11] It could be said in mitigation of the
Vatican financier's position that the fact that the Vatican did not own
directly any major manufacturing industry put the papacy at one remove
from the application of the ethics of industrial relations and such key concerns as wages and working conditions. Under Pius XII, the Church in
Italy had a closer relationship with the working masses through the Associ-
azioni Cattoliche Lavoratori Italiani, a workers' section of Italian Catholic
Action and later the Catholic-dominated trade union organisation, Confederazione Italiana Sindacati Liberi. Their primary role in the era of
deepening Cold War polarisation in Italy in the late 1940s was to combat
Communism on the shop floor, but they also served, in theory at least,
as the agents for the implementation of the principles of the great social
encyclicals.[12]

Paul VI was the first pope truly to comprehend the tension between the
thrust of Catholic social teaching and the Vatican's investment policies,
being particularly concerned about the bad publicity which the activities
of some Italian companies in which the Vatican had a share-holding had
generated for the Church.[13] He was also very sensitive to the needs of the
poor, Third World countries and on 13 November 1964, at the end of a
special mass celebrated in St Peter's for members of the Vatican Council,
Pope Paul took off the tiara which had been presented to him by the
people of his former archdiocese of Milan the previous year and placed
it on the altar, letting it be known that he had decided to give his tiara to
the poor, having heard 'many grave words about the poverty and hunger

[10] Pollard, *The Vatican and Italian Fascism*, p. 139; for the Charter of Labour, see
    P. Cannistraro (ed.), *Historical Dictionary of Fascist Italy* (Westport Conn., 1982), p. 114.
[11] Dwyer (ed.), *New Dictionary of Catholic Social Thought*, p. 116.
[12] P. Ginsborg, *A History of Contemporary Italy: Society and Politics, 1943–1988* (London,
    1990), pp. 50–1.
[13] Rees, *Inside the Vatican*, p. 220.

of the times'.[14] Appropriately, it was bought up by Cardinal Spellman of New York and is now displayed in the National Shrine of the Immaculate Conception in Washington DC.

Though the finances of the papacy as a whole may be heavily dependent upon the world's free-market, capitalist system, with all the moral and public relations risks which go with that situation, there is, ironically, no such problem inside the State of the Vatican City itself. Its economy, including the 'tourist' sector (the Vatican museums and postal services), the rented accommodation sector, transportation, including the one hundred metre length of railway line, the 'retail sector', the profits from the Annona supermarket and the provision of energy and fuel is totally owned by the state and run for the benefit of the state, with heavily subsidised prices for its citizens and employees and their dependants. Thus there was reproduced, in miniature, the *stato assistenziale*, literally the 'public relief state' of the last years of papal Rome. And in a broader sense, this was reproduced on a gigantic scale in Italy under the Christian Democratic regime which governed the country between 1948 and 1994, as a result of the application of the Catholic social doctrine of 'social solidarity', and the ruthless pursuit of the vote through clientelism.[15] So, after 1950, the Italian capitalist economy, in which Nogara had previously built up such a strong Catholic/Vatican component, co-existed with a social system with strong resemblances to Communist rule in Eastern Europe but which was in fact inspired in part at least by Catholic social teaching.

The tension between the theory and practice of capitalism and Catholic social theory endures, personified by the Polish pope John Paul II and his profound suspicion of liberal-democratic, individualistic, Western capitalistic society and expressed many times in his reign.[16] Nevertheless, the capitalistic element of Vatican financing remains.

The Italian dimension

The popes in the period of this study were as diverse as any could be, coming from noble (Pius IX, Leo XIII and Benedict XV), middle-class (Pius XI and Pius XII) and peasant (Pius X) backgrounds; there were great pastoral popes (Pius IX and X), those with a mixture of pastoral and curial/diplomatic experience (Leo XIII, Benedict XV and Pius XI) and

---

[14] *Times*, 14 Nov. 1964.
[15] For a brief account of the *stato assistenziale* under the Christian Democrats see R. Leonardi and D. A. Wertmann, *Italian Christian Democracy: The Politics of Dominance* (Basingstoke, 1989), ch. 8.
[16] D. Willey, *God's Politician: John Paul at the Vatican* (London, 1992), pp. 70–1.

purely curial/diplomatic experience (Pius XII); some came from a northern Italian background (Pius X, Benedict XV and Pius XI) and three from the centre, from the former Papal States in fact, Pius IX, Leo XIII and Pius XII, but they all had one thing in common, they were *Italians*. This was important, very important. As Vincenzo Gioberti, the Piedmontese priest who looked for Italian unification under the presidency of the pope, once remarked, the papacy was an *Italian* institution: 'the Papacy is supremely ours and our nation's because it created the nation and it has been rooted here for eighteen centuries; it is concrete, living, real not an abstraction nor a chimera, but an institution, an oracle and a person'.[17] Whether the papacy created the Italian nation is highly debatable, and whatever divine origins Roman Catholic theology may ascribe to the Holy See, nevertheless it was, as Gioberti says, an essentially Italian institution, and after 1523 all the popes themselves were Italian. So the cultural milieu in which the papacy operated, thanks to the Counter-Reformation institutions of Inquisition and Index, meant that Rome, like the rest of Italy, was 'sealed off' from external intellectual influences, and the early nineteenth-century popes sought to maintain this situation, despite the depredations of the Enlightenment and the French Revolution.

The rise of Italian nationalism, one of the many 'step-children' of that Revolution, meant that the relationship between the Holy See and Italy after 1861 also played a crucial role in the development of the modern papacy, and in the core of that relationship, the *dissidio* between Church and State, or the 'Roman Question' as it was frequently called, Pacelli and the Banco di Roma eventually played their part. Though some of his financial decisions may have been disastrous for the Vatican, Pacelli's influence in government circles was worth its weight in gold. His efforts contributed enormously to the composing of the *dissidio*. The slow and gradual process of reconciliation which took place between Italy and the Holy See after 1870, and especially from the early 1880s onwards, was greatly assisted by the Vatican's involvement in the Banco di Roma. Pacelli and the bank constituted a meeting point between Catholic Rome, and ultimately Catholic Italy, and royal, liberal-conservative Rome – the royal court in the Quirinale Palace, Parliament and government. The ecclesiastical governing elite of the Vatican entered into an indirect relationship with the Italian political class which, despite repeated alarms and excursions and the anti-clerical forays of the Italian press and die-hard elements of the Left-wing political groups, including increasingly

---

[17] As quoted in D. Mack Smith (ed.), *The Making of Italy, 1796–1870* (London, 1968), pp. 80–1.

the Socialists, became progressively more stable and secure. Pacelli's access to both worlds, as a rather independent-minded member of Rome's Catholic establishment, made it possible for him to act as an increasingly effective intermediary between them. His ability to win from the Italian government satisfaction of the Vatican's legal, financial and other needs (see Chapters 3 and 4), and the solution of potential problems, like the smoothing of the protocol difficulties involved in baptisms, royal marriages and funerals, for instance, as well as his efforts to bring the Church and the liberal-conservative political together against their common enemy, the Socialist working-class movement, helped pave the way for the improved relationship between the Vatican and Italy during the difficult period of the First World War,[18] and eventually the formal, legal *Conciliazione* between the Holy See and the Kingdom of Italy brought about by Pius XI and Mussolini in 1929.

Ultimately, the activities of Pacelli and the Banco di Roma symbolised the broader process of change taking place in Italy whereby Catholics were entering the country's economic and political life. The Libyan War gave rise to the first major manifestation of widespread Italian, Catholic patriotic enthusiasm (allowing for the minor displays of this over the defeats of Italian troops at Dogali, 1888, and Adowa, 1896), thanks to Pacelli's mobilisation of Catholic opinion through the newspapers of the Trust. As Webster describes it, Catholics and Nationalists came together in an alliance which was to be a forerunner of the clerico-Fascist support for Fascism a little more than ten years later.[19] And again, after the nascent Fascist regime had come to power following the March on Rome of October 1922, the problems of the Banco di Roma prompted the first one-to-one meeting between representatives of the Vatican and Fascism – Cardinal Secretary of State Pietro Gasparri and Prime Minister Mussolini. In return for Mussolini's promise to salvage the Banco di Roma from yet another financial crisis, and thus protect the Vatican's not insubstantial deposits in the bank, the Vatican agreed to abandon the Catholic Partito Popolare Italiano, and its leader Fr. Luigi Sturzo, one of the major obstacles to Fascism's complete political ascendancy.[20] As intended, this contributed in no small part to the early demise of the Popolari as a political force, preparing the way for the secret negotiations between the Vatican and Fascism which began in 1926 and led to the agreement three years later, which included the crucial financial settlement. During the 1920s and 1930s, in order to protect its interests, especially its financial interests, the Vatican continued its support

---

[18] See Pollard, *The Unknown Pope*, ch. 4.
[19] R. A. Webster, *Christian Democracy in Italy (1860–1960)* (London, 1961), p. 49.
[20] Molony, *The Emergence of Political Catholicism*, ch. 8.

of Fascism through three major crises of its rule – the Matteotti Crisis of 1924 when the murder of the eponymous Socialist MP nearly brought down Mussolini's government, the Great Depression of the early 1930s which had serious, if temporary, destabilising effects on the regime and the Abyssinian War of 1935–6.[21] The Vatican, however, stood aside during the crisis of 1943 which toppled the regime because Fascism was patently in terminal decline and consequently beyond saving as a result of defeats in war, the invasion of Sicily and the opposition within the Party, the Court and the Armed Forces, and the widespread demoralisation and alienation of the mass of the Italian population.

Nogara played his part, too, in the Church's evolving relationship with Italy after 1929. His very successful management of the Vatican's finances provided the economic underpinning to Catholic power in Italy in the twelve or fifteen years following 1948. How conscious was Pius XI of what the long-term consequences of Nogara's investment strategy in Italy would be? Did he indeed direct it? Is it conceivable that it formed a part of his strategy of a 'Christian restoration of Italian society in a Catholic sense', and consequently for Catholic power in Italy in the post-Fascist era? Was it just an accident? A remark he made to Nogara about the property acquisitions of British Grolux in November 1932, that this Vatican stake in the British economy 'will be useful for [the progress of] the Catholic camp', might just suggest that he did.[22] Whatever the answer, the consequences are clear. As Grilli has amply demonstrated, the Vatican's penetration and 'colonisation' of the Italian economy eventually provided one of the pillars of Catholic 'triumphalism', of Christian Democratic hegemony in the years of the Church's 'omnipotence' in Italy. From being an economic, social and, to a lesser extent, political 'condominium' with the Fascists in the 1930s and early 1940, Italy from the mid-1940s was under the social, political and *economic* hegemony of a Catholic block – something which is rarely mentioned in the historiography of the period. Catholic power and influence would not have been so strong in Italy in those post-war years without the dimension of Vatican financial involvement in the Italian economy. Finally, it has to be said that the Italian economy benefited enormously from the presence of the Vatican and the activities of its financiers, particularly in Rome, thanks to the steady influx of Peter's Pence after 1860, the capital invested by the Vatican in various economic sectors, especially after 1929, and the millions of pilgrims who visited the Eternal City and other religious sites.

[21] Pollard, *The Vatican and Italian Fascism*, pp. 28–30.
[22] AFN, Nogara's diary, entry for 3 Nov. 1932.

There can be no doubt that the successful management of the Vatican's finances after 1870 supplied the increasingly absolute papal monarchy with a key resource in its various efforts to exert its full authority and control over the world-wide Church-money. In addition, the ways in which this success was achieved to some extent influenced the directions in which that monarchy actually developed.

'The American connection' and the internationalisation of the Roman curia

The growth in the numbers of American Catholics and their wealth, and the consequent growth in the size of their contribution to Peter's Pence, and Vatican finances generally, is one of the most striking characteristics of the period under discussion. Whereas in 1850 Catholics had only numbered 2 million souls out of a total of 24 million, fifty years later they were 12 million out of 76 million, and nearly one hundred years later, 24 million out of 151 million, and as their numbers grew, they made an increasingly significant contribution to both Peter's Pence and the missionary outreach of the Church.[23] New York, Boston and Chicago, in that order, were by 1950, the wealthiest Catholic dioceses in the world, thanks to large numbers of Irish, German and other central European and Italian immigrants.[24] By 1949, the American Church was quite simply 'the richest and most lively branch of the Catholic Church in the world'.[25] American Catholics were also by now the leading contributors to Peter's Pence (a third), followed by Germany, Italy, France and Spain, and this position has been maintained ever since.[26]

As the years went by, the growing importance of US Catholicism, by now the new 'eldest daughter of the Church', was recognised in Rome. The appointment of American cardinals – there were four in 1939 and even with three deaths there were five after the 1946 consistory – was the clearest sign of this, but the whistle stop tour made by Cardinal Pacelli in 1936 emphasised that the Vatican now took cognisance of the importance of the American Church, as well as the diplomatic and economic strength of the great republic. Nogara's visit, a year later, also proves this point. Seen in the wider context of his travels in the late 1930s, which included Hungary, France and South as well as North America, Pacelli's visit also revealed Pius XI's increasing anxiety about the world situation and his desire that his 'chief minister', and probable successor, should be more

[23] N. Lo Bello, *Vatican USA* (New York, 1972), pp. 28–9.
[24] Gollin, *Worldly Goods*, p. 280.
[25] As quoted in Arthur Jones, 'The American Way', in *The Tablet*, 15 June 2002.
[26] Rees, *Inside the Vatican*, p. 224.

widely known in the Catholic world, a sign of the Vatican's concern that it should be seen as a more truly *international* institution.

Given the crucial contribution which American Catholics were making to the financing of the papacy, it is perhaps surprising that they did not have more impact and influence on the policies and procedures of the Vatican in the 1920s and 1930s. The problem was that big movers and shakers in the American Church, like Cardinal Mundelein of Chicago, the archetypal 'bricks and mortar' bishop, whose financial success was unparalleled in the 1930s, had no personal experience of Rome and no strong connections with figures in the Roman curia. Besides, his description of Hitler as a 'paperhanger, and a poor one at that'[27] made him *persona non grata* in both Nazi Germany and Fascist Italy, something of a handicap for anyone hoping to have influence in Rome. William O'Connell, cardinal archbishop of Boston was better placed; Cardinal Merry Del Val was a long time friend and ally, but he died in 1930. In any case, much of Merry Del Val's influence disappeared with the election of his rival, Giacomo Della Chiesa as Pope Benedict XV in 1914.[28] Though someone like Mundelein had a great deal to teach Vatican ecclesiastics about the efficient investment and management of the Church's money, like setting up a diocesan 'bank',[29] after 1929 Nogara ruled the roost as far as the Vatican's finances were concerned and had no more need of help from American ecclesiastics than he had from British banks.

Francis Spellman, who was appointed archbishop of New York in 1939, and then cardinal in 1946, had a rather a rather different career from either Mundelein or O'Connell. He was one of the first American priests, after his superior Cardinal O'Connell, to make a serious career in the Roman curia. O'Connell had been rector of the American College in Rome between 1895 and 1901, and as bishop of Portland was one of the leading enforcers of a policy of 'Romanisation' in the American Church. Spellman went much further than his former boss. He began in his inimitable way, by making a habit of photographing important curial officials and thus ingratiating himself with them. In consequence, he made powerful friends in the Secretariat of State in the 1920s and early 1930s, including Count Galeazzi, Msgr Borgoncini-Duca who became the first nuncio to Italy in 1929, and Cardinals Gasparri and Pacelli, and even earned recognition from Pius XI as his little American 'Benjamin'. He was so powerful in Vatican circles, as well as in ecclesiastical and political circles in his home country in the 1940s and 1950s that he was dubbed

---

27 Kantowicz, *Corporation Sole*, p. 53.   28 Pollard, *The Unknown Pope*, p. 68.
29 See also Gannon, *The Cardinal Spellman Story*, p. 153, where he describes how Spellman set up a diocesan 'bank' for New York modelled on that pioneered by Mundelein in Chicago.

the 'American Pope'.[30] The dollar power of US Catholicism obviously served only to reinforce his influence in the court of Papa Pacelli and *La Popessa*, whose favour he carefully cultivated.[31] As Ordinary for the US Armed Forces, with strong connections on Wall Street, and as a personal friend of both Pius XII and President Roosevelt, Spellman exercised enormous influence in the Vatican between 1939 and 1958.[32]

It is emblematic of increased American influence in the Vatican that after the end of the war no less than four Americans were working in its representative missions abroad: Msgr John Collins was *chargé d'affaires* in Liberia, Msgr Gerald O'Hara (bishop of Savannah-Atlanta) was nuncio in Romania, Msgr Joseph Hurley (bishop of St Augustine) was *regent* of the nunciature in Belgrade and Msgr Louis Muench (bishop of Fargo) was apostolic visitor, replacing the papal nuncio in occupied Germany.[33] Certainly, the corps of papal nuncios and apostolic delegates was generally speaking much less Italian than it had been by comparison with the pre-war period,[34] but among the growing number of non-Italians, the Americans constituted by far the largest group. At last, the Roman curia was following the Papal Court in becoming more international in composition.

However, while the Spellman-Pacelli axis served as the underlying link between the Vatican and USA in this period, the Vatican, like the USA, also had *economic* as well as political and religious interests to defend in Italy and elsewhere during the Cold War. This might have been perceived as an almost total economic, ideological and political identification with the West, and indeed was seen in this way from Moscow, but it does not mean that Vatican policy was always aligned with that of the United States and the West in the great struggle with Communism. Apart from the fact that the death of Roosevelt and succession of Truman in 1945 broke the personal link between Washington and Rome, as Peter Kent has demonstrated, the US policy of acceptance of Yalta, and consequently consigning Catholics in Eastern Europe to the tender mercies of Communist regimes effectively installed by the Red Army, was wholly at variance with Papa Pacelli's concerns.[35] It was in fact not until the Second Council of the Vatican in the 1960s that the overwhelming demographic and financial importance of American Catholicism was finally translated into real power and influence in the Vatican. In 1964, a crucial role was played by Cardinal Albert Meyer of Chicago and other American bishops

---

[30] Cooney, *The American Pope*, p. 1.   [31] Ibid.   [32] Ibid., p. 51.
[33] *Annuario Pontificio*, 1948, pp. 792–800.   [34] Ibid., 1939, pp. 789–96.
[35] P. C. Kent, *The Lonely Cold War of Pius XII: The Roman Catholic Church and the Division of Europe 1943–1950* (Montreal, 2002), pp. 5–6.

in getting the declaration on Religious Liberty through the last session of the Council.[36]

Given the increasing contribution of American dollars and business expertise to the finances of the Vatican over this period, and the consequent enormous growth of influence there, it was inevitable that sooner or later an American would play an important role in their management. Indeed, the fact that this did not happen until some time after the Second World War may be accounted for by the post-war dominance of Canali, Spada, Galeazzi and the Pacelli nephews, rather than Nogara. The first American to take up a major role in the management of the Vatican's financial affairs was Archbishop Paul Marcinckus, Paul VI's 'gorilla', who became secretary of the IOR in 1968, and president in 1971. He left in 1990 after the Vatican bank had made a loss of 241 million dollars.[37] Cardinal Edmund Szoka's experience of running the Vatican's finances was rather more positive. A mid-westerner like Marcinckus, Szoka was archbishop of Detroit before he was brought to Rome in 1990 to run the Prefecture of the Economic Affairs of the Holy See, the office created by Paul VI to oversee all of the Holy See's financial agencies.[38] So successful was he that in 1997 he was promoted to be president of the commission governing the Vatican City State.[39]

At the time of writing, the American Catholic primacy in the funding of the papacy is under threat. The spreading paedophile priest scandals, particularly those in the major archdioceses like Boston, have had a serious impact upon the capacity of the American Church to raise funds from the faithful. On the one hand, dioceses are likely to have to pay out large amounts of compensation to victims as a result of litigation, so much so that the Boston archdiocese is thinking of filing for bankruptcy. On the other hand, Catholics distressed by the scandals are more reluctant to put their hands in their pockets for the Church. This, in its turn, has impacted upon the flow of funds from the United States to the Vatican. Unless and until confidence in their priests, and above all bishops, is restored among the American Catholic laity, that very honourable primacy will be in peril, and the Vatican will have to face some serious financial problems. The pacifist position taken by the Vatican over the Anglo-American attack on Saddam Hussein's Iraq will also not have helped matters.

Romanisation

The other side of the coin of internationalisation was 'Romanisation'. If the Roman court and curia became less Italian and more and more

---

[36] Hebblethwaite, *Paul VI*, p. 41.   [37] Raw, *The Moneychangers*, p. 9.
[38] Rees, *Inside the Vatican*, p. 226.   [39] *Annuario Pontificio*, 1999, p. 90.

subject to influences from the world-wide Church, especially from across the Atlantic, then at the same time the world-wide Church was fashioned more and more uniformly in the Roman mould. As Cardinal O'Connell, the leader of the Romanising party in the American Church before and after the First World War, said: 'To know the Catholic Church, and to have those Catholic traditions that enable one to keep the faith intact, one must have been to Rome, to have had international experience.'[40] Internationalisation and Romanisation went together hand in hand, though clearly internationalisation moved more slowly, and they were driven in large part by the ways in which the Vatican financed itself after 1870.

The papacy's capacity to Romanise various national churches by means of key episcopal appointments, and the imposition and enforcement of uniform regulations and procedures, and in fact to transform the Roman Catholic Church into a sort of priestly bureaucracy, depended on the use of apostolic nuncios and delegates in the countries concerned. One of the consequences of the effectiveness of the new methods of funding the papacy was precisely its ability to build a growing network of papal nunciature in those countries with which it had diplomatic relations, and apostolic delegations with which it had not, non-diplomatic representatives of the papacy accredited to national churches rather than national governments. The apostolic delegates and the papal nuncios performed the fundamental task of supervising the national churches, settling internal disputes, and above all ensuring they conducted their organisational and liturgical life in conformity with the dictates of Rome, and all in accordance the Code of Canon Law after 1917.

Whereas there were twenty-three nuncios in 1870, by 1950 there were forty, and though there were only five apostolic delegates in 1870, that number had risen to twenty-four by 1950.[41] In 1870, the Holy See had diplomatic relations with a small handful of states, almost entirely restricted to Catholic countries in Europe and Latin America; in 1950 the Vatican maintained relations with all the great powers of the world except the Soviet Union and the People's Republic of China and with an increasing number of Third World countries, which were the product of the by now inexorable process of the decolonisation of the European empires.[42] This was a sign of the growing diplomatic influence and prestige of the Roman Catholic Church in nearly every continent.

But expanding the Vatican's diplomatic network cost money, lots of it, as Pius XI had pointed out in the preamble to the text of the Financial Convention in 1929 (see Chapter 6, p. 141). Theoretically, apostolic

---

[40] As quoted in E. O. Hanson, *The Catholic Church in World Politics* (Princeton, N.J., 1987), p. 171.

[41] *Annuario Pontificio*, 1950, pp. 791–80.   [42] Ibid.

delegations and nunciatures were supposed to be funded by the local, national church, as the US bishops were supposed to do, and did, when an apostolic delegation was set up in Washington in 1893 (see Chapter 3, p. 74). But in reality, from the early 1930s onwards, the Vatican was increasingly obliged to find the funds itself in those missionary or semi-missionary territories where the local church simply could not afford the expense of establishing and maintaining a papal representative. In 1938, for example, Nogara was given the task of finding the premises for the new apostolic delegation to the Church in Great Britain,[43] and by the outbreak of war, the Vatican was devoting a not insignificant part of its income to the support of its representatives abroad (see Chapter 9, p. 168).

As has been seen, the actual form which the Vatican's major new means of funding took from the 1860s onwards, the world-wide diocesan and parochial collections of Peter's Pence, played a formative role in the development of the modern papacy. It laid down the basis for a more direct relationship between the faithful and their spiritual head, and from the financial mobilisation of the Catholic masses, Rome passed to their social and political mobilisation, the mobilisation of the faithful in support of Pius IX and Leo XIII's battles with secular states, and the 'despoiling' of the Italian state in particular; thus the 'prisoner of the Vatican' syndrome was an absolute prerequisite to the success of financial mobilisation (see Chapter 2, p. 34, and Chapter 3, pp. 58–9). As Zambarbieri has demonstrated, soon papal approbation of all manner of Catholic activities and associations – pious sodalities and confraternities, charitable organisations like the Society of St Vincent De Paul, associations for the collection of Peter's Pence, mutual benefit associations, Catholic youth and general pressure groups and eventually Catholic trade unions and peasant organisations – in various countries was sought by the faithful, especially the laity, further reinforcing the links with Rome.[44] This 'Catholic movement' throughout the world grew rapidly between 1870 and the outbreak of the First World War. After that war, Pius XI, building on the work of Benedict XV in Italy (though arguably Pius IX and Leo XIII had also earlier contributed to this development), sought to extend the rigidly uniform and hierarchy-dominated Italian model of Catholic Action to parishes and dioceses in every part of the whole Catholic world as a way of providing for the defence of the Church and its values from the multifarious dangers which it faced in the various countries of the world.[45] Thus was yet

---

[43] AFN, memorandum of 12 Nov. 1938.
[44] Zambarbieri, 'La devozione al Papa', pp. 20–33.
[45] See for example, A. M. Crofts OP, *Catholic Social Action: Principles, Purpose and Practice* (London, 1933); L. Civardi, *A Manual of Catholic Action* (London, 1935); and Anon., *A Scheme for Catholic Action*, with a foreword by Cardinal Hinsley (London, 1935).

another centrally and uniformly organised and directed system imposed by Rome upon virtually the whole of the universal Church.

The ultimate form which the Romanisation of the Catholic Church took during the development of the modern papacy was the emergence of a powerful papal 'cult of the personality', which is still one of the defining features of Roman Catholicism today. The financial mobilisation of Catholics through regular Peter's Pence collections was the key to this new relationship between the faithful and their spiritual leader, and it was re-inforced by the development of an international postal and telegraph system which made it possible for the faithful to communicate directly and personally with the Roman pontiff, something which was encouraged, and sometimes orchestrated, in the Vatican.[46] Another factor which helped consolidate the relationship was the massive growth of pilgrimages to Rome, which were facilitated by the application of steam power to railways and shipping. But arguably the Vatican's need for the *financial* benefits of pilgrimages, the bringing of further collections and *purses* by the pilgrims was also a crucial factor (see Chapter 3, pp. 58–9, and Chapter 6, p. 135), helping to turn the Roman pilgrimage into the ultimate act of Roman Catholic religiosity. Thanks to Nogara's successful management of the Vatican's finances after 1929, it was possible to provide a worthy setting for these great encounters between pilgrims and pope. By 1950, the Vatican itself, the approach to it – the Via della Conciliazione – and the Borgo more generally had fused together into a kind of 'city-state shrine' to host the vast, oceanic crowds who flocked to see Pius XII in the spectacular ceremonies of Holy Year. All this had, in a sense, been pre-figured by Cardinal Nicholas Wiseman, first archbishop of Westminster after the restoration of the hierarchy in England. In his famous hymn, *Pilgrimage to Rome*, of the 1850s he wrote:

> 1. Full in the panting heart of Rome,
> Beneath the apostle's crowning dome,
> From pilgrims' lips that kiss the ground,
> Breathes in all tongues one only sound:
> 'God bless our pope, the great, the good'.
> 2. The golden roof, the marble walls,
> The Vatican's majestic halls,
> The note redouble, till it fills,
> With echoes sweet the seven hills:
> 'God bless our pope' &c.
> 3. Then surging through each hallowed gate,
> Where martyrs glory, in peace, await,
> It sweeps beyond the solemn plain,

---

[46] Zambarbieri, 'La devozione al Papa', pp. 31–3.

Peals over the Alps, across the main,
'God bless our pope' &c.
4. From torrid south to frozen north,
That wave harmonious stretches forth,
Yet strikes no chord more true to Rome's,
Than rings within our heart and homes,
'God bless our pope' &c.[47]

By 1950 the great Ultramontane project, of which, this hymn is a most powerful expression, had been made into a reality. Rome was now totally, completely and unquestionably the centre of the Catholic world as never before, and Vatican finances and financiers of the preceding one hundred years had played an important role in that achievement.

[47] *The Westminster Hymnal* (London, 1983), p. 243.

Appendices

Section 1: prerogatives of the Pontiff and the Holy See

1. The person of the Supreme Pontiff is sacred and inviolable.
2. Any attempt against the person of the Supreme Pontiff, or any provocation to commit the same, shall be punished with the same penalties as are established by law for a similar attempt or provocation against the person of the King.
3. The Italian Government shall render to the Supreme Pontiff in the territories of the Kingdom, the honours which are due to royal rank, and shall maintain the privileges of honour which are paid to him by Catholic Sovereigns.
4. The annual donation of 3,225,000 lire in favour of the Holy See is maintained . . . for the diverse ecclesiastical wants of the Holy See, for ordinary and extraordinary repairs to and custody of the apostolic palaces and their dependencies; for all allowances, gratuities and pensions to the guards . . . and to all persons attached to the Pontifical Court, and for eventual expenditure; as well as for the ordinary repairs and custody of the museums and library thereto annexed, and for allowances, stipends and pensions to persons employed for that purpose.
5. The Supreme Pontiff shall . . . have free enjoyment of the apostolic palaces of the Vatican and the Lateran . . . as also of the villa of Castelgandolfo.
6. During the vacancy of the Pontifical See, no judicial or political authority shall . . . offer any impediment or limitation to the personal liberty of the Cardinals. The Government shall take proper measures in order that the assemblies of the Conclave and of Oecumenical Councils be not disturbed by external violence.

---

[1] *Times*, 15 May 1871.

7. The Supreme Pontiff shall be at liberty to correspond with the Episcopate and the whole Catholic world, without any interference on the
part of the Italian Government. To this effect he shall be free to establish in the Vatican, or in any of his residences, postal and telegraph
offices, and to employ therein persons of his choice.

APPENDIX II
THE FINANCIAL CONVENTION OF 1929[2]

Considering that Italy and the Holy See, in consequence of the stipulation
of the Treaty with which the 'Roman Question' has been permanently
solved, have deemed it necessary to regulate in a separate convention,
forming an integral part of the Treaty, their financial relations: that the
Supreme Pontiff, considering on the one side the enormous damages suffered by the Apostolic See by the loss of St. Peter's Patrimony, consisting
of the ancient Pontifical States, and of the possession of ecclesiastical
institutions, and on the other hand the increasing needs of the Church if
only in the city of Rome, and at the same time taking into consideration
the financial position of the State and the economic conditions of the
Italian people, especially after the war, has decided to limit his request
for an indemnity to the strictest necessary amount, asking for a sum,
partly in cash and partly in Consols, which is greatly inferior in value to
that which the State would have had to pay up to now to the Holy See, if
only in fulfilment of the undertaking contained in the Law of Guarantees
of May 13th, 1871; that the Italian State duly appreciating the fatherly
sentiments of the Supreme Pontiff, has considered its duty to agree to
the request for the payment of such an amount; the two High Parties,
represented by the same plenipotentiaries, have agreed:

> Art. 1. – Italy pledges herself to pay to the Holy See, at the
> exchange of the ratification of the Treaty, the sum of Italian
> Lire 750,000,000 (seven hundred and fifty millions; equals
> about £8,152,000) in cash, and to deliver at the same time
> sufficient 5 per cent Italian Consols, bearer bonds, of the nom-
> inal value of Italian Lire 1,000,000,000 (one milliard; equals
> about £10,869,000), with interest falling due on June 30th,
> 1929.
> Art. 2. – The Holy See agrees to accept the said amounts as a
> final settlement of its financial relations with Italy caused by
> the events of 1870.

[2] From the translation in *Italy Today*, May 1929.

Art. 3. – All acts necessary for the execution of the Treaty, of the present Convention and of the Concordat will be exempt from any tax.

Rome, February 11th, 1929.
(Signed)   PETER CARDINAL GASPARRI
                                   Benito Mussolini

Bibliography

ARCHIVES, PRINTED PRIMARY SOURCES AND OFFICIAL AND PERIODICAL PUBLICATIONS

ARCHIVES

AAC=Archives of the Archdiocese of Chicago (Chicago)

AAES=Archivio Affari Ecclesiastici Straordinari. Archives of the Vatican Secretariat of State (Vatican)

ACMFA=Archive of the Czech Ministry of Foreign Affairs (Prague)

ACS=Archivio Centrale dello Stato. Italian Central State Archives (Rome)

ADP=Archive du Département de Paris (Archives of the Department of Paris)

AFN=Archivio Famiglia Nogara. Personal papers of Bernardino Nogara (Rome)

ASBCI=Archivio Storico della Banca Commerciale Italiana. Historical Archive of the Banca Commerciale Italiana (Milan)

ASBdI=Archivio Storico della Banca d'Italia. Historical Archive of the Banca d'Italia (Rome)

ASMAE=Archivio Storico del Ministero degli Affari Esteri. Historical Archive of the Italian Foreign Ministry (Rome)

ASV=Archivio Segreto Vaticano. The main Vatican archive (Vatican)

Bank of England Archive (London)

Companies House=United Kingdom national register of companies (London)

NARA=United States National Archive and Records Administration (College Park, Maryland, USA)

NCWC=Archives of the National Catholic Welfare Conference, including the papers of the US Bishops' Conference (Catholic University of America, Washington, DC)

PRO (National Archives)=Public Record Office (Kew, London)

R deCCV=Registre de Commerce, Canton Vaud, Switzerland. Cantonal records of companies (Maudon, Vaud, Switzerland)

WDA=Westminster Diocesan Archives (London)

PRINTED PRIMARY SOURCES

Acta Pio X, Positio e Summarium (Vatican City, 1949)

Actes et documents du Saint-siège relatifs à la Seconde Guerre Mondiale (12 vols., Vatican, 1968–74)

Catechismo della Chiesa Cattolica: testo integrale e commento teologico (Vatican City, 1992)

Ciano's Diary, 1937–8, ed. with an introduction by M. Muggeridge (London, 1952)

Ciano's Diary, 1939–45, ed. with an introduction by M. Muggeridge (London and Toronto, 1947)

Code of Canon Law: New Revised English Translation (London, 1983)

Documenti della Diplomazia Vaticana: il Vaticano e la democrazia italiana (Lugano, 1948)

Hachey, E. (ed.), *Anglo-Vatican Relations* (Boston, 1972)

Lai, B. (ed.), *Finanze e finanzieri vaticani tra l'Ottocento e il Novecento da Pio IX a Benedetto XV: atti e documenti* (Milan, 1979)

Martini, F., *Diario: 1914–1918*, ed. G. De Rosa (Milan, 1966)

Opera Omnia di Benito Mussolini, ed. E. D. Susmel (32 vols., Florence, 1952–)

Osio, B. (ed.), *Antonietta Osio Nogara, 1904–1987: diari e lettere sparse* (privately published, 1989)

Pacelli, F., *Diario della Conciliazione*, ed. M. Maccarone (Vatican City, 1959)

Scottà, A. (ed.), *La Conciliazione Ufficiosa: diario del barone Carlo Montei 'incaricato d'affari' del governo italiano presso la Santa Sede, 1914–1922* (2 vols., Vatican City, 1997)

Vaticano e Stati Uniti, 1939–1952: dalle carte di Myron C. Taylor, ed. with an introduction by E. Di Nolfo (Milan, 1978)

OFFICIAL AND PERIODICAL PUBLICATIONS

Acta Apostolicae Sedis. Official 'gazette' of the Holy See (Vatican City)

Annuario Pontificio. Papal Year Book (Vatican City)

La Civiltà Cattolica (Rome)

Il Corriere della Sera (Milan)

Financial Times (London)

L'Illustrazione Vaticana (Vatican City)

Mémorial du Grand Duché de Luxembourg. Official gazette of the Grand Duchy (Luxembourg)

New York Times (New York)

Notiziarie Statistiche. Annual report on limited companies in Italy (Rome)

L'Osservatore Romano (Rome, then Vatican City after 1929)

La Stampa (Turin)

Times (London)

SECONDARY SOURCES

Aarons, M. and Loftus, J., *Ratlines: How the Vatican's Nazi Networks Betrayed Western Intelligence to the Soviets* (London, 1991)

Unholy Trinity (New York, 1998)

Alexander, S., *Church and State in Yugoslavia since 1945* (Cambridge, 1979)

Alvarez, D., 'Vatican Communications Security, 1914–1918', *Intelligence and National Security*, 7 (1992), pp. 443–53

Alvarez, D. and Graham, R., SJ, *Nothing Sacred: Nazi Espionage against the Vatican, 1939–1945* (London and Portland, Oreg., 1997)

Anon., *A Scheme for Catholic Action*, with a foreword by Cardinal Hinsley (London, 1935)

Aubert, G., 'Documents relatifs au movement catholique italien sous le pontificat de S. Pie', *Rivista di Storia della Chiesa* (1958), p. 223

Il Pontificato di Pio IX, ed. G. Martina (2nd edn, Turin, 1970)

Ayrinhac, A. D., *Legislation in the New Code of Canon Law* (New York, 1930)

Banca Commerciale Italiana, Archivio Storico, Collana Inventari, Servizio Estero e Rete Estera, ed. R. Benedini, L. Contini and M. Zighetti (Milan, 1997)

Serie II, vol. 2, ed. A. Gottarelli, G. Montanari and F. Pino (Milan, 2000)

Barraclough, G., *The Medieval Papacy* (London, 1968)

Barry, R., OP, 'The Contribution of Thomas Aquinas', in J. A. Dwyer (ed.), *The New Dictionary of Catholic Social Thought* (Collegeville, Minn., 1994)

Bedeschi, L., 'Significato e fine del Trust Grosolano', *Rassegna di Politica e Storia*, 116 (1972), pp. 7–17

Belardelli, G., 'Un viaggio di Bernardino Nogara negli Stati Uniti (novembre 1937)', *Storia Contemporanea*, 23 (1992), pp. 321–38

Bell, D. Howard, *Sesto San Giovanni: Workers, Culture and Politics in an Italian Town, 1880–1922* (New Brunswick, N.J., 1986)

Bertini, C., *Ai tempi delle guaranteggie. Ricordi di un funzionario di polizia, 1913–1918* (Rome, 1932)

Binchy, D. A., *Church and State in Fascist Italy* (Oxford, 1970)

Blackbourn, D., *Marpingen: Apparitions of the Virgin May in Bismarckian Germany* (Oxford, 1993)

Blouin, G., *Catalogue of the Vatican Archives* (Vatican City, 1998)

Bolton King, G., *A History of Italian Unity* (2 vols., London, 1909)

Bosworth, R., *Italy and the Approach of the First World War* (London, 1983)

Italy and the Wider World, 1860–1960 (London, 1996)

Bouscaren, T. L. and Ellis, A. C., *Canon Law: A Text and Commentary* (Milwaukee, 1957)

Bradsher, G., *Holocaust-Era Assets: A Finding Aid to Records at the National Archives at College Park, Maryland* (Washington, DC, 1999)

Burgess, A., *Earthly Powers* (Harmondsworth, 1980)

Byrne, H., 'Investment of Church Funds: A Study in Administrative Law', PhD thesis, Catholic University of America, 1952

'The Financial Structure of the Church', in L. J. Putz, CSC (ed.), *The Catholic Church in the USA* (London, 1958)

Cameron, R. (ed.), *Banking and Economic Development* (Oxford, 1972)

Cameron, R. E., 'Papal Finance and Temporal Power (1815–1871)', *Church History*, 26 (1957), pp. 132–47

Cannistraro, P. (ed.), *Historical Dictionary of Fascist Italy* (Westport, Conn., 1982)

Caracciolo, A., 'La continuità della struttura economica di Roma prima e dopo il 1870', *Nuova Rivista Storica*, 38 (1954), pp. 182–206, 327–47

Roma capitale. Dal Risorgimento all crisi dello stato liberale (Rome, 1956)

Caravale, M. and Caracciolo, A. (eds.), *Lo Stato Pontificio da Martino V a Pio IX* (Turin, 1978)

Carlen, C. (ed.), *The Papal Encyclicals* (5 vols., Raleigh, N.C., 1990)

Caroleo, A., *Le banche cattoliche dalla prima Guerra mondiale al fascismo* (Milan, 1976)

Castelli, L., *'Quel tanto di territorio': ricordi di lavori ed opere eseguiti nel Vaticano durante il Pontificato di Pio XI (1922–1939)* (Rome, 1940)

Casula, C. F., *Domenico Tardini (1888–1961) e l'Azione della Santa Sede nella crisi fra le due guerre* (Rome, 1988)

Catholic Directory, Anno Domini 1999 (New Providence, N.J., 1999)

Cereti, G., 'The Financial Resources and Activities of the Vatican', *Concilium*, 116–20 (1978), pp. 3–116

Cerretti, E. (ed.), *Il Cardinale Bonaventura Cerretti* (Roma, 1939)

Chabod, F., *L'Italia contemporanea, 1918–1948* (Turin, 1961)

Chadwick, O., *Britain and the Vatican during the Second World War* (Cambridge, 1986)

A History of the Popes, 1830–1914 (Oxford, 1998)

Chernow, R., *The House of Morgan: An American Banking Dynasty and the Rise of Modern Finance* (New York, 1990)

Chimielewski, P. J., SJ, 'Nell-Brunning, Oswald Von', in J. A. Dwyer (ed.), *New Dictionary of Catholic Social Thought* (Collegeville, Minn., 1994)

Ciampani, A., *Cattolici e Liberali durante la trasformazione dei partiti. La 'questione romana' e la politica nazionale e progetti vaticani (1876–1883)* (Rome, 2000)

Cipolla, A., 'Due giorni in Vaticano', *La Stampa*, 16 and 22 Nov. 1931

Civardi, L., *A Manual of Catholic Action* (London, 1935)

Coleman Nevill, W., SJ, 'The Smallest State in the World', *National Geographical Magazine*, 75 (1939), pp. 380–92

Confalonieri, A., *Banca e industria in Italia (1894–1906)* (Milan, 1974)

Cooney, J., *The American Pope* (New York, 1983)

Coppa, F. J., *Pope Pius IX: Crusader in a Secular Age* (Boston, 1979)

Cardinal Giacomo Antonelli and Papal Politics in European Affairs (New York, 1990)

The Modern Papacy since 1789 (London, 1998)

Cornwell, J., *A Thief in the Night: The Death of Pope John Paul I* (London, 1985)

Hitler's Pope: The Secret History of Pius XII (London, 1999)

Cornwell, R., *God's Banker* (New York, 1983)

Crispolti, F., *Corone e porpore* (Rome, 1936)

Crocella, C., 'La crisi finanziaria dello Stato pontificio nelle trattative per l'adesione della Santa Sede alla convenzione monetaria del 1865', *Rivista di Storia della Chiesa in Italia*, 17 (1973), pp. 404–25

Augusta miseria: aspetti delle finanze pontificie nell'età del capitalismo (Milan, 1982)

Crofts, A. M., OP, *Catholic Social Action: Principles, Purpose and Practice* (London, 1933)

Dal Gal, G., *Il Papa Santo* (Padua, 1954)

D'Azeglio, M, *Gli ultimi casi della Romagna* (Turin, 1846)

De Cesare, R., *The Last Days of Papal Rome* (London, 1909)

De Felice, R., 'La Santa Sede e il conflitto Italo-Etiopico nel diario di Bernardino Nogara', *Storia Contemporanea*, 8 (1977), pp. 823–34

Della Cava, R., 'Financing the Faith: The Case of Roman Catholicism', *Church and State*, 35 (1993), pp. 37–61

De Leonardis, M., *L'Inghilterra e la questione romana: 1859–1870* (Milan, 1981)

Del Re, N., *La curia romana* (Rome, 1970)

J. Delumeau, 'Political and Administrative Centralisation in the Papal State in the Sixteenth Century', in E. Cochrane (ed.), *The Late Italian Renaissance* (London, 1970)

Demarco, D., *Il tramonto dello stato pontificio: il papato di Gregorio XVI* (Turin, 1949)

De Rosa, G., *Storia del Banco di Roma*, III (Rome, 1984)

De Rosa, G., *Una banca cattolica fra cooperazione e capitalismo: La Banca Cattolica del Veneto* (Bari and Roma, 1991)

De Rosa, L., 'Le origini dell'IRI e il risanamento bancario del 1934', *Storia Contemporanea*, I (1979), pp. 7–42

Storia del Banco di Roma, I–II (Rome, 1982–3)

De Zulueta, T., 'Is the Vatican Going Broke?', *Sunday Times*, 1 June 1980

Dizionario storico del movimento cattolico in Italia, I/I (Turin, 1981)

Duffy, E., *Saints and Sinners: A History of the Popes* (New Haven, Conn., 1997)

Dwyer, J. A. (ed.), *The New Dictionary of Catholic Social Thought* (Collegeville, Minn., 1994)

Einaudi, L., *Money and Politics: European Monetary Unification and the International Gold Standard (1865–1873)* (Oxford, 2001)

Eizenstat S. E. and Slany, W. Z., *Supplement to the Preliminary Study on US and Allied Efforts to Recover and Restore Gold and Other Assets Stolen or Hidden during World War II* (Washington, DC, 1998)

Enciclopedia cattolica, X and XVII (Rome, 1954)

Epstein, K., *Matthias Erzberger and the Dilemma of German Democracy* (Princeton, N.J., 1959)

Fadda, P., 'Il banchiere del Papa al capezzale della Montevecchio', *Argenteria*, new series, I (1992), pp. 101–17

Falconi, C., *The Popes in the Twentieth Century* (London, 1967)

Il cardinale Antonelli: vita e carriera del Richelieu italiano nella chiesa di Pio IX (Milan, 1983)

Farini, D., *Diario di fine secolo*, ed. E. Morelli (Roma, 1961)

Felisini, D., *Le finanze pontificie e i Rothschild 1830–1870* (Naples, 1991)

Ferguson, H., *The World's Banker: The History of the House of Rothschild* (London, 1998)

Fogarty, G. P., *The Vatican and the American Hierarchy from 1870 to 1965* (Collegeville, Minn., 1982)

Formigoni, G., *I cattolici deputati (1904–1918)* (Rome, 1989)

Forsyth, D. J., *The Crisis of Liberal Italy: Monetary and Financial Policy, 1914–1922* (Cambridge, 1993)

Gallagher, C., 'The United States and the Vatican in Yugoslavia, 1945–1950', in D. Kirby (ed.), *Religion and the Cold War* (London, 2003)

Gambasin, A., *Gerarchia e laicato in Italia nel secondo ottocento* (Padua, 1986)

Gannon, R. I., SJ, *The Cardinal Spellman Story* (New York, 1963)

Garvin, L., *The Calvi Affair* (London, 1984)

Ginsborg, P., A *History of Contemporary Italy: Society and Politics, 1943–1988* (London, 1990)

Giordani, I., *La Rivolta Cattolica* (Turin, 1924)

Giovagnoli, A., 'La Pontifica Commissione Assistenza e gli aiuti americani (1945–1948)', *Storia Contemporanea*, 9 (1978), pp. 1081–111

Gollin, J., *Worldly Goods: Pay Now, Die Later* (New York, 1971)

Grilli, G., *La finanza vaticana in Italia* (Rome, 1961)

Grissel, H. De La Garde, *Sede Vacante: Being a Diary Written at the Conclave* (Oxford, 1903)

Guanno, G. and Toniolo, G. (eds.), *La Banca d'Italia e il sistema bancario, 1919–1936* (Bari and Rome, 1993)

Guarino, M., *I mercanti del Vaticano, affari e scandali: l'impero economico delle anime* (Milan, 1998)

Hales, E. E. Y., *Revolution and the Papacy, 1769–1846* (London, 1960)

Hanson, E. O., *The Catholic Church in World Politics* (Princeton, N.J., 1987)

Harris, R., *Lourdes, Body and Spirit in a Secular Age* (Berkeley and Los Angeles, 2000)

Harrison, G., *I-ME-MINE* (Richmond, 1980)

Hearder, H., *Italy in the Age of the Risorgimento, 1790–1870* (London, 1983)

Hebblethwaite, P., *John XXIII: Pope of the Council* (London, 1983)

  Paul VI: The First Modern Pope (New York, 1993)

  'Pius XII: Chaplain of the Atlantic Alliance?', in C. Duggan and C. Wagstaffe (eds.), *Italy in the Cold War: Politics, Culture and Society, 1948–1958* (Oxford, 1995)

Hochhuth, R., *The Representative*, trans. with a preface by Robert D. MacDonald (London, 1963)

Hoffman, P., *Anatomy of the Vatican* (London, 1985)

Holmes, D., *The Triumph of the Holy See* (London, 1978)

Horaist, B., *La dévotion au pape et les catholiques français sous le pontificat de Pie IX (1846–1878). D'après les archives de la Bibliothèque apostolique vaticane* (Rome, 1995)

Insolera, I., *Roma moderna* (Turin, 1971)

Jacquemyns, G., *Langrand-Dumonceau. Promoteur d'une puissance financière catholique* (5 vols., Brussels, 1960–5)

Jankowiak, K., 'Benoit XV', in P. Levillain (ed.), *Dictionnaire de la papauté* (Paris, 1997)

Jemolo, C. A., *Church and State in Italy, 1850–1950* (Oxford, 1960)

Jones, A., 'Sixty Years of Inept Management, Bad Investments Lead to Vatican Deficit', *Republic*, 11 Mar 1988

Kantowicz, E. R., *Corporation Sole: Cardinal Mundelein and Chicago Catholicism* (South Bend, Ind., 1982)

Kent, P. C., *The Pope and the Duce: The International Impact of the Lateran Agreements* (London and Basingstoke, 1981)

  The Lonely Cold War of Pius XII: The Roman Catholic Church and the Division of Europe 1943–1950 (Montreal, 2002)

Keogh, D., *The Vatican, the Bishops and Irish Politics, 1919–1939* (Cambridge, 1986)

'Ireland, the Vatican and the Cold War: The Case of Italy', *Historical Journal*, 34 (1991), pp. 931–52

Kersevan, A. and Visentini, P. (eds.), G. *Nogara: luci e ombre di un arcivescovo, 1928–1945* (Udine, 1997)

Kertzer, D., *The Kidnapping of Edgardo Mortara* (New York, 1997)
   The Popes against the Jews: The Vatican's Role in the Rise of Modern Anti-Semitism (New York, 2001)

Kindleberger, C. P., *The World in Depression* (London, 1978)
   A Financial History of Western Europe (2nd edn, Oxford, 1993)

King, B. and Okey, T., *Italy Today* (2 vols., London, 1909)

Knox, M., *Hitler's Italian Allies: Royal Armed Forces, Fascist Regime and the War of 1940–1943* (Cambridge, 2000)

Lai, B., *Vaticano aperto: il diario vaticano di Benny Lai* (Milan, 1968)
   Finanze e finanzieri vaticani tra l'Ottocento e il Novecento da Pio IX a Benedetto XV (Milan, 1979)
   I segreti del Vaticano da Pio XII a papa Wojtila (Bari, 1984)

Lamberts, E. (ed.), *The Black International, 1870–1878. The Holy See and Militant Catholicism in Europe* (Leuven, 2001)

Lazzarini, L., *Pio XI* (Milan, 1937)

Leonardi, R. and Wertmann, D. A., *Italian Christian Democracy: The Politics of Dominance* (Basingstoke, 1989)

Levillain, P. (ed.), *Dizionario storico del papato* (Milan, 1966)
   Dictionnaire de la papauté (Paris, 1997)
   The Papacy: An Encyclopedia (3 vols., London, 2002)

Levillain, P. and Uginet, F.-C., *Il Vaticano e le frontiere della Grazia* (Milan, 1985)

Lo Bello, N., *L'oro del Vaticano* (Milan, 1971)
   Vatican USA (New York, 1972)
   The Vatican Empire (New York, 1976)

Logan, O., 'Pius XII, Romanità, Prophesy and Charisma', *Modern Italy*, (1998), pp. 237–49
   'The Clericals and Disaster: Polemic and Solidarism in Liberal Italy', in J. Dickie, J. Foot and F. Snowden (eds.), *Distastro! Disasters in Italy since 1860: Culture, Politics and Society* (New York, 2002)

Luxmoore, J. and Babuich, J., *The Vatican and the Red Flag: The Struggle for the Soul of Eastern Europe* (London, 1999)

McAvoy, T. T., CSC, *A History of the Church in the United States* (South Bend, Ill. 1969)

McKnight, J. P., *The Papacy: A New Appraisal* (London, 1953)

Mack Smith, D. (ed.), *The Making of Italy, 1796–1870* (London, 1968)

MacNutt, F. A., *A Papal Chamberlain* (London, 1936)

Magister, S., *La politica vaticana e l'Italia, 1943–1978* (Rome, 1979)

Majo, A., *La stampa quotidiana cattolica Milanese*, vol. II: *1912–1968 le vicende de l'Italia* (Milan, 1974)

Malagodi, G., 'Il Salvataggio della Banca Commerciale nel ricordo di un testimone', in G. Toniolo (ed.), *Industria e banca nella grande crisi, 1929–1934* (Milan, 1978)
   Profilo di Raffaele Mattioli (Milan and Novara, 1984)

Manfroni, G., *Sulla soglia del Vaticano, 1870–1901: dalle memorie di Guido Manfroni*, ed. C. Manfroni (2 vols., Milan, 1920)

Manhattan, A., *The Vatican Billions* (London, 1972)

Manuzi, M., 'Politics and the Italian State Industrial Sector, 1933–1980 – With Two Case Studies' (PhD thesis, Anglia Polytechnic University, 1999)

Margiotta-Broglio, F., *Italia e Santa Sede dalla Prima Guerra Mondiale alla Conciliazione* (Bari, 1966)

Maritain, J., 'A Society without Money', *Review of Social Economy*, 43 (1985), pp. 75–83

Martina, G., 'L'ecclesiologia prevalente durante il pontificato di Pio XI', in A. Monticone (ed.), *Cattolici e fascisti in Umbria (1922–1945)* (Bologna, 1978)

Pio IX (1846–1851) (Rome, 1974)

Pio IX (1851–1866) (Rome, 1986)

Pio IX (1866–1878) (Rome, 1990)

Mazzonis, F., 'Storia della Chiesa e origini del partito cattolico', *Studi Storici*, 2 (1980), pp. 363–400

'Pio IX, il tramonto del potere temporale e la riorganizzazione della chiesa', in B. Angloni et al. (eds.), *Storia della Società Italiana*, vol. XVIII: *Lo stato unitario e il suo difficile debutto* (Milan, 1981)

Miller, A., 'Banks and Banking', in J. A. Dwyer (ed.), *New Dictionary of Catholic Social Thought* (Collegeville, Minn., 1994)

Misner, P., *Social Catholicism in Europe: From the Onset of Industrialisation to the First World War* (London, 1991)

Mollat, G., *The Popes at Avignon: 1305–1378* (London, 1963)

Moloney, T., *Westminster, Whitehall and the Vatican: The Role of Cardinal Hinsley, 1935–1943* (London, 1985)

Molony, J. N., *The Roman Mould of the Australian Catholic Church* (Melbourne, 1969)

The Emergence of Political Catholicism in Italy: Partito Popolare, 1919–1926 (London, 1977)

Moretti, V. (ed.), *Le Auto dei Papi: settant'anni di automobilismo vaticano* (Rome, 1981)

Mori, G., *Il capitalismo industriale in Italia* (Rome, 1977)

Mori, R., *Il tramonto del potere temporale* (Rome, 1967)

Muhlen, E., *Monnaie et circuits financiers au Grand Duché de Luxembourg* (Luxembourg, 1968)

Murphy, P., *La Popessa* (New York, 1983)

Natalini, T., (ed.), *I diari del Cardinale Ermengildo Pellegrinetti (1916–1922)* (Vatican City, 1994)

Negri, P., *Le ferrovie nello stato pontificio (1844–1870)* (Rome, 1967)

New Catholic Encyclopedia, III (New York, 1967)

New Catholic Encyclopedia, XIV (Washington, 1967; 2nd edn, New York, 2003)

Noonan, J. T., *The Scholastic Analysis of Usury* (Cambridge, Mass., 1957)

O'Brien, A. C., 'L'Osservatore Romano and Fascism: The Beginning of a New Era', *Church and State* (Spring, 1971)

O'Neill, R., *Cardinal Herbert Vaughan* (London, 1995)

Owen, R., 'Pope's Divine Drives on Show', *Times*, 15 Dec. 1997, p. 11

Pallenberg, C., *Inside the Vatican* (London, 1961)
  Vatican Finances (London, 1971)
Passalecq, G. and Suchecky, B., *The Hidden Encyclical of Pius XI* (New York, 1997)
Perin, R., *Rome in Canada: The Vatican and Canadian Affairs in the Late Victorian Age* (Toronto, 1990)
'Pertinax', *Le Partage de Rome* (Paris, 1929)
Petriccioli, M., *L'Italia in Asia Minore: equilibrio mediterraneo e ambizioni imperialiste alla vigilia della prima guerra mondiale* (Florence, 1983)
Piluso, G.-D., 'Un centauro metà pubblico e metà privato. La Bastogi da Alberto Beneduce a Mediobanca (1926–1969)', *Annali della Fondazione Luigi Einaudi*, 26 (1992), pp. 347–91
  'Le banche miste', *Archivi e Imprese* 113 (1996), pp. 7–57
Pollard, J. F., *The Vatican and Italian Fascism, 1929–1932: A Study in Conflict* (Cambridge, 1985)
  'Conservative Catholics and Italian Fascism: The Clerico-Fascists', in M. Blinkhorn (ed.), *Fascists and Conservatives: The Radical Right and the Establishment in Twentieth Century Europe* (London, 1990), pp. 31–50
  'Fascism', in J. A. Dwyer (ed.), *The New Dictionary of Catholic Social Thought* (Collegeville, Minn., 1994)
  'Religion and the Formation of the Italian Working Class', in R. Halpern and J. Morris (eds.), *American Exceptionalism: US Working Class Formation in an International Context* (London, 1997)
  The Unknown Pope: Benedict XV (1914–1922) and the Pursuit of Peace (London, 1999)
  'The Papacy in Two World Wars: Benedict XV and Pius XII', in R. Mallett and G. Sorenson (eds.), *International Fascism, 1919–1945* (London, 2002)
  'The Vatican, Italy and the Cold War', in D. Kirby (ed.), *Religion and the Cold War* (London, 2003)
Raw, C., *The Moneychangers* (London, 1992)
Rees, T. J., SJ, *Inside the Vatican* (Cambridge Mass., 1996)
Regards sur la ville: Lausanne, 1900–1939, Catalogue of an exhibition at the city historical museum (Lausanne, 2001)
Renda, F., *Socialisti e cattolici in Sicilia* (Palermo, 1972)
Rendina, C. (ed.), *La grande enciclopedia di Roma* (Rome, 2000)
Rhodes, A., *The Vatican in the Age of the Dictators, 1922–1945* (London, 1973)
  The Power of Rome in the Twentieth Century: The Vatican in the Age of the Liberal Democracies, 1870–1922 (London, 1983)
Rienzi, W. A., 'The Entente and the Vatican August 1914–May 1915', *Historical Journal*, 13 (1970), pp. 491–508
Rossi, M. G., *Le origini del movimento cattolico in Italia* (Rome, 1977)
Romano, S., *Giuseppe Volpi: industria e finanza tra Giolitti e Mussolini* (Milan, 1979)
Rychlak, R. R., *Hitler, the War and the Pope* (Huntington, Ind., 2000)
Salvemini, G., *Chiesa e stato in Italia* (Milan, 1969)
  The Origins of Fascism in Italy (New York, 1973)
Scoppola, P., *La proposta politica di De Gasperi* (Bologna, 1977)

Seldes, G., *The Vatican – Yesterday, Today and Tomorrow* (London, 1934)

Seton-Watson, C., *Italy from Liberalism to Fascism* (London, 1967)

Sire, H. J. A., *The Knights of Malta* (New Haven, Conn., 1994)

Smit, J. O., *Pope Pius XII* (London, 1949)

Snider, C., *L'Episcopato del Cardinale Andrea Ferrari, Contributo allo Studio delle condizioni religiose nell'età contemporanea* (2 vols., Vatican City, 1974)

Soderini, E., *Il pontificato di Leone XIII* (2 vols., Milan, 1932–3)

Spadolini, G., *L'opposizione cattolica* (Florence, 1954)

  Giolitti e i cattolici (Florence, 1960)

Spadolini, G. (ed.), *Il Cardinale Gasparri e la Questione Romana. Con brani delle memorie inedite* (Florence, 1972)

Spinosa, A., *L'ultimo papa* (Milan, 1992)

Steinberg, J., *Why Switzerland?* (Cambridge, 1976)

Teeling, W., *The Pope in Politics* (London, 1937)

Theodoli, A., *A Cavallo di due secoli* (Rome, 1950)

Thierry, J.-J., *Le Vatican secret* (Paris, 1962)

Ticchi, J.-M., *Aux frontières de la paix: bons offices, médiations, arbitrages du Saint-Siège (1878–1922)* (Rome, 2002)

Toniolo, G., *L'economia dell'Italia fascista* (Bari, 1980)

Traniello, F. and Campanini, G. (eds.), *Dizionario storico del movimento cattolico in Italia (1860–1980)* (3 vols., Turin, 1981)

Tully, S., 'The Vatican's Finances', *Fortune International*, 116 (1987), pp. 28–31

Uginet, F.-C., 'Les finances papales', in P. Levillain (ed.), *Dictionnaire de la papauté* (Paris, 1997)

  'Le finanze pontificie', in P. Levillain (ed.), *Dizionario storico del papato* (Milan, 1966)

Vaughan, H., *A Lenten Letter on Penance and Other Good Works by Herbert Cardinal Vaughan, Archbishop of Westminster* (London, 1901)

Vecchi, A., 'Linee di spiritualità nei documenti pontifici da Pio IX a Pio XII sull' azione cattolica', in anon., *Spiritualità e azione del laicato italiano* (2 vols., Padua, 1969)

Viaene, V., *Belgium and the Holy See from Gregory XVI to Pius IX (1831–1878)* (Louvain, 2001)

  'Catholic Mobilisation and Papal Diplomacy during the Pontificate of Pius IX (1846–1978)', in E. Lamberts (ed.), *The Black International, 1870–1878: The Holy See and Militant Catholicism in Europe* (Leuven, 2001)

Von Aretin, K.-O., *The Papacy and the Modern World* (London, 1970)

Walsh, M., *Vatican City State* (Oxford, 1983)

Weber, M., *The Protestant Ethic and the Spirit of Capitalism* (2nd edn, London, 1976)

Webster, R. A., *The Cross and the Fasces: Christian Democracy and Fascism in Italy* (Stanford, Cal., 1959)

  Christian Democracy in Italy, 1860–1960 (London, 1961)

  Industrial Imperialism in Italy, 1908–1915 (Berkeley, Calif., 1974)

The Westminster Hymnal (London, 1983), p. 243

Who Was Who in America, 1 (Chicago, 1943)

Willey, D., *God's Politician: John Paul at the Vatican* (London, 1992)

Woolf, S., *A History of Italy: 1700–1860: The Social Constraints of Political Change* (London, 1979)

Woywood, S., *A Practical Commentary on the Code of Canon Law* (2nd edn, New York, 1926)

Yallop, D., *In God's Name: An Investigation into the Murder of Pope John Paul I* (London, 1985)

Zamagni, V., *The Economic History of Italy, 1860–1990: Recovery after the Decline* (Oxford, 1993)

Zambarbieri, A., 'La devozione al Papa', in E. Guerriero and A. Zambarbieri (eds.), *La chiesa e la società industriale (1878–1922)*, Storia della Chiesa, XXII/2 (Milan, 1996)

Zivojinovic, D., *The United States and the Vatican Policies, 1914–1918* (Boulder, Colo., 1978)

Index